Meet Me in the Middle

Barbara —
Thank you for ethics,
competence, creativity,
and leadership you
inspire in students
and colleagues every
day. We're lucky
to have you on this
wondrous journey!
— Rick Wormeli
Sept. 2002

Meet Me in the Middle

Becoming an Accomplished Middle-Level Teacher

Rick Wormeli

Rachel Carson Middle School
Herndon, Virginia

Stenhouse Publishers
Portland, Maine

National Middle School Association
Westerville, Ohio

Stenhouse Publishers
477 Congress Street, Suite 4B
Portland, ME 04101
www.stenhouse.com

National Middle School Association
4151 Executive Parkway, Suite 300
Westerville, OH 43081
www.nmsa.org

This book includes material that has been adapted from articles and columns first published in *Middle Ground* magazine and/or *The Crucial Link*. The author and the publisher are grateful to the editors of these magazines for their permission.

The following are registered trademarks of the respective companies:
Mindtrap, Mindtrap; Habitat Rummy, Project WILD; *Jeopardy!*, Columbia Tristar Television, a subsidiary of Sony Pictures Entertainment; Taboo, Milton Bradley, a subsidiary of Hasbro; Pictionary, Pictionary Inc., a subsidiary of Hasbro; Password, Pearson Television Ltd.; GameBoy, Nintendo; Rubik's Cube and Rubik's Revenge, Seven Towns Ltd.; HyperStudio, Knowledge Adventure, Inc., Havas Interactive; PowerPoint, Microsoft; SimCity, Maxis, a subsidiary of Electronic Arts; Toastmasters, Toastmasters International; Situational Leadership, Center for Leadership Studies, PDC and Associates; Band-Aid, Johnson & Johnson; Rolaids, Warner-Lambert, a subsidiary of Pfizer; Smartees, Ce De Candy, Inc.; LifeSavers, Kraft Foods, a subsidiary of Philip Morris.

Library of Congress Cataloging-in-Publication Data
Wormeli, Rick.
    Meet me in the middle : becoming an accomplished middle-level teacher / Rick Wormeli.
    p. cm.
    Includes bibliographical references and index.
    ISBN 1-57110-328-7 (alk. paper)
    1. Middle school teaching. I. Title
LB1623.W67 2001
373.1102—dc21   2001031173

Manufactured in the United States of America on acid-free paper
07 06 05 04 03 02 01 9 8 7 6 5 4 3 2 1

To my wife, Kelly, and my children, Ryan and Lynn,
for their laughter, imagination, and unconditional love.

Contents

Foreword

L et me say this simply—teachers need this book. At a time when only test scores matter, when pedagogy means "hand out more worksheets so students can practice for the tests," when teachers are reluctant to select curriculum and teach in a way they know is better for their students, Rick Wormeli lays out a clear vision of what responsive middle-level teaching should be. This is a book for all reasons—help for the novice teacher to focus on the essential, support for the mid-career teacher wanting to improve her craft, and inspiration and confirmation for the later-career teacher as well.

But make no mistake, this book is much more than an exhortation to do better for young adolescents. Wormeli does a masterful job pulling together seemingly disparate threads—connecting middle school philosophy with standards; current brain research with multiple intelligences theory. Wormeli's discussion of differentiated instruction may be the most powerful section of the book for any teacher.

After a fast start in the 1960s through the early 1990s, middle-level education is now under ever-increasing criticism and scrutiny. While some school districts claim that middle school philosophy and practices have not served them well, other schools recognize an essential truth—the middle school teacher is the most important element in creating a successful middle-level classroom. In *Meet Me in the Middle: Becoming an Accomplished Middle-Level Teacher,* Wormeli shows how this is so.

Many books about teaching consist of long to-do lists—to be an effective teacher one must be willing to take risks, enjoy ambiguity, and have a sense of humor. Important, yes, but not exactly words to get us through next week! Rick Wormeli doesn't waste time telling us what we must do; rather he shows us what we must be to be effective teachers of ten- to fourteen-year-olds. His ideas on motivating young adolescents are less prescriptive dos and don'ts than ideas about forming connections with kids and building strong learning communities. This book is definitely more strategy than technique, as it should be.

Anyone who sees Wormeli in his classroom, hears him present at a conference, or reads his work, in this book or his columns in *Middle Ground,* knows that he is an accomplished middle school teacher. He practices what he preaches. In *Meet Me in the Middle* we learn about Rick Wormeli and from Rick Wormeli at the same time. In this book, he does what many writers are not able to do: he demonstrates theory with rich examples from his own teaching.

Another measure of effectiveness for me is, Would I want my kids in Rick Wormeli's class? Without hesitation, I would say yes, given his commitment to teaching all children at high levels. He is obviously a caring teacher, and his excitement about working with ten- to fourteen-year-olds and his passion for what he does is infectious—and inspirational! And he doesn't expect you to pick these ideas up and run with them. He knows these ideas work for him. You have to figure out how to adapt them to make them work for you. Underlying everything he writes is a strong sense of what has worked for him and excellent knowledge of research about all aspects of teaching and learning with ten- to fourteen-year-olds.

Wormeli knows and cares about his students, and that commitment and devotion to kids is seen again and again in the book. You will laugh with Adverb Man as he crashes through the ceiling and nearly knocks himself out, but that only serves to demonstrate the lengths to which Wormeli will go to make learning meaningful, compelling, and fun. But the book is not about him; it is about tested ways to engage students in learning to the highest levels. Fittingly, the final chapter, The Truth About Middle School Students, caps his beliefs about teaching young adolescents in the best manner possible—through his students' thoughts about life and living. If ever one wondered about the abilities and capabilities of ten- to fourteen-year-olds, one should read this chapter. Above all, Wormeli is an advocate for young adolescents—those who will succeed in his classes and those who will not. He reminds us that even those students who do not always do so well in school generally go on to full and productive lives. Read this chapter first!

A key feature of this book is the comments by students addressing topics under discussion and letting us know how middle school students feel about such topics. When Corrina and Stephen comment on the unique qualities of teachers who inspire them, their comments give further credibility to Wormeli's comments about effective teachers.

Two chapters in particular are different from any I have seen in a book of this type. His discussion of active learning gives a new meaning to the term: "But beware, this chapter might expand your lung capacity and your instructional repertoire at the same time." An appropriate warning in an excellent chapter. Not afraid to take on any and all issues, Wormeli does an excellent job of applying brain research to the middle school classroom.

I really like the structure of this book. Part 1 creates a culture of learning, which leads to Part 2 and many specific ideas on promoting higher student achievement through innovative and accomplished practice. Part 3 cycles back to the middle school context—effective teams, teacher-student advisories, outdoor adventures, and working with parents. It offers two unique chapters, one on mentoring new teachers and one on the National Board Certification process. As one of the first Nationally Certified Board teachers, Wormeli speaks passionately about how important that process has been to improving himself as a middle school teacher. The appendixes are full of great resources and examples of teaching ideas.

Rick Wormeli's growing national reputation is well deserved because he talks the language of teachers, and we know that when he advocates for his students, he really means it. More important, he knows how to do it! He is in demand as writer, speaker, and consultant at conferences and in school districts around the country as he continues to refine the practices in this book. As you will see, this book offers sound and immediately practical advice for veteran, aspiring, and new teachers.

As a veteran middle-level teacher, he is well aware of the factors that influence his work, and he comments on them extensively; he is particularly concerned with the context of teaching in excellent middle schools and takes great pains to recognize that an accomplished teacher works in very different ways. This book does not pretend to be another treatise on what teaching should be, nor is it simply a bag of tricks. Wormeli incorporates both practical and theoretical ideas so they are immediately understood and usable.

If you know Rick Wormeli, you will not be surprised by the tone of this book for it is very readable and inviting. If you don't know him, you will feel as if you have known him all your life after finishing *Meet Me in the Middle*. He is the teacher you would like to have on your team or in the room next door. And this book will help all of us become the middle school teachers we need to be.

Ed Brazee, Professor of Middle-Level Education
University of Maine

Acknowledgments

There are not words enough to express my gratitude to the following people for their inspiration and direction in the course of my becoming a teacher. These comments will have to suffice for now, however, until such time as I can more fully thank them.

My greatest thanks goes to my parents, Paul and Nancy, and to my brother, Ben, and his wife, Natalie, for their love and their inspiration to give ceaselessly and graciously to the world.

I also wish to thank the students, parents, and staff at the following schools for their wisdom and patience with me: Rachel Carson Middle School, Herndon Middle School, Freedom Hill Elementary School, and Sterling Middle School in Virginia.

There are six people who deserve special thanks for helping me grow as a professional:

Dr. Tom Gatewood, a Virginia Tech University professor, middle school visionary, and one of the most encouraging and intelligent individuals I've ever known. During the past thirty years, he has trained an army of highly effective middle school teachers and administrators.

Dr. Clyde Roper, a Smithsonian Institution scientist, consummate story-teller, and talented teacher. His love for learning and the natural world have turned countless students into lifelong learners and protectors of the planet. He has been a mentor to me in more ways than he knows.

Cabell Lloyd, former principal of Freedom Hill Elementary School and my first mentor in this teaching journey. Cabell taught me that teaching was more than a job and that my students must come first.

Kathy Aronson, a colleague at Herndon Middle School, who taught me that "the truth is out there" if I am willing to fight for it. She showed me how to do what's right for students, not just what's easiest for the teacher.

A final thanks to the greatest editors and coaches on seven continents, Holly Holland and Philippa Stratton, who not only trusted me as a first-time author but demonstrated that you can be in the business world and still be compassionate, ethical, and stirring. Without their insightful and honest critique, this book would never have been published. I am particularly indebted to Holly for seeing enough in my rough drafts to warrant a regular column for *Middle Ground* magazine. She is the wise mentor most writers only dream of having. I am grateful for her tenacity and encouragement. She's still teaching me about conciseness and the active voice.

Introduction

I begin this book with the most influential statement I ever heard. It is the quote against which I compare all other declarations in books, teacher in-service workshops, and education journals. I heard it when I was in middle school myself, and I have never forgotten its potency: "Everything in this book may be wrong."

With these words, Richard Bach ended his book *Illusions: The Adventures of a Reluctant Messiah,* the sequel to his 1970 bestseller, *Jonathan Livingston Seagull.* Most of the book before that sentence is filled with wonderful lessons on life, such as, "What the caterpillar calls the end of the world, the Master calls the butterfly," and "Argue for your limitations and sure enough, they're yours." Multiple passages from these allegorical books have been printed in the margins of school and camp handbooks for years. I've seen excerpts printed on banners hanging in school dining rooms or above classroom chalkboards. I think the reason so many people find inspiration in Bach's words is that while he dares us to be great he acknowledges that the path to perfection is littered with failures. It's what we learn from these mistakes that will determine our growth. Bach argues against conformity and complacency. He urges us to challenge all that we hold dear to see if our habits are moving us closer to excellence or keeping us stuck in mediocrity.

I'm about to tell you things about middle school teaching that I believe fervently, and I want you to believe them, too. So why do I begin with the suggestion that everything in this book may be wrong? Because as accomplished practitioners, middle school teachers also should be intelligent consumers. We shouldn't take what any writer or educator says without examining it closely. With young adolescents, what works this week might not work next week but might work again in the future. What helps Ms. Smith across the hall might not help Mr. Green next door. What our communities wanted from schools five years ago is not what they want from schools this year. The shifting priorities of our profession demand that we continually seek new ideas but also be savvy when practicing them. In that context, I recommend that you take the pieces from this book that seem most useful to you now and leave the rest for another day. Find what makes you passionate and build on it.

I love being on the front lines of middle-level education. Sometimes I can't believe I'm paid to do my job. Being a middle school teacher is a combination of serving in the Peace Corps, organizing an amoebae circus, competing in the decathlon, and earning an Academy Award. In no other job do you laugh aloud, ignite someone's imagination, bring peace, pose conflict, kiss frogs, quell fears, affirm goodness, stand amazed, and read a crumpled love note that assures the end of the world by 3 o'clock that afternoon. And that's just the end of first period. I wouldn't miss it for anything.

Every day brings the chance to embrace absurdity while achieving substance. One day in class I dressed as Adverb Man, including tights, a cape, and a mask. In a mock rescue of someone learning how to modify adjectives, adverbs, or verbs, I misjudged the height of the classroom ceiling as I leapt from a desk and called, "Up, Up, and modify!" My head broke through the thin drywall and slammed into a water pipe. I fell onto a group of desks in a crumpled mass, while pieces of ceiling tile crashed on top of me. One of my students, standing nearby, brushed the dust away from his face and announced, "Hey, Adverb Man, you modified the ceiling. Wouldn't that make you Adjective Man?" The next day, another student arrived dressed as Pronoun Girl and a third showed up as Antecedent Boy. It was better than Schoolhouse Rock! The best news was that everyone aced the adverb test that week.

The desire to help people make such powerful connections has been with me since childhood. In fifth and sixth grades, I assisted my teachers in making tests, reviewed concepts with my classmates, and conducted reading groups. What a goody-goody! It gets worse. I organized my own after-school club, "Operation Sandbox," a two-hour program for youngsters who lived on my street. I cringe whenever I think about returning four-year-old Mark Thompson to his mother after a session of arts and crafts in my backyard and offering her this commentary: "Mark worked very hard today. He's still having difficulty with his alphabet, however. That's something to work on." I smiled knowingly, as if Mark's mother and I were professional colleagues concerned about his development. I was eleven years old. I'm sure it was hard for Mrs. Thompson to keep from laughing as she thanked me and took Mark inside for a bath. We had used a lot of blue paint in arts and crafts that day.

In high school, my interests turned to medicine. I became a lab assistant in the biology department, and I joined the school medical club. One Friday evening in October, I arrived home from a high school football game and received a telephone call informing me that a man had died that evening. The medical examiner wondered if I would be interested in assisting at the autopsy the next morning because my name was next on the volunteer list. I couldn't believe my good fortune! I told the caller I would be there, then hung up and tried to sleep. The following morning, I was at the examiner's office twenty minutes early, and I enjoyed every minute of the next three hours. We peeled back the dead man's rib cage and sliced samples of every organ. How often do most people get to touch a human spinal column from inside the torso cavity? I did that day. We also found a hole blown through the left ventricle of the heart; leaking blood had congealed around it. Under the medical examiner's tutelage, I became a scientist and a detective. My teenage mind exploded with questions and career goals.

A short time later I began my undergraduate work at Virginia Tech University, majoring in biology and aiming for medical school. During my sophomore year, however, I changed course. First, I fretted that spending up to twelve years preparing for a career would keep me locked away from the real world too long. Second, I encountered the formidable wall of organic chemistry and earned my first D. I reflected on my disappointing performance in chemistry and realized that details were not my strong suit. I loved biology with its systems of relationships, cycles, and evolutions, but I got lost when we began focusing on cytosine and guanine and the way they were arranged in the sixteenth strand of DNA. So I decided to find another way to serve others and stay in science—becoming a teacher. Eventually, I began teaching English, but that's another story.

Once I shifted to education, I never looked back. My professors were wonderful. They encouraged me to advocate for effective learning, even if it meant being a rebel. I remember the time Dr. Terry Graham told the story of a teacher who had been struggling with a challenging student and had tried a new strategy in class. It bombed, and the teacher became distraught.

"I want my own child in that teacher's class," Graham said, shocking our standard sense of good teaching. "She may have failed that day, but she was willing to do the research, take the risks, and try something new until she found what worked with that student. I'd much rather have my child in her hands than in the hands of someone who does the same thing with every student regardless of effect, and when students fail, assumes it's a problem with the student."

In my current teaching practice, I use Graham's example as a yardstick: Am I using what's effective, not just what's comfortable or familiar? Would experienced middle school teachers want their children in my class? If I want to be an excellent middle school teacher, I can't always play it safe. I've got to challenge myself as much as I challenge my students.

Some time after Graham related his story of the risk-taking teacher, I was preparing lessons about the skeletal system during my stint as a student teacher. In the midst of my preparations, Graham invited me to his home. After a few minutes of chitchat, he walked me out to his car, opened the trunk, and revealed a human skeleton. He had heard that I was looking for a way to make the skeletal unit more vivid. I wanted to hug him! When I asked where he had obtained the skeleton, he lowered his voice and turned the question back on me: "Where do you think?" I suggested hospitals and doctors' offices. He nodded and agreed that those were good places, but said that if I really wanted to be a good teacher I had to learn to think beyond the obvious.

"Fraternities, Rick, fraternities," he told me, leaning closer. "That's one of the best places to get a skeleton."

I laughed heartily at the fast one he had pulled on me, but I also grasped the seriousness of his message. At that moment, teaching became a lot more intriguing to me. It seemed less like a job that I hoped to hold in the future and more like an adventure that would challenge me physically, intellectually, and spiritually throughout my career. I realized that if I could dream something, I also had the power to make it real.

About this time, I was tutoring Bob, a blind student, in my computer class. I still remember sitting in the snack bar at Squires Student Center talking to Bob about programming in BASIC and FORTRAN. I bent, twisted, and attached about thirty plastic straws across two tables to set up a three-dimensional flow chart that Bob could feel with his hands. With only limited supplies, I had to communicate a concept. This episode showed me not only how but why teachers must be able to put theory into practice, constantly shifting between philosophy and pragmatism. All students need to find a way into the material, and teachers are their interpreters and guides.

I spent my first year as a full-time teacher working with seventh graders. The year was filled with eccentric behaviors, inanities, and wild misperceptions of the world. But each day I also found humor, brilliance, and grace in my students. In the following years, I attended seminars about Attention Deficit Disorder, learning disabilities, human growth and development, and self-esteem, but nothing spoke directly to my suspicions about the unique nature of the middle-grade child. Then I took some courses in middle-level curriculum as part of a graduate degree in Educational Administration at Virginia Tech. Those courses—and subsequent classroom experiences—confirmed my belief that children between the ages of ten and fourteen do not need either the protected coddling of elementary school or the alienating subject departmentalization of high school. They need a bridge between the two levels.

Young adolescents undergo rapid physical, intellectual, and moral growth. They move from concrete to abstract thinking, from absurdity to rationality, and back again. They deal with tremendous pressures from peers, parents, and society, all the while searching for identity, purpose, security, and acceptance. These shifts produce strong emotions. Acting out, feeling hurt, defining authority by defying it, and alternating between being a child and being an adult all create situations that demand guidance from compassionate adults who have lived through those phases.

"The task of the modern educator is not to cut down jungles, but to irrigate deserts," the writer C. S. Lewis once said.

I recognized early on that good middle school teachers must never forget that they are modeling citizenship every moment of every day. We must decide what kind of world we want twenty years from now, then help create it by demonstrating the right behaviors under the close scrutiny of tomorrow's impressionable leaders.

Good middle school teachers also must strive to be enthusiastic about their work, even if it's the eighth period of the school day. A positive attitude is contagious. Word will spread that manipulating databases is fun, that President Harry Truman's diplomatic talks present compelling drama, that determining whether something is an object or a subject pronoun can be as intriguing as solving a puzzle. Students will catch the spark.

My passion for teaching and learning was ignited by educators who worked with me as a student and as a colleague. Now I hope to start similar fires within others. This book includes much of what I've learned from research, observations, conversations, and experience. I approach my work as a mentor teacher by remembering the words of author, speaker, and education consultant Spencer Rogers: "There's nothing new in here. It's all been said before."

What do I offer then? I'm a conduit. I am a middle school educator halfway through his career. I take the wisdom of my teaching heroes, apply it in my classroom, and tell you how it worked. I throw in some things I discovered on my own as well. Although there are plenty of original ideas in this book, their genesis is in the readings and relationships I've developed during my nearly two decades in the profession. I invite you to take the perspectives presented in this book, put your own spin on them, apply them in your practice, then go to a teaching conference and present them as your own, saying, "Here's an idea I had." After you've used a strategy, it becomes part of your repertoire. This is one of the wonders of middle school teaching—the free exchange of practices that help us all.

Portions of this book originally appeared as columns in National Middle School Association's *Middle Ground* magazine or in *The Crucial Link,* published by the Virginia Middle School Association. Notice the practical tone, compared with more scholarly recitations. I encourage readers to look at these pages and say, "Well, if he can do it, so can I." I'm sure you can; I'll be your loudest cheerleader. There are middle school teachers out there right now who are waiting to hear your wisdom. Take up a pen or a computer keyboard and write your first article for a state or national professional magazine. Whether you're an undergraduate, a current practitioner, or a retired educator, writing about your experiences and insights will focus your thinking and prove cathartic after a long day of adolescent excuses. Consider this your catalyst.

If you read this book from cover to cover, you will find some ideas revisited. Teaching and learning are like that. One reading strategy, for example, can lead to different discussions about subject content, multiple intelligences theory, and assessment. One perspective can relate to many practices. Although each chapter is designed to stand alone, the cross-references had to be made. No aspect of teaching exists in a vacuum.

The first title of this book was *Stepping Off the Curb*. It conveyed the sense of marching from the sidewalk to the street, getting halfway across, and noticing that the traffic light is shifting to a cautionary color. Middle schools can be full of apprehensions, but that's not the whole picture. *Meet Me in the Middle* issues an invitation to observe the fuller ramifications of our work. This book asks pre-service teachers to join the journey of education, working teachers to revitalize their practice, and policymakers to recognize the critical importance of the middle grades. Besides that, I'm having so much fun that I'm going to bust if I don't tell someone about it!

Join me in becoming a middle school ambassador. It requires compassion, mental dexterity, content expertise, and visionary thinking not found in many professions. Feel more alive than you ever thought possible. Young adolescents are on the cutting edge of life, and you get to be their guide. So go ahead, turn the page. Come, meet me in the middle.

Stoking the Fires Within   1

Check out these well-known phrases on posters and coffee mugs in schools: "Wake me up when it's Friday." "School is what we sandwich between weekends." "I hate Mondays." "Homework causes brain damage." They might sound amusing, but they turn a sarcastic smile our way. They perpetuate a degrading stereotype, one of just surviving in our profession.

Fight the bromide that those who can't do, teach. It not only minimizes the skills and intelligence needed in education, it makes teaching seem like a refuge for rejects instead of a higher calling. Middle school teaching is not a cushy job with lots of time off. One of the worst bumper stickers I have seen states that the three best things about teaching are June, July, and August. It's clever, but it promotes the false impression that teachers are mediocre, that we want to do less than our full share. The reality is that most of us pack more into nine months than many people do in an entire year.

Some will argue that these satirical sayings provide a harmless way for teachers to poke fun at themselves. I contend that they present negative perceptions that damage our profession. We can replace these sayings on posters and mugs with ones that express the passion of teaching and the possibilities of learning. How about "What are the three-*squared* best things about middle school teaching? September, October, November, December, January, February, March, April, and May!"

It's a privilege to be in education. Not everyone is called to such a noble cause. We can practice indifference, blame others for the problems we encounter, or take what we find and improve it. A positive attitude can reshape a blob of sand into King Arthur's castle.

I've learned a lot about our profession by sitting next to people in airplanes. Everyone has an opinion about teachers and schools. When I first graduated from college, and people asked what I did for a living, I replied excitedly, "I'm a middle school teacher." After three or four years of listening to cynical colleagues and public outcry, however, I responded almost meekly by saying, "I'm a middle school teacher; don't hit me." Now, after nineteen years of teaching, my skin is thicker, my spirit is more resolute, and my dedication is deeper than ever. Today, when people ask me what I do for a living,

I summon all the forces within and exclaim in the voice of the great Wizard of Oz, "I AM A MIDDLE SCHOOL TEACHER!"

Taking a Look at Ourselves

Close your eyes for a moment. Imagine that you're attending your own funeral. As you hover over the pews, you listen to a family member, a personal friend, a co-worker, and a supervisor talk about you. If you're a teacher, maybe a student will speak as well. What do you want them to say?

Put their comments in the present tense, and you have a personal mission statement. Steven Covey, author of *The Seven Habits of Highly Effective People*, uses this activity to help us figure out the principles by which we want to live our lives. Everything we do should fall within that context.

Another way to clarify what we stand for is to identify our heroes. Who are they? What attributes do we admire? Which of those characteristics do we have, which do we still seek to embody, and how can we achieve them?

William Arthur Ward reminds us, "The mediocre teacher tells. The good teacher explains. The superior teacher demonstrates. The great teacher inspires." Do our actions and attitudes live up to that? We all know people who seem to have retired on the job. Yet every one of us, regardless of our role in the school building, has the capacity to inspire others. All jobs are important and can bring dignity to our profession. Each of us must be worthy of the task.

In his book *Reaching the Peak Performance Zone,* Gerald Kushel states that peak (excellent) performers take total responsibility for their work. They are intrinsically motivated, they share generously, they ask for mentoring when needed, and they continually find reasons to achieve excellence. Less than peak, or standard, performers blame others or conditions for their results. They are extrinsically motivated, stingy in sharing, and are overreactive to authority. Do we conduct ourselves in our jobs so that we merit others' cooperation and involvement? Are we worth listening to? With our children and our futures at stake, we can't afford to be anything less than distinctive. We can admit mistakes, make corrections, and learn from them. We can stop accusing and start assisting. We can clean up after our projects and rewind the videotape for the next person. We can stand up to waste and inefficiency and find room for compassion. In any capacity in our schools we can be a role model for others. It all stems from attitude.

A friend of mine used to run adventure trips for teenagers. I joined him on several outings. Every single morning, no matter how many obstacles the group had encountered the day before, he would call from his sleeping bag, "I feel gooooooood today!" And within minutes he would ask each of us, "How can I help you this morning?" He may or may not have felt as good as he said, but he knew it was important to keep everyone's spirits high and to set an example of approaching life with vigor and enjoyment. It wasn't a sacrifice for him. He kept his eyes on the goal: personal growth for each camper.

You might be lucky enough to work in a school where your supervisor focuses on helping you do your job well. Teachers should do the same for their students. In education, such service moves everyone closer to peak performance.

I've heard this story passed down from several educators over the years:

> Three construction workers were building the outer foundation wall of a new church on a hot and humid summer afternoon. I asked the first one what he was doing. He grimaced and spoke to me through clenched teeth: "I'm chiseling granite; what does it look like I'm doing?" I asked the second worker what he was doing. He turned quickly and growled at me, "I'm working hard for my wages!" I asked the same question of the third worker. He wiped the sweat from his eyes and smiled. "I'm building a monument to God," he said.

This story is a kick in the pants to reexamine our teaching motivation. Some days it feels like chiseling granite or just working for wages, but the goal should be building the monument. Taking up two class periods to show *The Lion King* and making a loose reference to ecosystems while we grade papers is not just a waste of time but an embarrassment to education. On the other hand, creating vividness and interest through carefully chosen video excerpts is a good use of time. When teaching suspense writing, for example, I show two minutes of *Jurassic Park*—the part in which the water-filled glasses begin to shimmer as the *Tyrannosaurus rex* approaches the car. I follow the excerpt with a discussion of how we can create the same suspense with words. Students read the related passage from Michael Crichton's novel of the same name. When I taught history, I used to show a disturbing scene from the movie *Glory,* in which the soldier played by actor Denzel Washington is whipped by officers for leaving camp to find some badly needed shoes. My students and I focused on each of the characters' perspectives on the flogging before we examined the effects of the Civil War on people's sensibilities. If what we're doing in our classrooms doesn't broaden our students' understanding and build connections to the world around them, then we're wasting everyone's time.

Good teachers come prepared to enlighten their students. They design the most effective lessons, not just time fillers. They enjoy themselves. They model making a positive contribution to the world.

Teachers can instruct by what they are more than by what they say. Young adolescents are in a developmental stage in which they can't separate the teacher from his or her attitude—the teacher *is* the attitude. If we want to know our impact on students, we can start by examining our attitudes. Are we modeling the virtues we're teaching?

I let students physically touch me. The power of touch is strong for young adolescents; it builds relationships and trust. Sometimes I think they touch me just to see if I'm real. They miss the earlier coziness they felt with their elementary teachers and their parents. It's not hard for a middle school teacher to stand still and say with body language, "Yes, I'm still here for you and I'm not going to stop believing in your ability to learn." I've had students slap me on the back for a job well done, shake my hand, and put their heads on my shoulders as we critiqued essays together during class. As long as their actions are not too extreme, I accept them because my students need to feel connected to adults in their lives.

I often walk into my classroom wondering what I will learn from students during the day and what they will learn from me. Will my planned activities present the best next step in the learning sequence? Have I presented the content accurately? Have I included a reference that will dull students' thinking or be considered insensitive? Will my students remember the key points after the bus ride home? Have I backed into the chalkboard and left white chalk imprints on my pants?

Eric Jensen says in his book *Super Teaching* that teachers with "high" egos want students to know when they (the students) make a mistake. These teachers need to be right about debates in the classroom. They hope students will like them. They want to be smart, witty, or charming in class, and they put their needs ahead of the needs of their students. They strongly resist change because change ruins the status quo for the strong ego. Teachers with "low" egos, on the other hand, let others shine. Their concern is for the students. They do whatever it takes to help out; pride doesn't get in the way. Such teachers admit mistakes and make it safe for students to admit theirs. They find satisfaction in helping others achieve.

Which kind of teacher do I want for my own children? One with a "low" ego. Which kind of teacher am I? Both, but being aware of my "high" and "low" ego moments can help me change my demeanor in the classroom and vary the strategies I use.

Listening

We can be more effective with our students when we make a sincere effort to listen to them. Every student has something to teach us, but we must be open to receiving it. I'm often guilty of forming my responses before students have finished making their points. I have to really concentrate to bite my tongue and keep my mind open. I try to let the student know that she was heard, either by paraphrasing her comments or asking a clarifying question that shows I was listening: "I understand that you're really upset about doing all the work when Jennifer did very little." Or I might thank the student for sharing: "It took a lot of courage to tell me this. Thanks for trusting me with the information." Or I might honor the importance of the request: "You make some good points. Let's take them one at a time and see what we can do."

Whatever happens, I try not to take the student's words personally. I've had students get terribly upset with me. Recently, a student accosted me in the cafeteria and demanded to know why I had humiliated him in front of the class earlier that day. He was breathing hard and wagging his finger at me in anger. He was on the verge of tears. I was taken aback; he had seemed fine in class.

"You're really upset with me," I said. "Let's find out what's going on."

I led him to the hallway outside the cafeteria. He told me that I had embarrassed him by publicly critiquing his PowerPoint presentation on a science fiction book. He thought I had been unusually cruel. I asked him to share the order of events from the day and describe his feelings at each point.

After he finished, his breathing calmed and his voice returned to a conversational tone. Before responding, I thanked him for confronting me. If he hadn't shared his feelings with me, I told him, I never would have known that I had offended him.

Next, I asked if I had treated him differently from other students. He shook his head, then said that I had told the class that he and his partner had failed to include many required items in their project. I agreed with that, reminding him that he and his partner had not presented the material required for a grade of A, as described on the rubric given to him two weeks prior to his presentation. He acknowledged that he and his partner had disregarded the requirements.

"Did I comment on you as a person?" I asked him. He agreed that I had not.

"Did I comment on your work?"

"Yes," he said.

"So you're upset because I held you accountable for doing good work and you chose not to do it?" I asked.

"It's not just that," he said. "You cut me down in front of everyone a few months ago."

This made me pause. What was he talking about? I apologized immediately if I had unfairly criticized him but assured him that I had not intended to do so. Then I asked him to describe the incident that had humiliated him. He explained that I had approached him in the hall between classes and hollered, "There's the *bad* puppeteer!"

Oh, I thought, suddenly remembering. I recalled the puppet show he had performed in class that day. It was a creative and substantive show, and I had praised him for it in front of his classmates. So when I spied him in the hallway later that day, I playfully called to him in a pirate's snarl, "Aye, there's the *mad* puppeteer!" I remembered that we both had laughed about it. Yet for months he had thought I was ridiculing him, telling everyone within earshot about his poor performance.

In the end, the student and I developed a greater understanding of each other. He realized that I would hold him accountable for meeting high standards. And he discovered that it is usually better to tell someone that their remarks hurt you than to let bad feelings fester and spread. I learned that what I say can have a profound influence on my students, in positive and negative ways, and that I need to weigh my remarks more carefully. Good intentions aren't always received that way, especially on the slippery slope of adolescence.

Speaking clearly and listening well are important skills for children and adults. All of us need practice from time to time. My students and I often practice responding to each other by paraphrasing what we have heard: "So what you're saying is . . ." or "So what the author is saying is . . . ."

Role playing and fishbowl activities are good ways for students to practice listening well. In a fishbowl activity, a group of students engages in an activity such as a discussion or mediation while the rest of the class observes silently. Afterward, the observers share their insights, which helps the class review the critical concepts from the lesson.

Such strategies can help teachers, too. Sometimes we will reach an impasse and find that we cannot continue working together constructively without a formal airing of grievances and a new plan for interacting. Chances are that if one of us is feeling tense, the other person is, too, and both would be better off speaking about it.

One time, when a colleague and I were having trouble communicating, we participated in a formal mediation session. I highly recommend it. Each of us had to repeat what the other was saying until satisfied that our positions were understood. We weren't allowed to take notes or make any comments while the other was speaking. As hard as it was, it was cathartic and enlightening. It taught me that listening well helps clarify messages, diffuses anger, and solves problems. We all want to be heard correctly, but our experiences and prejudices sometimes limit our ability to listen accurately and well.

First-year teachers and seasoned veterans both understand that academic enlightenment is not the only thing we have to be concerned about in middle school classrooms. Our attitudes are critical to building the strong relationships that enable a culture of learning to flourish.

Educational systems are people-centered. Survival in this world requires good people skills. Positive attitudes can change the world—one young adolescent, and one middle school teacher, at a time.

Motivating Young Adolescents | 2

Some days I think I would have it made as a teacher if I could blend my grammar lessons with a surround-sound speaker system that played hot music tracks with vibrating bass lines. As students completed research projects, lasers would shoot through the backlit, mist-filled classroom, forming red graphic organizers that would hover in the air above their heads. One wall of the classroom would slide open, revealing a twenty-five-foot movie screen featuring filmed versions of students' narratives. We'd eat popcorn and pizza, and everyone would earn an A.

Getting young adolescents to pay attention and learn is 80 percent of our battle in middle schools. The rest is pedagogy. However, I believe there are ways to motivate middle school students short of turning our classrooms into multimedia playgrounds. I've heard the testimonials about zero brain growth in this age group, and I don't buy it. Young adolescents are moving through one of the most dynamic stages of development of their lives. As teachers, we might have to bushwhack through the hormonal tendrils on a daily basis, but it's worth the effort to find the gold inside each child.

If you want students to invest in your lessons, you need to be able to answer yes to most of the following questions:

Are you interested in knowing and being with your students?
Have you created a classroom where students feel safe enough to share their emotions?
Are your lessons vivid?
Are you enthusiastic about your subject?
Do you build suspense by giving them something to look forward to?
Do your lessons take into account the varied learning styles of students?
Can all students succeed in your classroom? Nothing motivates like success.
Is the material relevant to your students' lives?
Do your lessons maintain momentum?
Do you clearly communicate instructions and expectations?
Do your students know why they are learning certain concepts and skills?

A room such as my English teacher's that is decorated with miscellaneous objects is not only interesting, but a comfort. When I come into the room, I feel relaxed and prepared to enjoy myself. Being comfortable in a teaching room is important because it is easier to learn.
■ Kara, seventh grade

Are the assessments authentic? Do the students know how they're going to be tested? Do they get regular feedback from you?

Do the students play a role in the teaching and learning? Do they occasionally have choices?

Do your students have proof of your belief in their ability to learn?

If you answer no to any of these questions, your students will probably lose interest and lack motivation for learning. Think back to when you were in middle school—what would have worked for you? The next time you make an assignment, sit at an absent student's desk and complete the task yourself. Look around the room and ask what would make the assignment, the lesson, and the room more inviting.

Express Interest in Knowing and Being with Your Students

Do what it takes to learn about their cultures. Read literature with characters similar to them. Visit them at home. Such visits have never failed to open my eyes.

Satisfy their question, What's in it for me? as you begin each lesson. Demonstrate how content or skills have direct connections to students' lives. Ask a colleague about the relevance of the material if you can't find a connection.

Hand out cards at open house events and ask parents, What is important for me to know about your child? Or ask the students, What is it that you enjoy most about school? What can I do to help you learn?

My sixth-grade teacher, Mr. Stanley, was an amazing teacher. He was such a good teacher because he was extremely fun and energetic. He would almost make learning entertainment. He would be very serious but funny at the same time, and I still don't understand how he pulled it off. Also, another reason why he was such a great teacher was because he would let kids be kids but still have the class under his control. He would be so energetic and fun he would have everyone listening to him without yelling or telling the kids to listen.
■ Stephen, eighth grade

Create an Emotionally Safe Environment

Students will attempt to answer a teacher's questions if they know they won't be ridiculed or considered slow by the teacher or their peers. Dr. Richard Lavoie, an education consultant from Boston, equates this to gambling with poker chips. A parent can build up her child's supply of poker chips with a favorite breakfast, a compliment, or words of encouragement as her child leaves for school in the morning. But one sarcastic comment from an adult at school ("What are you, stupid?" or "Look, you're not going to understand this any-time soon, so just stop trying.") can scatter those poker chips. A student with a limited number of emotional poker chips will hold on to the ones he has, rarely taking chances, to preserve his stake at the end of the day. A compassionate and motivating teacher can add to a child's pile of chips, create classrooms that minimize their loss, and encourage a student with few chips to risk one for the chance to gain more.

There are many ways to boost the confidence levels in our middle school classrooms without getting lost in self-esteem hoopla such as putting up "happy" posters. Be pleasant to students. Call them by their first names. Greet them at the door. Smile often. Catch them doing something well. Crack a few jokes. Ask questions that show your interest. Applaud risk taking. Share excellent homework or test responses with the rest of the class. Allow occasional democratic voting in the class. Refer one child who is an expert on something to another child who needs help, and make sure you rotate the expert's role. Ask students to tutor their peers after school. Give them responsible jobs in the classroom or school. Ask them to serve as hosts for guest lecturers. Point out moments of caring among peers that occur in class. Post news articles about their accomplishments in the room. Make at least one positive phone call or note home for each child per year.

Use Stories

Professional presenters know that audiences perk up and become more attentive when presenters use stories to illustrate their points. Stories provide meaning and analogies that clarify our perceptions. Besides that, stories entertain us. They present a natural tool for middle school teachers, no matter what subject they specialize in.

When teaching geometry, for example, make up a story about the beautiful Area (pronounced Ah-ree-a), who lives in a castle, and her boyfriend, Peri, who walks around the *outer edge* of the grounds, calling her name to the *center* of the grounds. He wants to meet her (Peri meet her, perimeter). In science, turn the energy cycle into a story. In history class, dress up as an army colonel who returns to his plantation after the Civil War and describe how he found his home and his family in ruins.

> Saying hi to kids in the hall, or having a casual conversation with students really makes the teacher seem relaxed. This then lets the students feel that they are in a (somewhat) relaxed environment. For me it is easier to learn when I am with friends or people I can talk to about what we're doing in class. It helps me understand difficult concepts or ideas. When the teacher dresses and talks casually, but is still strict about turning in papers and deadlines, students are more able to learn because they don't feel uncomfortable.
>
> ■ Carrie, seventh grade

> History, it's never come easily to me, and I've never enjoyed it until this year. Mrs. Moritz makes history interesting, yet challenging. I think the reason her teaching piques enthusiasm is because she really knows the material, and gives us exciting assignments such as creating our own plays and songs. Mainly though, it's the way she stands at her podium and can tell us stories from history like she was chatting with a friend about a funny story that happened to her. She uses inflection in her voice, shows enthusiasm, and does not read word by word from a textbook. This catches student interest because it gives it emotion, and we want to learn more.
>
> ■ Corrina, seventh grade

Offer Vivid Lessons

Teachers sometimes need to think unconventionally. While being dramatic or artistic helps in some situations, there are many different ways to be vivid with students. For example, use masking tape design on the floor. This design could be a flow chart for a math algorithm, an outline of the human heart, or a historical time line.

When teaching the order of operations in mathematics class, dress up as Aunt Sally. Stumble a bit and apologize to the class for your clumsiness: "Please Excuse My Dear Aunt Sally" (parentheses, exponents, multiplication, division, addition, subtraction).

When discussing the spelling of the phrase *a lot,* let students lean each way to say the words. Or, better yet, let them get out of their seats, walk to one side of the classroom and say "a," then walk to the other side to say "lot." Place *a* and *lot* on either side of the front chalkboard so they get the message that there should be a space between these two words.

Start a pronoun-antecedent lesson with questions such as, What is it? Did she like the gift you gave her? and Give it to me. Don't identify the antecedents. Ask students why they are so confused by your questions.

Put on scuba gear, soak yourself, and fall from an eyeball before you begin to tell a summary of Isaac Asimov's *Fantastic Voyage.* Melodramatically romance the librarian with Shakespearean sonnets.

I heard about a teacher who comes to class wearing coats and long shirts covered with strips of Velcro. She attaches props and supplies for her presentations to the Velcro spots and pulls off each item as needed. Everything's at her fingertips and visually interesting. And by replacing everything on the Velcro, she's set up for the next class period. Joseph and the Amazing Technicolor Velcroat! I'm thinking of a way to use this.

Express Enthusiasm for Your Subject

We respond emotionally to everything—we receive and react to the tone of a message long before we respond to the content. When we're excited, we hang on every word. If not, we don't hear the information.

Think about your power. Your words and actions have a dramatic impact on your students. When you publicly acknowledge the wisdom of a quiet, shy student, that student's status rises. If you do something embarrassing in class, students will feel comfortable doing the same. By being enthusiastic about the day's topic, you give permission to others to be enthusiastic.

The reverse is true; the surest way to turn students off is to express indifference toward your lesson. Check your body language and verbal intonations to see what signals you're sending. Better yet, ask someone to videotape you in class and help you analyze your performance.

Work with a colleague to build drama and interest into the day. Gayla Moilanen, a former teacher leader in my school district, uses a mock videotape format (see Appendix A). In the midst of her partner's presentation, she pulls out a remote control, presses a button, and calls out, "Pause." The partner freezes while Gayla debriefs, summarizes, or rewinds "the tape" to make sure students understood the important points. Another time their roles might be reversed.

Startle students. Dropping a book or standing on top of a desk works well when done selectively. Play a review game with students. If you win, a student has to run down the hall, yelling, "English is great! English is great!" If you lose, you have to run down the hall, yelling "[Insert a student's name] is great!" Chase tardy students with a six-foot inflatable shark. Walt Grebing, former president of National Middle School Association, used to roll a huge, gold-painted tire down the hallways and into classrooms to honor students and teachers who demonstrated "tireless effort."

Build Suspense

Foreshadow what is to come; pique interest. Drop hints on upcoming class activities. Put a strange, seemingly unrelated object in the middle of the room a day or two before its use. Students marvel when I throw a softball-size glob of clay through the room, especially when it smacks a clean chalkboard. I do this to demonstrate the similarity of sculpting to writing and the frustrations that often follow the creative process. Their eyes are wide, their hearts are racing, and their minds are deeply curious about what will happen next.

The teacher on the 1980s television show *Head of the Class* used to make statements such as, "Tomorrow we find out how a baseball started World War II." I've used this same approach; it gets students thinking beyond the classroom walls.

Meet Learning Needs

With your students, conduct learning inventories to determine such things as proper lighting, sounds, furniture, room layout, and group interactions that individuals prefer. The Dunn and Dunn Learning Style Inventory has been particularly effective with my students. Following is a letter I wrote to a student after I conducted such an inventory with him.

Dear Wes,

Thank you for letting me conduct the Dunn and Dunn Learning Style Inventory with you last week. Your cooperation helped me figure out what you need from a teacher in order to learn. There were four areas I studied about the way you learn. These include physical factors (using your senses and the way the classroom is arranged), psychological factors (what motivates you and how you deal with assignments), perception factors (how you like to get information), and the time of day in which you like to learn. On some of these factors you were very definite. On others, you were somewhere in the middle. In the case of these "middle of the road" results, you are probably still exploring what you think works well for you. You'll decide which ways are better as you move into high school. Let's begin with the learning factors that are very clear.

The kind of place in which you study best is warm and quiet. This means that any music playing in the background may distract you. You like to have one place in which to do all of your schoolwork. You are a very motivated individual, Wes. In fact, if you had your choice, sometimes you would like to work at a faster pace and set your own goals. You seem to create your own internal sense of reward for a job well done. You indicated, however, a need for teachers to be around you when you are learning. Getting good comments from teachers seems to "spark" your efforts and make you want to get involved more.

Wes, it seems easiest for you to do assignments when the directions are clear and definite. You like things to be organized when presented to you or when you work on something. It bothers you if a lot of choices are given in an assignment. You'd rather the teacher said straight out how to do it, and then let you do it. You learn best when studying alone. Learning with friends seems to distract you more than help you. The same could be said for having a variety of learning situations—you seem to know what you like and you stick with it. You really value having the opportunity to explore things creatively on your own.

In looking at your senses, your needs are very clear. You like to hear the information, and you like to participate in the learning. Sitting back looking at a diagram doesn't help you nearly as much as working with your hands, doing some kind of movement during the lesson, or listening and discussing the knowledge. Finally, during the course of the day, your mind is most ready for learning in the afternoon. Morning times are more of a challenge for you and an evening preference is still undecided.

There are several areas in which you are undecided about how they affect you. These are areas to explore this coming school year to see what really works for you: Do you like to have a lot of light or just a little? Are you learning more by sitting in soft furniture such as a pillow or a couch, or in a straight-backed chair? Can you finish things on your own, or do you need someone to remind you? Do you need to eat something every two hours or so, or can you make it between meals? Let me know what you find.

So what does all this mean for a specific subject? Let's choose science. Your teacher could offer the following things to make learning for you easier:

- A quiet, warm room (in fact, wear headphones to tune out distractions if necessary)
- The freedom to move at a faster pace if you desire
- Praise and encouragement
- Opportunities to work individually on assignments
- An atmosphere that doesn't allow you to get off-task when working with others
- Clear instructions and expectations
- Opportunities for you to learn by listening and responding
- An atmosphere that encourages creativity
- Opportunities to get involved in learning, such as working at the chalkboard, moving around the room, participating in discussions, labs, and artwork
- More difficult topics in the afternoon

I hope all this information is helpful to you and your learning. Please remember that these characteristics are neither right nor wrong. They are like fingerprints—they just *are*. These results do not show you are strong in one area and weak in another. That would be a misinterpretation. You are unique and special as you are. You are capable of learning in almost any situation. These factors merely indicate your preferred learning style, not the only way you learn. If you have any questions, please give me a call.

Sincerely,

Mr. Wormeli

You can use other learning style predictors, such as the Myers-Briggs Personality Survey (see Keirsey 1998); Bernice McCarthy's 4-MAT learning styles, which focuses on right and left brain dominance and four styles of learning; and Howard Gardner's theory of multiple intelligences. Chapter 7, Differentiated Instruction, offers a more detailed explanation of the multiple intelligences theory and its applications in the classroom. I mention it here because of its tremendous power to motivate young adolescents. When we teach students in ways that address their learning preferences, we can inspire them to participate and express themselves more fully.

Maintain Momentum

Robert Canady of the University of Virginia recommends a 75:25 ratio of time that students are actively engaged in learning versus being managed by the teacher, as in maintaining discipline, reading announcements, and collecting homework. It's surprising how much time we spend in management tasks compared to direct teaching. Chapter 3, Brain Research, and Chapter 9, Planning for Block Scheduling, both explain why what happens at the beginning and end of our lessons is more important than what happens in the middle.

We shouldn't squander our valuable instruction time with routine management tasks. Immediately upon arrival, students should be engaged in some form of learning or preparation for learning. Take time later, during the middle of the lesson sequence, to deal with administrative tasks. Plan ahead so you will have all your provisions ready. Rearrange the classroom to decrease bottlenecks near supply areas. Anticipate possible interruptions, too. Teach students what to do if you are not available. It's worth the time away from content to teach students to be autonomous with procedures. It will keep the learning flowing.

For openers and throughout the lesson, I often use Sponge activities (see Appendix B) regardless of the length of the class period. These activities soak up loose time with purposeful experiences. They start and maintain momentum. Some suggestions:

- Write three questions on the board related to today's lesson.
- "There are four questions on this quiz. What would be a good fifth question?"
- In-out game. Don't reveal the category. Just start giving clues, such as the parts of a cell: "Mitochondria are in my club, but Mighty Mouse is not. Endoplasmic reticulum is in my club but endoskeletons are not. A nucleus is in my club, but nuclear warfare is not." Students determine the classification, then confirm their hypothesis by offering an example of their own. If it fits the pattern, the teacher invites them to be part of the club. The game continues until everyone is a member.

In my sixth-grade year, our school organized an opera that the fifth and sixth graders participated in. For this opera our school worked closely with people from George Mason University. The opera was written, performed, and run by the students. Every Monday, part of the day was spent working with students from other classes and learning how to perform a job that interested us in the opera. This opera gave students a chance to meet new people. By working constantly with a group of students and teachers you learn cooperation skills. Every job in the opera required tremendous amounts of responsibility and commitment, considering that there were often after-school meetings. By participating in this opera, students had fun while learning skills that would benefit them every day of their lives.

■ Rochelle, seventh grade

Communicate Goals Clearly

Many middle school students lack the motivation to complete assignments because they don't understand what they're supposed to do. If they have a clear picture of the outcome and how they can achieve it, they will be more inclined to try. Students can hit a target when it's well defined and stationary. To communicate your expectations, you can share the objectives of each lesson, relate current content to previously learned material (this shows the big picture of learning), model how to complete an assignment, and provide samples of student work from previous years.

After I teach a lesson, I often portray a novice-level learner and ask the class to guide me as I work through the task from the beginning. If students can break down the instructions for a younger student or someone who hasn't been in class all week, they can demonstrate their understanding of what I taught them.

Use Games

Games are intrinsically motivating. Make sure your games actively engage as many students as possible at all times, and give clear directions with well-defined rules. Allow the students to help solve problems if they arise. Make sure prizes or rewards for winning are quick and fair, with ample opportunity for all students to earn something. (I use summer camp cheers—one for the winning side, one for the losing side.)

If you're stuck for a game idea, consider television game show formats such as *Jeopardy!, The $25,000 Pyramid, Password, Hollywood Squares,* and *To Tell the Truth.* We don't have enough money for buzzers in my school, so we use squeaky pet toys when players want to signal their answers.

"Guess the Fib" is another example of a motivating game. Young adolescents tend to be very focused on what is true and what is false as they make sense of the world. Here's the procedure:

1. Let students try to figure out which figures, data, or information is false. I might provide three facts about a topic; two facts are true and one is false.
2. At the end of a presentation, ask students to guess which of the related facts was false, providing evidence to back up their opinions. You might want to let them research their answers and point out their true/false picks the following day.

Chapter 5, Games in the Classroom, and Appendix C offer more ideas.

Use Authentic Learning and Assessment

Having someone from the outside observe or evaluate classroom projects and presentations can be highly motivating to students. They like having a real audience for their work. For example, I get nearly 100 percent participation from all my students when they know their literary magazines will be displayed in hospitals and doctors' offices throughout our community. Working on a school newspaper motivates students to write, investigate, measure the effects of their words, meet deadlines, and work as a team. Students who design their own Web pages are motivated not so much by the technology as by the fact that others will see their work.

I used to have a teacher who handed back graded schoolwork in the order of A's, B's, C's, etc. Everyone in my class despised her for this. Normally, if your name wasn't called in the first thirty seconds, that usually meant you had a C. It's like breaking someone's privacy by virtually announcing their grade. Currently, however, I have a teacher who instructs students to fold graded papers when they are completed. That way, when she passes them out, not a single wandering eye can see your grade.
■ Kara, seventh grade

Use Frequent and Formative Feedback

We need to provide evaluations along the way, giving students time to correct their mistakes and revise their work while they're still learning. An end-of-unit grade for a six-week project does little to motivate middle school students, especially if the mark comes two weeks after they have completed the project. On the other hand, multiple confirmations of success or redirection can keep them going during the most challenging parts of an assignment. If possible, opt for using mandatory checkpoints on long projects, grading sections as they are completed, and using a variety of assessments.

Don't overuse grades. While grades might serve as initial inspiration, they are extrinsic and elusive symbols, and their effectiveness deteriorates with time. When students focus on mastery of concepts and skills rather than on the number of problems they answered correctly, they are motivated from within; the results last longer. Learning misses the point when it focuses on whether or not a grade is a 93 or an A. Consider the difference between a student who says, "I need to know how the lack of sunlight affects the habitat of the giant squid," and one who says, "I need to get four more problems correct." Middle school students seek meaning, and meaning is motivating.

Use PQRST to Motivate Reading

Use the PQRST method and similar devices for making sense of reading assignments, for instance, from textbooks (see Appendix D). I found the PQRST method during a training session offered by my school district several years ago. The basic format that students should follow when reading a chapter is

P   *Preview* to identify the main parts.
Q   Develop *questions* to which you want to find answers.
R   *Read* the material.
S   *State* (or *summarize*) the central idea or theme.
T   *Test* yourself by answering questions, or *teach* it to a classmate.

Methods such as these are motivating because they give students an identifiable structure to follow for reading and interacting with material. When left to their own devices, many students find textbook chapters overwhelming or boring. They don't know how to get the most from them, and when success is elusive, motivation decreases. The PQRST method provides security and specific directions.

Provide Background

Successful reading has more to do with a student's background and experiences than with his ability to decode or define words. I can read many passages that I can decode but that might confuse me. Understanding material makes us comfortable, and that which is comfortable is motivating.

Before giving students a reading assignment, we can show them pictures or video excerpts to provide context. We can ask them to role play, listen to testimonials, or watch demonstrations. The idea is to create some familiarity about the content before encountering it at a challenging level.

Another strategy is exclusion brainstorming, which I also learned at a school district training session. Here's the process:

1. Write the topic on an overhead projector or chalkboard.
2. Write a series of words, some that pertain to the topic and some that do not.
3. Ask students to draw a line through the excluded words, circle those that relate to the topic, and explain their choices.

This is a motivating activity because it's like solving a puzzle. Middle school students enjoy finding patterns and drawing connections. They will isolate critical attributes and categorize items all day long. Check out the teen magazines and their plethora of lists of what's "in" and what's "out" for further evidence. Middle school students judge everyone according to arbitrary criteria. In their insecurity, they want to know what's considered cool and important. Exclusion brainstorming appeals to that need.

Use Cooperative Learning Strategies

Give everyone an important role in the learning process. A shared burden is easier to accept. Don't forget the old standbys: "jigsaws," in which everyone brings a piece of the information puzzle to teach the members of his or her group, and "think-pair-share," in which everyone first thinks individually, then shares with a partner, and finally reports to the larger group.

Learning works best when the teacher makes it fun. They don't just make you take notes all period. They get you thinking about the concepts, and you get into the material more. The students also remember the material better when they have to take a test on it. One of my teachers made learning fun by getting the students involved. He asked us to come up with an acronym for something. He said we could make it as funny as we could as long as it made sense. Everyone in class enjoyed that. He also let us listen to music while we were working. One time he got so into the *1812 Overture* that he knocked a desk over. It was very funny, especially because my friend was in the desk at the time. He went with it.

■ Geoff, eighth grade

Use the Boom Box

Music goes a long way toward motivating middle school students.

Let Students Use Their Bodies

Young adolescents are very interested in their own anatomy. Ask them to create a life-sized outline of their bodies, then draw and color in "Characteristics of . . ." in the corresponding locations. For example, you may want to focus on the characteristics of a good writer, reader, scientist, mathematician, artist, historian, or citizen. The parts of the body can symbolize the attributes of the character.

I know it's not always easy trying to motivate today's young adolescents. But if we vary our techniques and tap into their instinct for fun, we can arouse even the most apathetic students. They will take risks, complete assignments, and most important, achieve.

Brain Research Applied to Middle School

3

I was in middle school in the mid-1970s when I first saw the film based on Isaac Asimov's *Fantastic Voyage*. Finally, I thought, I'm going to find out what the human mind looks like from the inside. Who cared that it was only Hollywood's interpretation of the brain's inner workings? The movie won an Oscar for special effects; that was good enough for me.

In the movie, scientists shrink a team of surgeons to microscopic proportions and send them in a submarine to the interior cavities of a critically ill patient. I remember watching the submersible *Proteus* maneuver through the brain tissue while little flashes of light moved along blue-gray strands surrounding it. One of the scientists claimed that the lights were thoughts traveling as impulses along neural pathways. How badly I wanted to reach in with some kind of scope and read those thoughts! To see the physical essence of the human mind, or even the metaphorical brain drawer in which the thoughts were held, would be the greatest thing in the world. All I had to go on up to that point was an illustration from an encyclopedia and what I could see of a pig's brains at the local butcher shop. Small, wrinkled, lifeless—those physical representations of the brain didn't seem majestic enough for an organ that has generated complex languages, created a method of space travel, and advanced medicine to such a degree that our life expectancy rates are double what they were one hundred years ago.

As we enter a new millennium, we have keener observations about the workings of the human mind than at any time in history. We have discovered more knowledge in the last ten years, for example, than in all of the centuries up to this point. As teachers, the flurry of brain research might seem overwhelming at times, but understanding it can help us improve our practice and develop new insights about adolescent learners.

Memory is the big issue for many teachers. Will students remember what they've learned in our classes? How can we get them to complete their homework, let alone recall President Hoover's dealings with big business during the Depression? It turns out that memory is a very coherent process, and it's an easy tool to use in our classrooms.

All information enters the brain through the five senses of sight, sound, smell, taste, and touch, and we store these memories in pieces. One brain researcher, David Sousa, has a unique way of explaining this. Everything we associate with a slice of lemon meringue pie, for example, can be found in different sections of the brain. The lemon smell will be in one place, the image of the pie in another, the delicious taste in another, and the memory of the restaurant where we last ate some pie in still another. All these memories are activated at the same time when triggered by one of the senses. The important thing to know about this process is that it provides many different opportunities for people to access information and create meaning for what they learn.

Think of it this way: When we make the right kind of connections for students, we can help the content catch a ride on one of the senses as the thoughts enter their brains. In the process, we can increase the likelihood that students will remember what they heard or saw or touched. It sounds fanciful, but it's true. Much of what we remember for the long term comes not just from the initial instruction but from interacting with new information. If we want to be effective in middle schools, we need to provide structure and opportunity for students to apply and reflect on their expanding pool of knowledge. For example, when we let students physically manipulate mixed number divisions in a unit on fractions or listen to a tape recording of a conversation in Spanish to reinforce vocabulary words, we give them the means to retrieve new concepts later with far more accuracy than traditional instructional methods such as lecturing allow.

Without some kind of application or reflection, new ideas shoot right to our limited short-term memory channels. Short-term memory holds data for about thirty seconds, long enough to remember a phone number while you dial it. Working memory is for temporary storage and processing, and lasts for twenty to thirty minutes. According to researchers, young adolescents can function with up to nine items in working memory, retaining these concepts for up to twenty minutes, depending on the interaction with the material. Long-term memory is where they keep information for recall days, even weeks, later.

Brain researchers have found that memories remain remarkably intact over time, but our access to those memories gets cluttered with neural debris. Every time we think of a specific fact stored in our memory, the neural pathway to that fact is reconnected, as if we're learning it for the first time. The more we access the fact, the more solid the route becomes. But if we don't access information for a while, other pathways grow through it, limiting the ability of the electrochemical impulse to reach the storage site. It's like getting lost in a large city because of increasingly complex traffic patterns.

In our classrooms, we can help students create more solid routes to memories by letting them ponder information as long as possible. Usually, whenever we call on one person to answer a question, the rest of the class tends to relax, and students no longer build those neural pathways. To prevent this, I often conduct a triad response:

1. I call on Casey to answer a question. He responds.
2. I call on his classmate, Kyle, and ask if he agrees or disagrees with Casey's comments. Kyle can add, argue, or clarify points with Casey. The second student must support or refute the point with evidence.
3. I ask a third student, Anna, to evaluate Kyle's comments and add her own opinions.
4. Casey gets the last word. He can revise his earlier comments, agreeing or disagreeing with his classmates.
5. If appropriate, I offer my response as teacher.

Because students never know whether a classmate will ask them to support, refute, or clarify their comments, they must keep their neural pathways open to the topic until the end of the discussion.

We can further extend processing along the neural pathways by increasing wait times. Research shows that the quality, complexity, length, and frequency of students' responses in the classroom increase in an atmosphere of expectation and patience. In each interaction, there are several possible points of waiting:

- The time between announcing a question and asking it
- The time between asking a question and calling on someone to answer it
- The time between calling on someone and requiring the answer
- The time between a student's answer to a question and the teacher's response to the question

Do we extend all of these wait times with each question? Not if we want to finish the lesson this decade. However, we should try to provide some extended wait time every day. It will improve students' responses and teach them the habit of thinking before speaking.

Recent research suggests that the brain continues to grow through puberty. During these years, the brain is hard-wired for tasks. To build on that framework, adolescents need engaging and relevant learning experiences and typically must repeat concepts and skills until the ideas become permanent additions to the basic structure. This brings up the idea of brain elasticity, which suggests that the brain changes physiologically as a result of experience. The more we learn, the more the brain adapts to receive the learning. In other words, the more we learn, the more we *can* learn.

Pat Wolfe and Ron Brandt, former editors of *Educational Leadership*, discussed this in a 1998 theme issue of the journal, "How the Brain Learns." I've found this theory in almost all the brain research books from the last five

A good way to learn things is to talk about it. That is why I like intelligent arguments about the certain topic you are learning about. In the argument you hear others' opinions, learn about the topic, and you learn that just because someone else says something you don't agree with doesn't mean they're wrong. It teaches you that your opinion/reason is much stronger if you back it up with reasons and/or examples.

■ Kaitlin, seventh grade

years as well. On a recent television news show, I watched as a medical scope showed real neurons growing and multiplying, branching off in different directions over time as the people learned new information. In another video documentary, different areas of the brain lit up as people solved problems together and interacted. In each instance, there was a sharp ebb and flow of neural energy that invigorated portions of the brain when it was thinking and a noticeable lack of inertia when the brain was not stimulated. If a pathway wasn't used for a while, it shrank and other pathways grew through it, thereby blocking impulses that might have wanted to connect with something at the end of the original pathway.

Wolfe and Brandt also tell us that the brain is innately social and requires interaction to remain elastic. In low-stimulus environments, a person's ability to think is diminished or never develops. In interaction-rich environments, thinking ability and memory increase. If we want young adolescents to keep learning, we have to keep those neural pathways limber through interpersonal exercises. I *knew* those peer critiques, debates, and collaborative projects were doing something positive all those years. I just couldn't identify it. Now I can. The brain needs these social experiences to mature properly.

The questions we use in class discussions can give students different ways to communicate with each other and commit new concepts to memory. Through engaging and challenging inquiries, they learn to keep their neural pathways open and put new and difficult concepts into long-term storage. To help them think through ideas and connect them to previous experiences, try some of these open-ended questions:

Why? Why not?
What are the important characteristics?
What will happen next?
How is it similar to . . . ?
How does it differ from . . . ?
Justify your opinion.
Provide more than one way to solve it.
Think of all the ways to use a . . . .
Under what conditions would this not work?

Chunking

Researchers say the ability to retrieve information immediately from long-term storage is related not to our intelligence but to the way we originally stored the ideas. Students who struggle to remember details may not have stored them in an efficient manner, and consequently they cannot find them as fast as the next person.

Chunking is a good way to help students preserve information. It's a simple idea with almost endless potential. Chunking occurs when our minds perceive discrete details as one item. For example, when we think about Albuquerque, we might recall its rich cultural plazas, the Sandia Mountains to the east, or the wonderful food for which the city is famous. Its name is composed of eleven letters. In one chunk, when we store the name in our minds, all those images and letters are stored with it (Sousa 1995).

Theoretically, then, we could store almost limitless amounts of information if we could connect all the pieces to meaningful chunks. Think of everything associated with the word *family* and you get an idea of the potential advantages of using this strategy. We can chunk things according to relationships, similarities, differences, functions, and classifications, among others.

Be careful, though. Many veteran educators have discovered that teaching two similar concepts at the same time confuses students and thwarts brain processing. By teaching similar concepts weeks apart, however, we can make sure that one concept moves to long-term memory before adding the second, thus reducing the confusion. If that's not possible or appropriate, we can teach the differences between the concepts first, then the similarities.

Practice is critical to learning for the long term. Many brain researchers call this phase the rehearsal period. Practice causes us to store information permanently, even if it is inaccurate. As middle school teachers, we need to check students' understanding frequently to make sure they are rehearsing only correct concepts. This might mean starting with structured practice at first, then letting students rehearse independently as their accuracy improves.

One type of practice that should not be construed as aiding long-term recall is parroting. Students who can recite something immediately after hearing it in one of our lectures are not demonstrating mastery of the material or original thoughts. They're parroting, which by itself will not add the concept to their permanent brain storage.

Emotions

Angry? Curious? Proud? Excited? Calm? Passionate? Emotions are powerful allies in middle school learning. Students respond well to emotional cues and retain information as a result. It turns out that brain research supports this theory. Teachers who turn up the emotional context of their lessons help students achieve more.

Let me give you an example. Not long ago, I took a risk with my students by staging an act of plagiarism in the classroom. I did this for several reasons.

First, cheating is a concept that adolescents tend to think about only in the abstract. They don't always know when they have crossed the line. If they have worked in cooperative learning groups before, where teachers encourage them to share ideas and resources for the group's benefit, they might not see anything wrong with copying another's work when they are completing projects independently in school. We can help them make clear distinctions by explaining the goals of each assignment, the responsibility of each person involved, and the acceptable methods of using available resources.

Second, the social stigmas attached to lying and cheating are less severe than they once were. Children today regularly hear about people who exaggerated their accomplishments, committed perjury, and twisted the truth with few repercussions. Small wonder that the *2000 Report Card: The Ethics of American Youth,* published by the Josephson Institute of Ethics, found that 70 percent of the 8,600 students surveyed said they had cheated on a test at least once in the past year, and nearly 80 percent said they had lied to a teacher. In a 1998 survey conducted for *Who's Who Among American High School Students,* eight out of ten top students admitted cheating on an exam, up ten points from fifteen years ago, and only 5 percent of the cheaters said they got caught. In my student advisory classes, I always include several sessions on cheating. When I think the atmosphere has become relaxed and trustful, I informally survey my students to find out who has cheated within the past month. Almost every hand goes up in the room, including those belonging to students I consider the most innocent and ethical among the group. In our discussions, they say they didn't consider copying someone else's homework or giving someone the answers to a test as cheating. I remember conducting a similar survey with my students ten years ago, when no more than half the hands in the room went up in response to my question. All of which is to say that as middle-level teachers in the new millennium, we have a great deal of work to do in helping students become honorable and ethical adults.

Third, ownership of property stands on an increasingly shaky foundation. Witness the rise of song-hijacking site Napster and other businesses that thrive on skirting copyright laws, the proliferation of Web sites offering ready-made term papers, and the greater ease of cutting and pasting information from the Internet into a report for school. Add to that the general lack of media literacy among students—if it's printed, it must be true—and you have the ingredients for a potent counterfeiting cocktail.

Finally, middle school students have finely tuned antennae for real or perceived injustices, which often cause them to cast about for blame. Helping them to accept responsibility for their own actions while directing their acute sense of outrage toward important social problems is among the best guidance teachers can provide. That's why I believe it's more critical than ever that we connect students to the feelings that cheating and plagiarism can evoke, not just in the person whose work was stolen but also in the person caught "borrowing" it. Watching a respected person's reputation become tarnished through an act the students might have considered benign can build a powerful bridge between emotion and intellect in students' brains.

To make this point, I pretended to share part of this chapter with my students on the pretext of seeking their critiques. I actually read a published article on teaching that someone else had written, hiding it in a notebook that I held in front of me like a script. A parent "plant" was in the room for the class period, pretending to observe the lesson. I often invite parents to drop by, so the students didn't take much notice of her.

As I started reading the passage, reminding my students that the words were my own, the parent became visibly uncomfortable. Finally, she interrupted me. She claimed that she had read in another book the exact ideas that I had passed off as my own. I assured her that she must be confused and resumed reading. A few minutes later, she interrupted me again, this time angrily. She said she was sure that I had lifted the material from another source. At this point, I blushed and appeared anxious. The parent's irritation increased until I finally admitted that I had borrowed the material from other authors.

Then she let me have it. Standing and gesturing dramatically, she said that I was a terrible role model for my students and that I had violated their trust in me. My actions constituted a breach of professional ethics, she said, and would have to be reported to the principal.

Throughout this exchange, I countered with many of the excuses students often make when they are caught plagiarizing: I had used only a small part, the rest of the chapter was original; what does it matter that those few lines are not my own if nobody suffers from it; I've never done something like this before, I won't do it again, so what's the harm?

My students' jaws fell open in disbelief. They were uncomfortable watching me become ensnared by a lie and having to listen to someone damage my reputation. At the height of the emotional tension between the parent and me, I paused and asked the students, "Have you had enough?" All thirty heads cocked to one side and mouthed, "What?"

With a smile and a thank-you to my parent assistant, I asked my students if they would like to hear five ways to avoid plagiarizing material. Then I went to the chalkboard. Their notebooks flew open and their pens raced across the page to jot down everything I said for the rest of the class. I taught them how to cite sources, how to ethically paraphrase another's words, and how much "borrowing" was considered permissible. We discussed the legal ramifications of plagiarism, and later we

> When my teacher got "caught" plagiarizing by my mom, I know I'll never forget it. The sensations were simply too real. . . . Although my teacher is extremely moral, it was frightening how close to home it struck. The moment when my teacher admitted it, the room fell silent. It was awful; all my life teachers have preached about plagiarism and it never really sunk in, but when you actually experience it, it's a whole different story.
>
> ■ Laura, seventh grade

> My English teacher's lesson on plagiarism was the most memorable lesson I'll have in his class all year. I'll never forget that tension we felt in the classroom.
>
> ■ Pam, seventh grade

applauded the acting talent of our parent assistant. It was an emotional lesson that I feel certain had resonated with them.

Water, Water Everywhere

It turns out that water is one of the great brain foods. Research shows significant increases in conductivity along the myelin sheath that surrounds the neuron when people drink water. Put another way, the more hydrated the neuron is, the faster and stronger the electrochemical pulses will be.

Water is suddenly a teacher's new best friend. I'm getting a water cooler or something similar for the room this year. It will increase student thinking (and my own!) and reduce the need for students to leave the room when they get thirsty (well, okay, it might increase the need for bathroom breaks, but I'll deal with that later). As for the wet mess underneath the water cooler, I'll place a mat and a bucket there. Any inconvenience will be worth it if it improves my students' ability to harness the power of their intellects.

Drinking water doesn't benefit just students. During lengthy paper-grading sessions after school, I used to drink two cans of caffeinated cola to stay awake. I discovered that caffeine acts as a diuretic that dries you out and makes you feel tired after the initial stimulation. Last year, I switched to drinking bottled water throughout the day. The result? No more waking up with the imprint of a student's essay on my cheek or forehead. I'm not sleepy anymore. My written comments to students seem more cogent, too. This might not be a scientific discovery, but it's enough proof of water's benefits for this paperwork-saturated teacher.

Additional Brain Techniques

When I show my students how to write persuasive essays, I tell them that research and anecdotal experience prove that the reader remembers most what is presented first in an essay, remembers second best what is presented last, and remembers least well what comes in the middle. That pattern applies to instruction as well. Unfortunately, most middle school classes begin with clerical matters—attendance, announcements, and homework—and the substance of our lessons often doesn't start until about fifteen minutes into the period. In such an atmosphere, students will be more likely to remember who was absent that day than recall the origins of Walt Whitman's poem "Oh Captain, My Captain" or the best way to determine compound interest on a loan.

We can change this classroom culture by presenting the lesson's most important points, the big truths, within the first five to ten minutes of each period. We can explain how we discovered those truths later. The important thing is to expose students to the essential and enduring knowledge when they are most likely to remember it—at the beginning. And don't forget to provide summarization and reflection activities at the end so students will take the learning with them.

Another successful technique that finds support in brain research is using metaphors and analogies. Such comparisons illuminate concepts by forcing students to think about the material long after they first heard it. There's one phonics program I know of that teaches children about "peanut butter and jelly sandwich" words; the consonants are the bread, and the vowels are the peanut butter and jelly between the slices of bread. For example, in *boat* the *b* and the *t* are the bread, the *o* is peanut butter, and the *a* is the jelly. In my history class one year, I asked students to draw an outline of the human body on paper and make analogies between the role of business in Depression-era politics and different parts of the human body. One group of students connected Boss Tweed's complex and often shady dealings in Chicago with the human heart. At first, I was confused by this link because of the heart's association with spirit and pluck. The students explained it beautifully, however. Boss Tweed was a powerful figure in Chicago politics, responsible for both good and bad events in the city, just as the human heart can be a force for positive and negative emotions. The students made a strong analogy that involved abstract thinking through an exercise that proved far more stimulating to their brains than memorizing a list of names and dates from early twentieth-century U.S. history.

Finally, don't forget Benjamin Bloom's taxonomy of higher-order thinking skills, an ascending scale of knowledge that builds from basic recall to the full evaluation of a concept or skill. Following is a brief overview of the taxonomy and some suggested applications. There are many books (e.g., Bloom 2000) and Web sites that describe the taxonomy and demonstrate its applications.

> It is far easier to remember an unusual or exciting event than it is to remember a list of facts. So how do you get students to remember what they've been taught? Good teachers get around this problem by associating facts with an interesting event.
>
> ■ Matt, seventh grade

Knowledge. Recalling basic facts. Students are asked to describe what they remember about a topic.
> What was the setting of the story?
> What are the basic steps in the Kreb's cycle?
> What are the main exports of Chile?
> What is the formula for determining the volume of a cylinder?
> Name the first three amendments to the Constitution.

Comprehension. Students are asked to demonstrate their understanding.
> Translate the passage from French to English.
> What's the difference between osmosis and diffusion?

Give a clear example of each system: socialism, communism, capitalism, tyranny, democracy, republic.

Classify the items according to their origin.

Explain how any whole number with an exponent of zero is equal to 1.

Summarize the contract.

Which part/word doesn't fit?

Why did the material retard the flames?

Which comments support the President's position?

Application. Students are asked to use their knowledge and skills in a different situation.

Predict what would happen if we changed the temperature in the terrarium.

Use the formulas for area to determine the surface area of the object.

Given what we learned about the factory labor atrocities in the early 1900s, create a proposal for a new business law in Chicago that protects the rights of workers aged ten to fourteen.

Explain how the music changed the tone of the film.

Offer resolutions to the conflict.

Analysis. Students are asked to break down topics into various components, analyze them, and see how they fit together.

Identify the mistake the student made as he solved the math problem.

In the news article, which comments seem politically motivated?

Determine which variables will affect the experiment's outcome.

How did the writer arrive at her conclusion?

Defend the character's decision to sell the guitar.

Justify your answer.

What was the relationship between big business and politics during this time?

What's the logical fallacy in his argument?

Synthesis. Students are asked to bring together seemingly contradictory aspects or topics to form something new.

Add Harry Potter to the conflict in the novel. How would his presence change the outcome?

Write a song that teaches students the differences between subjective and objective personal pronouns.

Create and present a television commercial that persuades viewers of the value of good personal hygiene, using the persuasive techniques we discussed in class.

Propose an alternative plan of action.

Create a cartoon that depicts two choices.

Write a constitution for your new underwater city that reflects the politics of ancient Rome.

Design a better inventory system.

Evaluation. This is the most complex level because it requires students to utilize all the other levels in addition to their own opinions. Students are asked to judge the importance of something, given specific criteria.

Which persuasive essay is most convincing? Why?

According to the standards set forth in the treaty, is the country in compliance? Explain.

Can you find inconsistencies in their arguments? Do the inconsistencies detract from the message? How?

Judge the value of the character's contributions.

Which decision is more ethical?

Which algorithm is the most efficient? Why?

Critique the performance.

Discussions of Bloom's taxonomy are so commonplace these days that people have become a bit indifferent to its potential. That's unfortunate because it's a valuable hierarchy to keep in mind for developing students' thinking skills. If we truly want to extend processing time and maximize meaning for students, we need to strategically use the varying levels of the taxonomy. There's a time and a place for knowledge, comprehension, application, analysis, synthesis, and evaluation experiences in every middle school classroom.

Teaching Young Adolescents to Reason

"Students need a basic core of knowledge, a general literacy about things, so they can be prepared to make decisions," Jane Doe argues.

John Roe, her teaching colleague, doesn't agree: "In our fast-paced information age, 'facts' become obsolete in three years. There's no way we can teach them everything. We have to teach them how to learn for themselves, how to look things up."

"Not so," Jane counters. "You have to start with that basic core of knowledge, and it should be standardized for the whole state. That way we build a minimum competency for our citizens and their decisions."

With "standards of learning," such as we have in Virginia, and high-stakes accountability tests, many middle school teachers are wondering how best to spend their instructional time. Don't get caught up in the cross fire of extremist thinking. All students need a basic core of knowledge *and* a solid set of reasoning strategies to find additional information that they will need over time. They need both basic skills and research capabilities. Neither is sufficient without the other. How do we ensure that they learn both? It takes vigilance and a great deal of reflection.

First, some context. From 4 B.C.E. to 1900, human knowledge doubled. From 1900 to 1950, human knowledge doubled again. It took only a decade, from 1950 to 1960, for knowledge to increase at the same rate, and only five years more to double again. From 1965 to 1985, human knowledge doubled every three years, and through the mid-1990s the escalation rate was every eighteen months.

These statistics come from *Ideas That Really Work!* by Cheryl Thurston, and I've encountered them at teacher conferences and in education periodicals. If we accept those facts about the growth of knowledge, we wonder how we can possibly keep up with our own learning, let alone guide hundreds of students to acquire theirs. Either we dissolve into a heap of quivering jelly, or we tackle the job with resolve and give it our best teaching. There's no time to spare.

Logical Fallacies

To start, we can teach students to think critically. Our students will encounter many false beliefs as they make their way in the world. Caveat emptor ("let the buyer beware") is only one of the important practical lessons they must understand.

Here's one idea that can help. Get a class set of the *National Enquirer* or a similar sensationalist tabloid newspaper. Try to find a publication that routinely makes scientifically, historically, and mathematically wild claims. After teaching logical fallacies to your students, let them rip up the reasoning in the publication. This would go a long way toward relieving us of *X-Files* paranoia and fantasies like *Buffy, the Vampire Slayer*.

Jim Norton, on his Web site *Practical Skepticism*, identifies some common fallacies. Other good sources are Carl Sagan's *The Demon-Haunted World: Science as a Candle in the Dark,* James Randi's *Flim-Flam!,* and Michael Shermer's *Why People Believe Weird Things.*

Here are some logical fallacies to discuss with middle school students. They are adapted from Jim Norton's *Practical Skepticism* Web site, and I thank him for giving me permission to include them in the book.

Ad Hominem *(Argument to the Man)*

You attack the person instead of attacking his argument. For example, "Von Daniken's books about ancient astronauts are worthless because he is a convicted forger and embezzler." (Von Daniken might be a crook, but that doesn't necessarily mean his books are worthless.) Or you attack the speaker's sincerity: "How can you argue for vegetarianism when you wear leather shoes?"

Straw Man *(Fallacy of Extension)*

You attack an exaggerated or caricatured version of your opponent's position. For example, you claim that evolution means a dog's giving birth to a cat.

Another example: "Senator Jones says that we should not fund the attack submarine program. I disagree entirely. I can't understand why he wants to leave us defenseless like that."

Argument from Adverse Consequences

You claim that an opponent must be wrong, because if he is right, then bad things will ensue. For example, the defendant in a murder trial must be found guilty, because otherwise husbands will be encouraged to murder their wives. Wishful thinking also falls in this category: "My home in Florida is six inches above sea level. Therefore, I am certain that global warming will not make the oceans rise by one foot."

Special Pleading (Stacking the Deck)

You selectively use arguments that support your position but ignore or deny the arguments against it. "The Ford Pinto was a great car because it got superior gas mileage and fit easily into most people's garages." Well, okay, but let's not forget the problem with the fuel tank exploding.

The Excluded Middle (False Dichotomy, Faulty Dilemma)

You assert or assume that there are only two alternatives when in fact there are more. For example, atheism is the only alternative to fundamentalism; being a traitor is the only alternative to being a vocal patriot.

Burden of Proof

You claim that whatever has not yet been proven false must be true (or vice versa). Essentially, you claim that you should win by default if your opponent can't make a strong enough case in defense. There are two problems here. First, you claim priority: Why should you be the one who wins by default? Second, you are impatient with ambiguity and want a final answer right away. Think of it this way: "Absence of evidence is not evidence of absence."

Poisoning the Wells

You discredit the sources used by your opponent. For example, "The report was prepared by a liberal think tank. We can't trust the statistics." Political opportunists of all kinds often make this argument. If the research or methodology is unsound, fine, show us. But a group's political leanings should not automatically disqualify the work it produces.

Begging the Question (Assuming the Answer, Tautology)

You reason in a circle. You include the thing you're trying to prove as one of your assumptions. For example, "We must have a death penalty to discourage violent crime." Wishing that something would lead to a result is no substitute for proving that it does.

Argument from False Authority

Remember the television commercial that started with, "I'm not a doctor, but I play one on TV"? Viewers wonder what they are supposed to conclude from that statement. Should we trust an actor's medical advice because he portrays a physician? No more than we should have listened to the Nobel Prize–winning physicist who claimed years ago that black people were biologically inferior to white people. Win a Nobel Prize for biology and we might pay attention, but your skill with atoms and particles doesn't qualify you to make claims about biological destiny.

Appeal to Authority

"Albert Einstein was extremely impressed with this theory." But a statement made by someone long ago could be out-of-date, or perhaps Einstein was just being polite, or perhaps he made his statement in some specific context. A variation of this fallacy is to appeal to unnamed authorities. You might hear phrases such as "scientists say" or "they say." It is possible that if you challenge the speaker, she will be able to clarify just who "they" are. However, it is also possible that she cannot.

Bad Analogy

You claim that two situations are highly similar when they aren't. For example, "The solar system reminds me of an atom, with planets orbiting the sun like electrons orbit the nucleus. We know that electrons can jump from orbit to orbit, so we must look to ancient records for sightings of planets jumping from orbit to orbit also." Um, is this speaker related to that Nobel Prize–winning physicist?

False Cause

You assume that because two things happened, the first one caused the second one. For example, "Before women got the vote, there were no nuclear weapons." Or, "Every time my brother Bill accompanies me to Fenway Park, the Red Sox lose." Sequence is not causation. Don't confuse correlation and causation.

Appeal to Widespread Belief (Bandwagon Argument, Peer Pressure)

You claim, as evidence for an idea, that many people believe something, or used to believe it. In the 1800s many people believed that bloodletting cured all kinds of illnesses. Clearly, the popularity of an idea is no guarantee that it's true.

Fallacy of Composition

You assume that the whole has the same simplicity as its parts: Atoms are colorless. Cats are made of atoms, so cats are colorless.

Slippery Slope Fallacy

There is an old saying that if you allow a camel to poke his nose into the tent, soon the whole camel will follow. The fallacy here is the assumption that something must be wrong because of its proximity to something that is wrong or could become wrong. For example, "If we legalize marijuana, then more people will try heroin."

Argument by Half-Truth (Suppressed Evidence)

This is hard to detect. You have to ask questions. A book on the Bermuda Triangle might tell us that the yacht *Connemara IV* was found drifting without its crew, southeast of Bermuda, on September 26, 1955. But the book might not mention that the yacht had been directly in the path of Hurricane Iona, with its 180 mph winds and 40-foot waves.

Argument by Selective Observation

The enumeration of favorable circumstances, or as the philosopher Francis Bacon described it, counting the hits and forgetting the misses. For example, a state boasts about the U.S. presidents it has produced but is silent about its serial killers.

Non Sequitur

Something that doesn't follow. For example, "Tens of thousands of Americans have seen lights in the night sky that they could not identify. The existence of life on other planets is fast becoming certainty!"

Euphemism

You use pleasing words to make a situation sound better or more emotionally palatable. "The lab rat wasn't killed, it was sacrificed." "The Holocaust wasn't genocide, it was ethnic cleansing."

Weasel Wording

You use word changes to claim a new or different concept when what you're really doing is trying to soften an old concept. For example, an American president may not legally conduct a war without a declaration of Congress. To get around that, various presidents have conducted "police actions," "armed incursions," and "protective reaction strikes." Orwell's classic *1984* has some particularly good examples of this logical fallacy.

Argument by Fast Talking

If you move from one idea to the next quickly enough, your audience won't have time to think about what you're saying so as to challenge your assumptions and claims.

Least Plausible Hypothesis

You ignore the most reasonable explanations, making the desired explanation the only possible one. For example, "I left a saucer of milk outside overnight. In the morning, the milk was gone. Clearly, my yard was visited by fairies."

Students love detecting logical fallacies in daily newspapers, television news shows, and infomercials. After they practice these reasoning skills, they will start examining other arguments in their classroom interactions and writings.

Suspicious by Nature

We need to teach students to be intelligent consumers of information and to understand voice and perspective. Every author is trying to manipulate the reader to feel particular emotions. Every teacher must make his subject seem worthy of studying. Every piece of music is written to evoke a response in the listener. In these cases, we suspend autonomy, submitting ourselves to manipulation because what is offered is considered healthful for us. Sometimes, however, we are not aware of the manipulation and its potential for harm. Advertising, peer pressure, and some social doctrines fall into this range at times. Being aware of both positive and negative manipulations serves students well and helps them learn how to run internal monologues: "Where is the author taking me in the next chapter?" "Why would the teacher say that?" "Where's the evidence?" "How does this fit with what we learned before?" "Is this useful to me?" "Am I safe with this person/topic/situation?"

> Don't think your students can't think for themselves. You never know if you're doing something wrong with your teaching skills unless you listen as much as you teach.
> ■ Ankur, eighth grade

Here's a useful exercise to help students become more aware of possible slant and bias in the media. Distribute copies of three different newspapers' stories on the same current event, and ask them to look for differences among the stories. What information was included in each story and what information is unique to each story? What information is emphasized in each story, by location in the column or by space allotted to it? Was any important information left out, and if so, how would it change the story's emphasis? What seemed to be each reporter's angle on the story? How did she hook readers and frame the story? Was the story presented in an evenhanded and fair way? Explain your answers. Examine the word choices: Were any words particularly effective, destructive, vivid, biased? What do you think the reporter wanted readers to take away from each story? Was she successful? How do you know? How did the reporter's personal opinion of the event affect the story? You also can use this exercise effectively with magazines and clips from television news shows.

More Reasoning Techniques

Middle school students can learn to reason deductively (if the premise is true, then so is the conclusion) and inductively (the premise gives some evidence for accepting the validity of the conclusion). We can teach them to examine arguments and claims in every subject.

One idea to pose conflict and enrich the learning is asking students to argue for and against something relevant to their lives. For example, they can argue for middle schools as they are currently structured, against the use of calculators in math class, for environmental protections in local habitats, or against children's receiving allowances from their parents. By examining both sides of an argument, particularly with topics or situations they might be inclined to take for granted, students can learn how to make better decisions.

To further develop their cognitive skills, try a few lateral-thinking puzzles with students. Lateral-thinking puzzles do not at first appear to have a successful solution, but creativity illuminates a simple answer. You can examine one puzzle per day or one per week, or post some puzzles on your classroom

Web site. No matter which subject you teach, you will help your students exercise their brains with these activities. Here are some examples:*

1. Henrietta entered a museum and toured a new coin collection. She passed by the display cases, viewing coins from around the world, including a very rare one dated 64 B.C. When she was finished, she went to the information desk and asked to see the museum director. When the director arrived, Henrietta informed her that the coin collection was a fake. It turns out she was right. How did she know?
2. What letter comes next in this sequence: J, M, M, J, S, N?
3. Place two equal-sized cups about six inches apart on a flat surface. Lay a piece of notebook paper across them. Find a way to use the paper to support a third cup placed in the space above and between the bottom two cups without the paper sagging under the weight of the cup on top.

One final idea to keep students' minds in high gear: Buy the game Mindtrap, and use it daily. The game includes cards with thoughtful puzzles, such as the lateral-thinking puzzles, and logic problems. (You're in a house that has a southern exposure on all four sides. A bear walks by the front window. What color is it? *Answer:* white. It's a polar bear because the only place a house could have a southern exposure on all four sides is the North Pole.)

Laminate the cards, if you like. Put small stacks of the cards in the centers of your desk groupings or tables. Throughout each class period, as students finish work early, let them try to solve the puzzles on the cards. I know this sounds distracting, but for some students it's not. They won't pay attention to every detail of our lessons anyway. Let's be honest: our minds wander when others are talking, and so do theirs. If I orchestrate that wandering so students will contemplate logic puzzles instead of creating distractions, then learning will happen even when their attention lapses. The puzzles start up and maintain the intellectual juices they need to solve problems, participate in discussions, and analyze and synthesize the day's topic.

*Answers to lateral-thinking puzzles:

1. The coin's date was 64 B.C., which suggests it was made sixty-four years before the birth of Christ. This is impossible, of course. How did the coin makers know that Christ would be born sixty-four years hence and that his birth would be the year marker for B.C. and A.D.?
2. J is the next letter. These are the months of the year, counting every other month. January would be the next month.
3. Fold the paper like an accordion, with as many folds as you can. The paper now acts like corrugated cardboard and can easily hold the weight of the third cup.

I also place manipulative puzzles such as the Rubik's Cube and Rubik's Revenge on tables. Being able to fidget with something unobtrusively seems to focus students and ease their stress. Classroom management concerns went down, not up, when I started doing this a few years ago.

Misconceptions

To be able to think for themselves, students must be able to monitor their misconceptions. This is hard work. Many of us leave high school harboring deeply rooted but significantly incorrect ideas about how things work in the world. The Annenberg/CPB Math and Science Project has produced an eye-opening, twenty-minute video called *A Private Universe* that uses a basic science topic as the catalyst for examining how students learn misconceptions. In the video, graduates of Ivy League colleges explain that warmer summer temperatures occur when the earth moves closer to the sun. In fact, this seasonal change happens because the earth is tilted 23.5 degrees off the polar axis; part of the earth is turned more directly toward the sun, but the earth's orbit does not change its proximity to the sun. In other words, high scores on standardized tests do not guarantee that students have accurate and deep knowledge of all subjects. Refer to the earlier sections in this chapter about chunking and rehearsal to understand why.

In the video, we see a teacher communicating to ninth graders the concepts of solar and lunar eclipses, seasons, and phases of the moon. Researchers interview one of the highest-achieving students (who also performed well on the unit test) after the lesson. She explains her thinking about those concepts, revealing serious misconceptions. In one example, the student states that the earth's orbit is elliptical (an elongated circle) because she saw a side view of the earth's orbit around the sun instead of a bird's-eye view from above. The earth actually has a very round orbit around the sun. At one point, the student draws a multiple figure-eight pattern around the sun to show the earth's orbit.

The video demonstrates how students develop their own ideas about how the world works. They filter the information we give them in science, math, foreign languages, English, history, art, music, technology, and physical education classes through their internal lenses, and they may or may not remember what we said to help clarify their distorted thinking. What should we do to prevent misconceptions from taking root in a student's mind? I put that question to a group of teachers in my school district. They came up with this list of suggestions:

- Ask simple, straightforward questions.
- Identify objectives early, and focus on the essential and enduring knowledge.

- Teach students how to monitor their own accurate learning.
- Teach students to be skeptical of information so they don't accept concepts at face value.
- Reward questioning.
- Require students to explain their reasoning.
- Revisit topics frequently.
- Teach students how to summarize accurately.
- Videotape class discussions and analyze them afterward. What did you miss that you will need to address or re-address? Did students express any misconceptions, and did you deal with these effectively? If so, what's your evidence that the misconceptions no longer exist?
- Integrate concepts and skills with other subjects to reinforce them and catch misconceptions.
- Ask parents to help. You can send home projects and activities designed to enlist parents in reviewing skills and ideas.
- Activate prior knowledge before continuing so students will make connections to what they know.
- Complete diagnostic assessments before teaching the unit so you can focus on what students need.
- Use plenty of writing activities. As students clarify their thinking through writing, their misconceptions become more evident.
- Establish a system that includes confidential letters to the teacher, learning logs, feedback forms, and exit cards that ask students to summarize what they have learned from each lesson and pose questions about things they still do not understand.

Watching the video *A Private Universe* has transformed my instruction. I no longer take it for granted that a student has learned a concept just because he performed well on my test. I want to know whether he truly understands it.

Final Thoughts

We should strive to give our students good mental workouts every day. As teachers, we can show students how to garden, or we can give them dried-flower displays. Whether we choose to ask probing questions instead of providing immediate answers or require students to find multiple solutions instead of accepting the first idea that pops into their heads, we can hold them accountable for well-reasoned thinking and demonstrate this kind of inquiry on a regular basis. We can publicly and repeatedly affirm intellectual achievement, reminding students that learning to struggle through challenges is a sign of strength, not weakness.

This kind of instruction might take more time initially, but with practice we can teach students how to think without slowing the curriculum. Be radical. Boldly teach what's best for today's young adolescents—how to question, investigate, interpret, create, dream, analyze, synthesize, evaluate, reflect, take initiative, and act ethically.

Remember that what we know about the human brain today could become obsolete tomorrow. As we make changes in our instructional practice, we should do so with the knowledge that new discoveries might dramatically alter our understanding of the most effective techniques. The best advice I can offer is to read about brain research, attend related workshops, start conversations at school, and reflect on classroom practice in light of what we know now. If we want our classrooms to truly reflect the knowledge we've gained in the past decade of research, we must be informed practitioners of brain-compatible learning. Although we can't imagine what opportunities and insights new research will bring, we can prepare our students well for the journey.

I'm still fascinated by the possibility of actually being able to see or touch a person's thoughts as the crew aboard the *Proteus* almost did. But for now I'll make do with the outward manifestations of those thoughts as expressed by my students in the classroom.

4

Active Learning

Students arrive at their history class alert and ready to work. They speak animatedly, and their rosy cheeks suggest that they have just engaged in a moderate workout.

"Just coming from P.E.?" the teacher asks.

"No, English," a student replies. "A new unit on punctuation."

Perhaps you haven't given much thought to incorporating movement in subjects other than physical education. If not, I urge you to consider it. From experience, I know that physical activities can create high-performance classrooms, improving student achievement and reducing discipline problems. Need more persuading? Then read on. But beware, this chapter might expand your lung capacity and your instructional repertoire at the same time.

Middle school teachers who maximize the exer-side of their lessons can advance student learning, no matter the subject. The brain functions at peak levels with a plentiful supply of oxygen. Oxygen gets to the brain through the bloodstream, which needs a periodic lube job to keep it from becoming sluggish.

In addition, the growth plates on the ends of a young adolescent's rapidly lengthening bones are under constant stress. While they may not be able to verbalize it, middle school students are uncomfortable sitting in almost any position in school desks and chairs. As a result, they squirm and get distracted. If we want them to care about what they're doing in class, we need to help them relieve the discomfort. If we don't give them a chance to relieve those pressures now and then, they will find their own ways, including roaming around the room and getting into trouble. I suggest letting them move every ten to fifteen minutes to relieve the stress. This can be as simple as letting them get up to turn in their papers, change seats to work with someone behind or beside them, or move their chairs into a circle. Let students stand up at regular intervals to briefly summarize with a partner what they just heard. Standing up gets oxygen to the brain.

Many young adolescents are concrete thinkers who haven't reached the stage where they understand symbolic and abstract concepts. The vividness of a physical experience can transform an abstract idea into a tangible, sensory impression that students can remember for the long term.

For those who are afraid of abandoning structure, remember that making your lessons more physical doesn't mean inviting pandemonium. Movement is only a means to an end—inspiring excited, energized learners—not the focus of our work.

Some Ideas for Active Learning

Sometimes we can make connections with students just by leaving the four walls of our classrooms. An example of this occurred a few years ago when I was teaching ratios as a way to determine tree heights. A student of mine, Fasih, couldn't comprehend the chalkboard drawings I presented. He had a learning disability, and this was one of many times that he couldn't understand new concepts as easily as other students.

As I considered my next step, I looked out the window and saw the late autumn sun sparkling on the school grounds. "Come on," I told my students, urging them to follow me. "Bring your notebooks, pencils, and calculators." I grabbed the yardstick.

We went outside and gathered on the grass near an old dogwood tree. "Let's be the ratio," I told the class.

"Fasih, you be our marker and stand over here." I took him about fifty feet away from the tree, out of its shadow.

"Okay, Fasih, stand straight. Good. How tall are you?" I asked.

"About five feet," he said.

"Everyone open your notebooks and draw a picture of the tree, then of its shadow extending from its base. Then draw a picture of Fasih standing in the field near the tree and draw his shadow extending from his feet across the grass. Write 'five feet' near the drawing of Fasih."

The students made their drawings. Fasih stood straight with a big grin on his face. When students were finished, I spoke again.

"With ratios, we need three of four pieces of information to determine the answer. Fasih, we have you, your shadow, the tree, and its shadow. What do we want to find out?"

Fasih didn't hesitate. "How tall the tree is."

"Good. What information do we have?"

"How tall I am."

"What do we need to get?"

One of the most effective teaching methods that I have experienced is acting out the material. This helps to lessen the feeling of doing work, and motivates the student to learn more about a subject. One example of this is an activity I did in seventh-grade history, where we simulated Ellis Island, an old immigration screening post. All students were given a separate role to participate in the process. Some were Ellis Island employees, with different jobs, such as health screeners and deportation officers. Others were immigrants, some with characteristics that would change their chances of entering America—diseases, rashes, previously in jail. This method helped to deepen our understanding of the immigration experience, showing us not only what occurred but also the perspectives and feelings of the immigrants. By acting this out, it was not only memorable but meaningful as well.

■ Kellen, eighth grade

Fasih hesitated. Some students began to murmur in the silence. I faced them, placing my finger on my lips. They understood and became still. After an appropriate wait time, I asked Mike to show Fasih his drawing. I leaned over and asked Fasih what else we knew. He looked up. "The shadows," he said.

"Excellent," I encouraged him. "Do we know the length of the shadows?"

Fasih shook his head. I handed Jennifer the yardstick. "Measure both shadows, please."

Jennifer measured Fasih's shadow (three feet) and the shadow of the tree (ten and a half feet). Students recorded the measurements next to the corresponding drawings in their notebooks.

"Do we have three of the four pieces of information for our ratio?" I asked Fasih. He nodded. "What are they?" I pressed.

"Me and two shadows," he said.

"Good. What are we after, again?"

"How tall the tree is."

"Yes," I almost shouted. "How do we set up the ratio—keep corresponding parts of the ratio on the same level with each other?"

Fasih wasn't sure. I didn't wait very long this time before offering guidance.

"Fasih, are you more like that tree or more like its shadow?"

"The tree," he answered.

"So what parts are similar to each other in the ratio?"

"The two shadows and the two standing things, me and the tree."

"Right. So what's the ratio?"

"My shadow is to me as the tree's shadow is to it?"

I touched my finger to my nose, our class's gesture for "you got the answer on the nose" (correct). I told the class to set up the ratio with the proper numbers. When they were done, I asked Maureen what the ratio was.

"Three is to five as ten-point-five is to X," she said.

I nodded. "Do you agree, Fasih?" He nodded too, showing me his numbers. I patted him on the back and spoke to the whole group. "Okay, work in partners and determine the height of that tree by solving for X."

Fasih and his classmates made their calculations while I watched. When they finished, I called on Fasih for the answer.

"Seventeen and a half?" he asked hesitantly.

I smiled. "There you go again, thinking like a true mathematician! Seventeen and a half feet is correct." I asked the rest of the class, "Who else matched Fasih's calculation?" Almost all hands went up. "Great! Okay, let's review the sequence. Fasih, how do you determine the height of a tree using a math ratio? Describe the process while pointing to the four objects that you used."

As he pointed first to himself then to the tree, Fasih said, "I am to the tree as"—then he pointed from his shadow to the tree's shadow—"my shadow is to the tree's shadow."

"Excellent. Let's join him, class," I said. We all gestured to each object of the ratio as we described the process. We repeated the gestures to memorize them. Afterward, I gave them one last challenge.

"There are five more trees in this area of the field. Determine their heights. You have fifteen minutes. Go!"

I stood in the center and answered questions as they arose. With only a few errors that were easily corrected, everyone arrived at the same correct answers. I confirmed their thinking with a calculator and we went back inside. There wasn't any homework that night; they didn't need it.

The next day, Fasih sent a report to the principal on the height of the six trees in the schoolyard as well as the height of the school. He had measured the height of the building using ratios and a yardstick on his own. During the rest of the year, Fasih became an expert on ratios and, later, on analogies in his language arts class. I also saw him frequently staring at shadows and their sources. You could see the gears clicking in his head.

As you can imagine, there are many ways to make learning more physical. But first, a caveat: before you determine how to teach, consider what you must teach. A physical activity will be nothing more than an outlet for adolescent energy if you don't tie it to the curriculum. Always keep in mind the essential and enduring knowledge that you're trying to convey. For example, when I taught mitosis in life science, I stressed that students must learn the basic phases of prophase, metaphase, anaphase, and telophase. There are other important phases, such as interphase, but the four main stages composed the foundation for the curriculum I was teaching.

Once you determine the essential information, consider the characteristics of the human body. What parts of the anatomy will best exemplify or amplify the concepts for the students? Young adolescents are fascinated by their bodies and will gladly pay attention to activities that enable them to use them in creative ways. More important, by incorporating their bodies into a lesson, you give them a natural study aid. If they can use their body parts to help them remember information for a test, then by all means let them.

In the case of cell division (mitosis), the hand and fingers can become reliable study aids. In prophase, the chromosomes are floating around in the cell's cytoplasm, getting geared up to split from one another. Ask students to hold their hands so that their fingers intermingle playfully like guests at a pool party. Suddenly, a lifeguard blows a whistle and asks everyone to line up along the median of the pool. Explain that this is metaphase, where the chromosomes line up along the central axis. Next, one of the fingers named Ana says good-bye to Gene (a weak but humorous reference to the topic of study) and the fingers pull apart, each hand moving to the side. This is anaphase, in which the chromosomes split in half and pull away from each other to form the new daughter cells. As the new cells form, they enter the stage called telophase. Of course, Ana and Gene promise to call each other on the

In a science class I once had, we always did a lot of worksheets and watched movies. I think it would be better if we had more hands-on activities or if we did physical activities to learn our lessons. Sometimes we end up watching a movie a week and doing lots of worksheets. Almost none of the kids enjoy that.
■ Christie, seventh grade

telo(tele)-phone just before splitting entirely in two. The split occurs, and two new daughter cells are formed. Students do this by holding two fists out to their sides.

After students learn the basic finger positions to represent each stage of chromosomal development, they can have fun calling out the stages in correct and incorrect order, using the corresponding hand movements. Purposefully make mistakes and let them correct you. Or let them perform a mitosis finger dance to music for a really vivid experience.

The examples of physical activities that follow can get you started, but you undoubtedly will think of many other applications. At your next department meeting, ask your colleagues to brainstorm for twenty minutes and come up with different ideas for turning abstract concepts into physical experiences. When I speak on this topic at education conferences, I ask the audience to do the same thing. Without fail, the group will suggest activities that are as creative as they are challenging. Don't believe me? Ask your colleagues to consider different ways to turn these concepts into physical movements:

- The molecular formula for photosynthesis
- Quadratic equations
- Socialism versus capitalism
- Nuance in poetry
- Conjugating verbs

I guarantee that you will want to jump out of your seat with the exploding possibilities for physical teaching. Your students will, too.

Additional Ideas for Making Subjects Physically Engaging

- For classrooms with no windows, install a huge mirror. It will create the illusion of more space. When used sensitively, the mirror can be a powerful instructional tool for young adolescents. They can rehearse skits and oral reports in front of it and use it for demonstrations. Don't forget the fun students will have posing in the mirror during free moments.

- Use adding machine tape and butcher paper freely. Let students write tall tales on floor-to-ceiling lengths of paper, then display their writing with illustrations. Or encourage them to use the paper for creating historical time lines or scale models of the relative distances between planets.

- Instead of asking students to pass their papers to you, let them get up and turn in their papers by tossing them into a basket in the back of the room. Make it a hard-to-reach basket to induce stretching. If you don't mind wrinkled papers, let them crumple their papers into balls and shoot their homework into a basketball net above the turn-in tray, or let them fold their papers into airplanes that they can glide into a homework box. Nominate a different student each week to smooth out the papers after everyone has had a turn.

- With colored chalk, draw a huge interior diagram of the heart on the school parking lot or a sidewalk. Better yet, let your students do it, then let them walk through the diagram as you demonstrate how blood flows from the body into the heart through the chambers and valves, to the lungs, back to the heart, then out to the body again. They can narrate the process while walking, or race to different sections by traveling the way the blood does. They can hold different colored cards to represent oxygenated and unoxygenated blood. They can do crazy movements or dances in the lung area to simulate the oxygen–carbon dioxide exchange.

- Play "Simon Says" as you reinforce the correct anatomical names for human bones, such as the clavicle, scapula, femur, and ulna.

- Let students stretch at least every thirty minutes. Traditional stretches are fine, but consider some different activities. For example, you might ask students to reach for "the Milky Way bars you stapled to the ceiling and the free movie passes you taped to the floor." Ask them to imagine they're standing at the top of a ski slope. In ready stance (pretend skis, poles, and all) they can push off the top of the mountain and swoosh back and forth down the course. Call out various obstacles so they can navigate around trees, jump over hills, and attempt various stunts on skis.

- Ask students to design their own graphic organizers on walls, floors, ceilings, or sidewalks. They can use tape, yarn, paint, or chalk. Give them the data for each portion of the floor's graphic organizer on sturdy cards, and let them race as a team to stand accurately in the correct spaces/sequences/subsets.

- Let students create a rap song about the lesson, using a defined beat they can keep time with using their bodies.

- Encourage students to represent concepts and terms artistically. They can draw science cycles, dramatically portray atomic interactions, and sculpt with clay while describing the stages of the writing process. The last example is one of my favorites. As the students sculpt, I ask them to explain what they are doing by using writing terms. For example, if a passage is boring (blah), it might need more texture (students chop at the clay with a tool), and in writing we call these details or descriptions. If a passage is based on a weak argument, we have to strengthen the reasoning (students can create an arch or other extensions with the clay). We might move the clay pieces around or throw them against the chalkboard, just as a writer might crumple up a piece of paper and start over with a different idea.

- Let students make and maintain your classroom bulletin boards.

- Encourage them to form "the wave" whenever a classmate does something well, or to applaud each other's efforts.

- Adolescents love camping and campfire songs. Ask them to rewrite some traditional tunes using the content or skills you've been teaching. I've used "Going on a Lion Hunt," "Green Grass Growin' All Around," "Head, Shoulders, Knees, and Toes," "My Aunt Came Back," and "Boom, Chicka-Boom" on many occasions.

- To review material, throw a large beach ball (the Summary Ball) into the classroom and let students toss it around. Each time someone catches the ball, he must call out one fact from the lesson. You can alter the rules to maximize involvement. For example, students can pass the ball only to someone who hasn't yet contributed; students must add something within three seconds of catching the ball or pass it on; or if a student cannot offer a new fact, she must sit down. Another alternative is letting each student call on a friend to help out. For Summary Eyeball, use one of those squishy plastic eyeballs encased in water for the prop. A plastic frog or something similar will work just as well.

- Use body outlines. Let small groups of students trace the outline of one member's body on mural paper, then ask them to label the parts of the body using analogies for the day's topic. For example, anything associated with passion, feeling, pumping, supplying, forcing, or rhythm can be listed near the heart. Anything associated with the intellect or imagination can be listed near the head. Fingers and hands can be associated with dexterity, working in unison, or artwork. Feet can relate to things requiring "footwork" or a journey. The position of the body can suggest part of the message as well. Imagine the parts of the human body representing the causes of the Civil War or the characters in a novel. Discussing the various proposed analogies will help them internalize the lesson.

- Turn something that students normally experience symbolically or abstractly into a physical act. For example, in science you can ask students to portray the earth, the moon, and the sun in a darkened room with a single light source, watching the changing shadow patterns on the students' bodies as they rotate and revolve.

- Set up an Olympics course with an academic focus. For the sixty-yard dash, create three stations, such as a wall or a portable chalkboard, to represent the sides of an equilateral triangle. Print a decimal number on each of fifteen large cards hanging at the first station, and post the equivalent fractions for each decimal at the second station. The third side will be the starting point. Team members must race one at a time to the far corners, pulling off equivalent values before returning to the starting point. For the finale, teams must add the total of all the cards and give the answer in both decimal and fraction forms. The winning team will have done so in the shortest amount of time.

- Make a three-by-three grid. After ten or twenty minutes of direct teaching, ask students to record three things they learned in the squares. Next, ask them to get up, move around the room, and talk with other students. They can share facts, giving one of the ideas in their squares to another student and receiving an idea they hadn't considered. When they have filled the squares, the students sit down and continue with the lesson.

- Carousel brainstorming. Post three to six sheets of newsprint around the room with a single concept or quote on each sheet. Students must move in groups and read the prompts, writing their responses on the newsprint.

- Another idea comes from Frost Valley YMCA in New York State. Ask teams of five students to run a mile and, when they return, to pick up an ice cream stick or tongue depressor with a fraction written on it. The sticks will be placed on a table in sequence, smallest fraction to largest. Each runner picks up what she considers to be the smallest fraction. Team members will arrive at different times, of course, so they'll get five different fractions. After all team members have taken sticks, they can work together to add the fractions. The team with the lowest sum wins.

- Instead of a normal spelling bee, try the "de Strange" version in which students spell the words aloud but substitute agreed-upon sound effects (usually animal or nonsense noises) to represent vowels and phonetic patterns (see Appendix E). For example, if a word contains a short *E* sound, give it a juicy "thpht!" sound (think of a Bronx cheer and ripple the cheeks and lips as you execute this one). An *O* might be represented by "oink!," an *I* could be a frog's "ribbit!," an *A* could be "achoo!," and a *U* could be "ooh-la-la!" To spell *receive,* the student would call out, *r,* thpht!, *c,* thpht!, ribbit, *v,* thpht! While one team makes sure that the other team has correctly spelled the words and given the correct sounds in the proper sequence, the other team must try to spell the words without laughing too hard. In order to do well, a team must know the correct spelling of the words in addition to the phonetic patterns. To keep students on their toes, add points to the listening team's score if the students find phonetic mistakes in the presenting team's submission, and subtract points if their assertion is wrong. The faster the presenting team can spell each word, the more outrageous the sounds and the more difficult it is for the other team to detect an error.

- In English classes, adopt Victor Borge's idea of each punctuation mark representing a particular noise, but instead make each punctuation mark a physical movement. Bending over, twisting, or throwing both hands into the air above your head can substitute for commas, question marks, and quotation marks, respectively. Ask students to read dialogue between two characters aloud and, every time they come to a punctuation mark to make the representative movements.

- Go to the school library for a presentation on demonstrative pronouns (*this, that, these, those*). Students can carry signs with demonstrative pronouns written on them, for instance, "Up with this, down with that!" "Give us these, get rid of those!" Librarians can counter with signs of their own: "Take this out of here!" (Be sure to ask for permission ahead of time.)

- Use drama. Skits help students summarize, personalize, and dramatize important concepts. One I've used to good effect in English class includes the dastardly villain Aintno Grammar, who ties a helpless student to a railroad track (two desks put together, with some rope around the student). Four students holding on to each other's belt loops choo-choo into the scene as the approaching train. Dudley Do-well Grammarian arrives on the scene and tries to save his friend from certain disaster. He pulls on the ropes but they won't budge. Dudley calls for Adverb Man, who flies in and assesses the situation. Adverb Man pulls out a large card with the correct adverb and says, "You need to pull *strongly* [or *together*], sir!" Dudley uses the card and pulls his friend free just as the train of students plows through the scene. Dudley and the rescued student thank Adverb Man in melodramatic fashion. But soon Adverb Man hears another distress call and must fly off to save another student. Along the way he hands out not-so-typical adverbs such as *not, now, very,* and *there.* I know this script seems contrived, but it really works. The best learning, of course, comes when the students write their own skits. The learning doesn't happen in the presentation; it happens while they are creating the skit.

Motivation and Learning and *The High Performance Tool Box,* by Spencer Rogers and colleagues, are excellent resources for more physical movement ideas.

Although it might take time to find activities that suit your style, you really can't go wrong when you try to make the abstract more physical for students. To get in the right frame of mind, put down this book and get some oxygen to your brain by doing several stretches. How about a walk outside? Moderate exercise and time to reflect—something we all need daily. So what are you waiting for? Get going, or I'm going to break out the punctuation unit with push-ups for every misplaced comma.

Games in the Classroom 5

Habitat Rummy," Milton calls out. "I have all five pieces of a red-tailed hawk's habitat."

"Prove it," Jenny says.

Milton lowers his cards so everyone can see. "Take a look—I have the correct food, water, space, shelter, and proper arrangement. Check the chart, if you don't believe me," he says.

The students glance at the chart they made with twenty animals' habitat factors. Sure enough, everything Milton has included for the red-tailed hawk's habitat is correct.

"Dang it," Jenny concedes. "I almost had a full habitat for a freshwater eel! Let's play again."

I learned to play Habitat Rummy in my first year of teaching. It comes from the Project WILD environmental protection curriculum available in most states. Project WILD has many other games and simulations that teach substantive content while entertaining students. Dr. Terry Graham, a professor of education at Virginia Tech University, gave those of us in his undergraduate education course the idea of using games to introduce, review, reinforce, or apply content. Games were intrinsically motivating, he said. When people have fun, they don't realize they are learning. He used a wide range of games to teach us. Each time we played, our spirits picked up, we focused instead of dozed, and we learned. Years later, when I was completing a master's degree in educational administration, one course on special education administration was taught entirely through a simulation game. Each student acted as a coordinator in charge of special education for a mock school district. The issues we confronted were the very ones I had witnessed in my own district. My classmates and I collaborated, applying techniques and perspectives learned through our readings. Often we were humbled by the common sense and wisdom of seasoned veterans who shared their successful actions after we gave our initial responses. To this day, I remember those lessons vividly. The simulation pushed me, too. Reading and discussion are fairly passive ways to learn, but taking action and having to cope with consequences is much more challenging.

Over the years, games have become a regular part of my teaching repertoire. They've proven to be an outstanding use of instructional time when I apply them. I ask myself three questions before deciding whether to use a game or simulation. First, does the game involve enough substantive content to justify the use of classroom time? Second, have I set up the game to maximize participation? Games in which two people compete might be fun for a while, but they don't engage everyone in thinking about the content, which is the first goal. I try to increase engagement by allowing contestants to receive help from their teammates, waiting until the last moment to choose the person who must respond, rotating everyone through the hot seat, and making the game something in which everyone must contribute for the team to advance. Third, are the rules of the game simple enough to understand? If I have to spend half the class period explaining the rules, my students will have limited time to play and little motivation to do so. Once students understand the rules, they can run the game while I monitor it for fairness and control.

I also try to put some flair into my classroom games. I might wear a crazy hat or a coat if I'm the emcee, play the theme song from the television show *Jeopardy*, bring small prizes, or lead crazy cheers at the end. Squeaky toys make great buzzers for respondents. Additionally, I try to build suspense with comments such as, "Will he answer correctly?" and "Is that your final answer?" Instead of requiring students to write something immediately on the chalkboard, I let them race across the room to get to the chalkboard (two points off if they run into the chalkboard because they were moving too fast). I also keep a tally sheet of scores for all my class periods, and post them for each class to see. Sometimes I invite staff members to stop by and join one of the teams; having an adult as a teammate raises the level of excitement for young adolescents. For team names, I try to make wild connections to students' names, such as Sensational Serena versus Jazzy Geena or Mighty Manuel versus Cowabunga Carrie. I recommend using the names of students who usually don't get much attention in class.

Before playing any new game with your class, play it once yourself or with another person to make sure you have all the pieces and have thought of all the problems that might arise. Visualize in your head every facet of the game to be played in your room. Be organized and prepared. Nothing is worse than building up excitement for the day's big event and having it turn sour because students ran out of questions, the point system didn't work, or the room was too small for students to move around as intended.

Talking about games has made me eager for the real thing. So let's move on to some really cool games that are successful with young adolescents. Most of the suggested games can be used with any subject. Borrow the format and insert your own content. As always, add your own rules and enhancements to improve them for your particular teaching situation.

Tic-Tac-[Topic]

Examples would be Tic-Tac-Grammar or Tic-Tac-Fraction.

Props

Tic-tac-toe grid, nine topic areas, questions for each topic area, X and O markers (chalk markers or posterboard cutouts with magnet strips or masking tape on the back)

How to Play

Set up your chalkboard (or similar surface) with a huge tic-tac-toe grid. In each square, place a topic you want students to review. Sometimes, I use review topics from units we completed months earlier, not just the recent ones, to fill in all nine spaces. Divide the class into two teams. One student at a time calls out a topic square and answers a review question. Students love to repeat phrases from popular television game shows, such as, "I'll take Objective Pronouns for the block." One team can be the X's and the other team can be the O's.

If the student on the responding team answers the question correctly, his symbol (X or O) gets marked (or placed) across the square. If he gives an incorrect answer, the next person from the opposing team gets to answer the question. During the first team's attempt, the opposing team's members are allowed to review their notes, discuss the answer (not so loud as to be heard by the responding team, of course), and get the next person in line ready to steal the square with a correct answer. If the opposing team's member guesses correctly, her team's symbol is marked on the topic square. If she answers incorrectly, throw the question out.

Teams take turns choosing a square and answering the questions. This means that a team could steal a square from the team that started a topic area and also start the next topic. Three X's or three O's in a row win the game. In situations in which no one wins, tally the number of X's and the number of O's and apply those numbers of points to each team. Tie games usually yield big scores. Let one student be the scorekeeper.

Taboo

Props

Taboo cards (made by you or the students), a timer, a buzzer (or pet squeaky toy to use as a buzzer), a small box for keeping the cards hidden, a discard bin

How to Play

To prepare, make up fifty or more Taboo cards about a unit of study or several units of study. To make a Taboo card, turn an index card vertically and write a vocabulary word at the top. Place a thick line underneath that word. In the remaining space under the line, write four or five words/concepts your students would normally associate with the vocabulary word. For example, under *Decimals* I would write *tenths, point, place value, base ten, hundredths*. To make this a particularly effective game, let students make up the cards based on a vocabulary list you give them. Place all the cards facedown.

Call up a representative from each of two teams. The two students can sit at a table in the front of the room. Set the timer for one minute (two minutes, if you think they need the time), and ask one representative to flip over the first card and give clues to her teammates. Her goal is to get them to say the vocabulary term at the top of the card without using any of the related terms listed below the line on the card. She is not allowed to use any portion of the vocabulary word. However, if one of her team members says one of the taboo words listed on the card, the team's representative can use the term in her clues. The representative may not use any gestures, sound effects, or rhymes in her clues. Here's an example.

The word is *mitosis*. The taboo words are *chromosomes, nucleus, two, separate,* and *cell*. A student might say, "This is the process in the smallest unit of living life, in which this thing divides into new daughter things. It happens in the brains of this smallest unit of living life. There's another word that sounds like it and starts with the same letter that confused Johnny yesterday in class. [The student is thinking of *meiosis*.] We did finger plays to represent this process."

The team can call out the answer at any point. If the team members guess correctly, their representative puts that card to one side, pulls up the next one from the pile, and starts giving clues. The process continues until time is called.

The opposing team has a buzzer (or squeaky toy), which team members can use if the person accidentally uses a taboo word or any portion of the intended vocabulary term in his clues. When that happens, the card is given to the opposing team's card pile and a point is awarded to the opposing team (the one with the buzzer). If a team's representative can't seem to communicate a vocabulary term successfully, she can pass on the card, but a point is awarded to the other team for each passed card. Keep playing until both teams have had the same number of opportunities to give clues or time runs out. To add a little more pizzazz, throw in a few cards relating to students' interests.

Rummy

Props

Index cards with specific content pieces you want students to put together

How to Play

Follow the rules for Rummy or Gin Rummy with playing cards, but instead of a run, such as the four, five, six, seven of spades, students get the components of a sequence you've taught, such as the steps in photosynthesis, the process for dividing fractions, or four things that led to the Civil War. Instead of getting sets, such as three sevens or four queens, students get four equivalent fractions or four verbs in the past perfect tense. Students work off a central pile, drawing and discarding cards just as they would do in a real card game until they achieve a winning hand. For example, a winning hand with seven cards would be a set of three and a run of four. Or, with ten cards, it would be a run of seven and a set of three. For added learning, let each student make his own deck of fifty cards with a unique design on the back based on the unit of study.

Charades

Props

Pieces of paper with concepts or terms recorded on them

How to Play

Play it like regular Charades except use concepts from the unit of study. My students and I have played it in some subjects in which we were using a jigsaw approach. Each member of the team would learn a different aspect of the concept presented, then the group would gather, and each student would perform a Charade to communicate the idea to the rest of the group.

Pictionary

Props

Drawing surface and tools, cards with concepts, timer

How to Play

Like the commercial game, participants draw doodles representing the intended word and try to get their teammates to state the word within a time limit. In this version, insert your concepts and vocabulary. Allow one minute, sometimes only thirty seconds if there are a limited number of concepts and terms. Give three points for each successful guess, and subtract one point for each unsuccessful guess. I usually divide the class into two teams. Each team has a spokesperson whose guess is the only one I will count. The rest of the team members can be poring over their notes or text looking for the answer and offering their ideas to the spokesperson.

Human Bingo

Props

Bingo cards with categories written in the squares (see Appendix F), edible markers, pens/pencils, the students' name written on individual pieces of paper, a small box or hat

How to Play

Give each student a bingo card, which includes a five-by-five grid. Label the center space "free." In the other twenty-four spaces, list the content you want students to review as well as a few things to add interest. For example, a math teacher could list math problems or terms in each of the spaces, English teachers could list grammar terms or concepts from a novel, and science teachers could list terms or lab protocols. For fun, insert phrases such as "Has seen [insert latest popular movie]," "Plays basketball," "Has traveled more than five hundred miles away," or "Is under six feet tall."

Give the students about ten minutes to move around the room getting their classmates to sign the squares on their bingo card. A classmate may sign a square only if she can do, solve, or respond to the prompt on the square she signs. For example, if the square says, "Knows three changes in the government as a result of the Spanish-American War," the student will have to recite them if the cardholder uses that person's name in the bingo sequence. If the students cannot do what they claimed, the cardholder does not earn a bingo. The cardholder can sign his name to only one of the squares.

Once all squares are filled with signatures, everyone sits down, and you start calling names of students from the slips in a hat or box. Students place a sunflower seed, an M&M, a piece of popcorn, or something else edible on each square in which the identified student's name appears. The first student to get five in a row hollers, "Human Bingo!" You then ask the caller to name each square's prompt as well as the name of the student who said she could respond to that prompt. As names are called, the student who signed the square must make an accurate response. If all five students respond accurately, declare it a successful bingo, and let the class eat the markers placed on their boards. If one or more of the five students does not respond accurately, the game continues.

Password

Props

"Clue-meter" line, vocabulary terms or concepts to review

How to Play

Call a representative from each of two teams to the front of the room. Ask the players to turn around and face their respective teams. Write the word on the chalkboard behind them or hold it up on posterboard so they cannot see it but the audience can. Once the teams have seen the word, put it away. Choose a team to start and ask if the representative wants to pass or play. If he passes, he will have the benefit of two clues before guessing the word, as long as the other team doesn't get lucky and guess the word in the first clue. If he chooses to play, his could be the lucky team and guess the word in the first clue, earning a higher number of points.

To start, allow all the members of the person's team to use their notes or textbooks and look for one-word clues. The clues cannot be proper nouns, sound effects, or gestures. Any of the seated team members can raise a hand, and the team's representative will call on her to share the clue. If the representative can guess the word with just this first clue, award ten points to the team and move on to a new word with the other team. However, if the representative incorrectly guesses in response to the team's clue, the chance now goes to the other team. This team gives a second clue to its representative, but now a correct answer is worth only nine points. If the player doesn't respond correctly, the chance goes back to the other team, and the correct answer is worth only eight points. This sequence continues until a player guesses correctly or the team hits the fifth clue. If neither team representative can guess the word at this point, throw it out and begin with another word.

To emphasize correct spelling, let the team that answered correctly earn five points by spelling the word. For example, if one team guesses "surface area of a cylinder" correctly on the third clue, the students get eight points, but the other team can spell it correctly and receive five points. If one team fails to spell the word correctly, let the other team try for the full thirteen points.

Slap!

Props

Overhead projector, screen or wall for projection, flyswatters, content questions and answers

How to Play

Write the answers to questions in separate spaces on an overhead transparency sheet. Project those answers on the screen or wall in your room. Let competing students stand near the projection, holding the flyswatters.

Read a question aloud. The first person to slap the correct answer with her flyswatter wins a point for her team. A colleague of mine, Pai Rosenthal, uses this in her foreign language classes. She said she used to have students run to the board and slap the answers on the screen, but the students were not able to stop themselves before slamming into the chalkboard behind the screen. She now has them stand on either side of the screen.

It's good to have several different transparencies with answers for variety's sake. There are many ways to use Slap! Teachers can call out definitions and students can slap the matching word; call out sequences and slap the next item in a sequence; call out incomplete analogies and slap the best choice for completing the analogy. However you use it, this game gets students moving and thinking.

Jeopardy!

Props

A *Jeopardy!* board, index cards with answers on them, enough cards for five categories, squeaky toys or buzzers

How to Play

First, make a *Jeopardy!* board. There are several ways to do this. Here's my poor man's version: Get about thirty pockets that librarians glue to the inside cover of library books. Put a magnetic strip or masking tape on the back of each pocket and post it in a five-by-five grid on the chalkboard. Write money or point values on the front lower half of each one—500, 400, 300, 200, 100. Into each pocket, slide an index card with an answer on it. Put the most difficult answers in the higher-point-value pockets. (When I make these, I usually write out five questions, rank them in order of difficulty, then label each one with a tiny 500, 400, 300, 200, or 100 so I know where they go on the board.) Do this for each of your five categories.

At the top of each row, write or post the title of the category. Call up a representative from each of three teams. Ask the students to sit at three desks in the front of the room. They must place their hands palms down on either side of the squeaky toy or buzzer you've provided. Choose a person to start a category.

"I'll take Three-Dimensional Solids for $200," Kelly says.

You pull the card out of the $200 pocket and read it: "This is a three-dimensional solid with fifteen edges, ten vertices, and seven faces."

Jesse is the first to use his squeaky toy. You call on him, and he says, "What is a pentagonal prism?"

"That's correct," you say. "$200 to Jesse's team. Choose another one, Jesse."

"I'll take Great Literature for $500."

And so it goes, just like the television game show. Make sure to have enough cards for at least two full boards of questions. Include audio and video daily doubles. For these, play a segment from a song or movie video that students have to identify. If they guess correctly, give them double the point or money value. When you have finished, stack the cards according to the category, then according to the difficulty of that category. This way, before the next class arrives, you can quickly redistribute the cards into the pockets.

Post an extra pocket with an index card off to the side. This is the final *Jeopardy!* answer. At the end of regular *Jeopardy!*, tell students what the category will be ("Today's category is Civil War Reconstruction"). They confer with their teams about how much of their earned money or points they should bet on the final answer, then write down the figure. Collect these papers and reveal the final answer. Whoever squeaks in with the correct answer first gets to make the bet. If it's the wrong answer, then the team members lose anything wagered. Compare final totals and pronounce the winner.

These games are starting points. Your colleagues and students will have many more ideas, so be sure to ask them. In today's GameBoy world where recreational use of technology seems to isolate us, an old-fashioned game in which folks compete face-to-face good-naturedly with rigorous content can build camaraderie and cognitive connections.

Accountability for High Standards | 6

Jared was presenting an oral report on Aristotle's rhetorical triangle (ethos, pathos, and logos), and he was floundering. Embarrassed because he kept forgetting his memorized speech, he begged me to let him take an F and sit down. Instead, I asked Jared to take a few deep breaths and try again.

He did, but he bombed anew. To help him refocus, I explained that an oral report is not just about delivering information; it's also about taking risks and developing confidence. After his classmates offered encouraging comments, Jared tried a third time and got a little farther before stopping his speech. I suggested that he repeat the presentation in short segments, resting between each one. This approach worked better. Jared finished and moved to take his seat, but I stopped him and asked him to repeat the entire presentation, this time without the rests.

As his classmates grinned and nodded, Jared returned to the front of the room. This time he made it through his presentation without a mistake. His classmates cheered. Jared bowed, smiled, and took his seat. It was a wonderful exercise in perseverance, risk taking, and accountability.

Many educators dismiss accountability as a bothersome buzzword, a futile paper chase, or a political gambit, yet it is—or should be—an essential part of education. Being held accountable for high standards shouldn't be synonymous with documenting academic deficiencies or pushing adolescents to pass politically motivated standardized tests. The real purpose of accountability is making sure that students achieve authentic learning goals and that teachers have valid measures of their effectiveness in helping students reach those objectives. It's a reciprocal equation: both students and teachers are responsible for meeting high academic standards.

Holding Students Accountable

If we want to hold students accountable for achieving at high levels, we must provide models of what such success looks like. In the classroom, we can post examples of outstanding projects and papers, discuss the characteristics

I once had a teacher who was very lenient on homework. A project supposed to be due on Monday could be turned in two weeks later and still get an A, with no consequences. At the time I thought this was a good thing. It allowed me to get A's though I turned things in a couple of days late every time. Now, however, if you turn in something late, there are consequences. They will bring your grade down very quickly. Now I realize it wasn't a very good thing this teacher did. It established a habit for me that affects me negatively now.
■ Andrew, seventh grade

of excellent work, and encourage students to think about how they can reach the same benchmarks. Then we can give them appropriate tools, such as scaffolding assignments, breaking larger projects into smaller tasks, and creating calendars of completion. It's a good idea to negotiate checkpoints so you can review their progress along the way, offer encouragement and constructive comments, and help them stay focused on the goal. What we discover during these individual and small-group encounters can help us design mini-lessons to fill any gaps in comprehension. We can't expect students to explain three ways to solve a multistep math problem if they've never practiced solving math problems three different ways before.

Another effective strategy is to tell them well before a deadline that you plan to display some of their assignments publicly. If they know their science essays or pen-and-ink drawings or math tesellations might be hanging in the main entrance to the mall, they will learn to be accountable to their community, friends, and family and put greater effort into achieving the high standards we've set.

To that end, I recommend reducing or eliminating extra-credit assignments. Instead of letting students complete additional projects to raise their grades, ask them to revise their original work based on the standards outlined in your rubric or the comments written in the margins of their papers. I have not allowed extra-credit projects for five years. As a result, students do a much better job the first time around. The difference is dramatic.

Sometimes holding students accountable involves risk taking—yours and theirs. One year, I had a student with Tourette's syndrome. He made strange noises in class and had frequent facial and body tics. These problems caused him to be insecure and shy and, sadly, the butt of jokes. He also had a learning disability in language arts. So what did I do? I encouraged him to take the lead in a school production of *Romeo and Juliet*. He had to memorize a tremendous number of lines, learn to fight with a sword, come to rehearsals every day, and put up with adolescent teasing about "being in love." He met all the challenges brilliantly. Not only were the tics and strange noises absent during his performance, but he demonstrated acting talent well beyond his years. His classmates marveled at a side of him they had never seen. Was casting him in the play a risk? Without a doubt. Was it worth it to hold him accountable for a higher level of performance than he had ever reached before? You bet.

Roger Lewin, a journalist and the author of several books about the human mind and evolution, reminds us that "too often we give children answers to remember rather than problems to solve." Let students struggle a bit, but back them up with a classroom culture that honors intellectual stretching and offers praise for more than being the first to have the right answer.

Accountability is not just an academic issue. It's also a benchmark of behavior. Most adolescents want to do the right thing, but they are highly susceptible to peer pressure, good and bad. Carol G. Freeman summarizes their erratic stages in her useful book *Living with a Work in Progress: A Parent's Guide to Surviving Adolescence*:

> These are the years in which they learn how to interact with the world around them. At times they will lie, cheat, bully, and make you want to volunteer them to test bungee cords. However, keep in mind that they are a work in progress and may be super-gluing their tongue to their locker one day and organizing a recycling effort the next. Therefore, we must view their indiscretions as opportunities for growth. But we must make it absolutely clear that we place a high value on respect and be prepared to stand by this priority.

That's where behavior standards come in. To help students act responsibly, start by asking them to describe an ethical issue they're considering, or will need to consider in the future, then put that decision through this five-question test:

> Am I making this choice with the hope that no one will find out?
> How will I look back on this choice ten years from now?
> Am I doing to others what I would want them to do to me?
> If [an admired person] were in the same situation, what would he or she do?
> If everyone were about to do what I'm going to do, would I want to live in the world shaped by that decision?

See Appendix G for a sample behavior analysis form.

Michael H. Popkin, author of the book series *Active Parenting of Teens,* says that responsibility is the process of making choices and accepting the consequences of those choices. Ask yourself who owns the problem. Who is raising the issue or making the complaint? Whose purposes are being thwarted by the problem? If the answer is the child, then the adults should let the consequences teach, if at all possible. Popkin encourages us to let children handle their own difficulties while offering them encouragement and support. How we communicate our standards will affect whether and how children live up to them, Popkin says. For example, we discourage accountability when we have negative expectations, focus on mistakes, expect perfection, and provide too much protection. We encourage accountability when we show confidence in a child's behavior, resist the temptation to rescue her, build on her strengths, value her, stimulate her independence, and separate her worth from her accomplishments and misbehaviors.

Try to get a telephone in your classroom. If a student doesn't have an assignment or continues to misbehave, ask him to call his mom or dad right then. For those tough behavior issues, ask mom or dad to come to your classroom and sit next to the student. It will help everyone be more accountable for improved outcomes.

I have found that denial tends to be the first response when a student is corrected for misbehavior, so I try to make it easier for the student to accept reality. I videotape the class with the camera focused on the student who can't control himself, then ask him to stay after school to view the tape with me. I focus on nonemotional questions, such as, What were you doing? What was the effect on your learning? What was the effect on the learning of those around you? What was the effect on the teacher? I often use this approach with a prop—posterboard screen covers with different-sized windows cut in them. The first time, a small window reveals just the student in action. The second time, I use a larger window to reveal the student and those immediately around him, which shows quite plainly that misbehavior by one affects all the others. This process is particularly effective when mom and dad come for a conference about the student.

Holding Ourselves Accountable

We might not like all the public pressure to boost students' scores on standardized tests and meet the requirements of various state mandates, but too many teachers are using that pressure as an excuse to stop trying anything innovative in the classroom. They claim that administrators, or the tests themselves, require rote memorization and workbook practice, not complex projects and high-level thinking activities. Besides, they say, innovations take too long; if we let students work on interdisciplinary projects, we won't be able to cover all the material in time for the test.

Hogwash. What parents and the public want students to do is *master* the material, not just *cover* it. Many of those "innovative" practices are the best teaching tools for learning and retaining new concepts.

In a recent report, *How Teaching Matters: Bringing the Classroom Back into Discussions of Teacher Quality,* Harold Wenglinsky of Educational Testing Service expanded on the work of William Sanders and others who have examined the impact that "good" and "bad" teachers have on student achievement. Wenglinksy found that "students whose teachers emphasize higher-order thinking skills (math) and hands-on learning activities (e.g., lab work in science) outperform their peers significantly." At a recent educational conference I attended, author and assessment expert Grant Wiggins cited additional research that students who are exposed only to workbooks and test-preparation skill sheets instead of imaginative, cross-disciplinary lessons usually perform poorly on state assessments. That makes sense. Students can't possibly memorize every fact that might show up on a state exam. And most states have moved away from strictly multiple-choice formats anyway. Instead, state exams increasingly ask students to explain their reasoning, to compare theories, to persuade an audience, to provide evidence for their conclusions—a wide range of applications of basic skills.

Here's how I look at it. I can teach comma placement in quotations using drills, but deeper, lasting learning will result when I ask students to write meaningful dialogue between a black student and a white student in South Africa during apartheid or to write a pretend interview with political leaders from the nineteenth and twentieth centuries. When adolescents *use* a new skill, they will be more likely to retain it. And when they remember it because they've applied it, or synthesized it, or evaluated it, they will know what to do when confronted with more difficult and perhaps unfamiliar material on tests.

As middle school teachers, we must take responsibility for adapting our instruction instead of blaming other people or unexpected conditions for the poor performance of our students. We must recognize that people learn in different ways, and we can't assume that our preferred instructional method is the only one worth using. We must be accountable for helping all our students learn. This might mean varying our techniques, providing extra resources, simplifying the steps of a problem, obtaining more professional training, adjusting the complexity of our assignments, or giving students different placements entirely. But whatever we do, we should not pass on our problem students and hope someone else will figure out how to help them.

A sports analogy comes to mind. Living in the shadow of our nation's capital, I read and hear a lot about the Washington Redskins pro football team. And I remember always marveling at how former Redskins Coach Joe Gibbs modeled accountability for his players and fans. Although he led his team to several Super Bowl titles, Gibbs's teams lost games people thought they should have won. Yet, after each defeat, the coach went out of his way to deflect attention from his players' mistakes on the field. Instead, his first response under questioning from reporters was to share what he had done wrong and how he planned to fix it before the next game.

We can learn from Gibbs's example, I think. Rather than acting like that hackneyed sage on the stage, we should position ourselves as the chief learners in our classrooms. If students see us stretching our intellects—learning from them and from others—they will be more willing to follow our lead, knowing that the reward will be more lasting than a good grade on a test.

Try apologizing sincerely to your students when you fail to live up to your standards. Vow to make corrections, and keep your promise. Come prepared to teach each lesson well instead of just trying to get by. Follow through on the little things, such as remembering the book you promised to share with Maria, making accommodations for Geoff's new family arrangement, or writing large enough on the chalkboard so Omar can see from the back row. In this way, you will model the commitment you expect from your students.

We also can invite students to catch us making mistakes. Require them to find evidence to support their claims, then reward their critical thinking. Learning how to point out mistakes in a responsible manner and defend a position honorably is another exercise in meeting a high standard of behavior. To take this to another level, let your students complete a teacher report card and grade your performance during the semester. Or let them design the report card based on what they consider to be good teaching. Together, you will demonstrate educational accountability. A sample of the teacher report card my students designed and use with me each quarter is provided in Appendix H.

Nothing should be so sacred in our classrooms that we are afraid to critique it. If we can't explain the relevance of a topic or an assignment so our students can construct meaning from it, then something's wrong. We have several choices. We can

- Stop teaching it.
- Talk to others and see if they can help us explain the significance in terms that adolescents will understand.
- Research the topic more extensively.
- Tell our students we don't know the answers to their questions and ask them to help us find out why the topic or assignment is required by the school/district/state curriculum. Their investigation might teach them more about the topic than we can.

If I'm having trouble rationalizing an assignment or topic, chances are that I haven't presented it well or considered it from a thirteen-year-old's perspective. In such cases, I try to examine my lesson plans and identify places where I failed to build sequential steps for understanding, or provide appropriate context, or make relevant connections. The school day is too short to waste time on activities that students can complete more easily at home or that ask little more of students than staying busy. Anyone can assign the questions at the end of a textbook chapter. But only an expert in young adolescent development and the food pyramid can make the topic of balanced and nutritional food choices so meaningful to middle school students that they will remember to make intelligent decisions when eating after school. That's the kind of standard I want to set.

Responding to Standards

Wouldn't it be great if people rallied in support of academic excellence as much as they do for athletic accomplishments? Imagine receiving advertising endorsements for your science research skills, having your photograph printed on cereal boxes for your ability to solve math problems, or signing an autograph for fans of your artistic performances. Imagine being hailed as a hero in an Academic Olympics. I can hear the television commentators now:

> Good morning, and welcome to the Millennium Games. We're focusing today on Marjorie Younger from Proud Middle School in Teamtown, U.S.A. In Sydney, Australia, she brought home a gold medal in the Women's four-by-one-hundred Science Investigation Relay, a silver medal in the Women's Academic All-Around Excellence Pentathlon, and a bronze medal in the Persuasive Writing category. Four years later, she's already earned one gold medal in the Civics competition, and she's getting ready to bring home the gold for the Academic All-Around Pentathlon for the United States. Her competitors have finished their rotation and now all eyes are on Ms. Younger. Let's welcome her to our Olympic venue. [Applause] [*Olympic theme music played.*]

Well, it *could* happen. I'm waiting for the moment when all the countries of the world can find common ground through intellectual achievement. We'll cheer sacrifice and adversity and cooperation and brilliance, all of it combined into television programming so compelling that we won't want to miss a single minute of it.

To reach such high goals, however far-fetched they might seem today, we need standards. They help us consistently move *every* child ahead, not just those who respond quickly to our assignments and tests. Standards spell out what our communities consider essential and enduring knowledge. They provide a guide rope that we can return to if we swim too far away during our investigations and a path to follow as we map the curriculum, creating intellectually rigorous and developmentally responsive experiences in each year of middle school.

The political pressure for standards—and the high-stakes accountability tests some states are using to measure our progress in meeting them—came about because some of us weren't performing well or weren't continually communicating the rich achievements in our classrooms. So standards we have and standards we must address.

Let's affirm a few things about state standards and their impact on us:

• Standards do not dictate instruction. They show us the goal, but we can devise the game plan.
• Standards are not limits; they are minimums. Our students can surpass them.
• Standards do not require students to sit only in straight rows, memorizing textbook chapters. Students must be able to process and apply our

subject content over time, not just know basic facts for a multiple-choice test at the end of the week.

- Standards don't force us to march in lockstep without regard for the individual student. They do not represent the end of teacher creativity. The last thing today's students need is a disillusioned or distraught teacher who trips over the books about differentiated instruction on her way to retrieve the books about lecturing.

I know there's no such thing as a model middle school teacher, but some of our colleagues come close. So let's keep that vision in mind as we examine the steps that will help us meet state standards.

- Put the student first. Focusing on a standard without regard for an individual's strengths and weaknesses is a prescription for failure. We must know our students well before we can teach them well.
- Keep up with the latest developments in our fields. Ongoing training keeps us enthusiastic about our work and accurate in our choice of instructional approaches. Standards-based assessments require more staff development, not less. Research proves it—highly trained teachers are more effective at increasing student learning.
- Maintain the image of school as a place to learn instead of a place where students must be controlled. We can't meet higher standards of learning if classroom management is our primary focus. Successful instruction, which addresses students' developmental and intellectual needs, is the highest form of classroom management. When students are actively engaged, they rarely create havoc. We must show our students that middle school is a place to explore, investigate, dramatize, and relate, not a place to stand in line, sit in rows, and fill in the blanks.
- Think unconventionally. Coverage is not mastery. If students don't comprehend something, we can't say, "Sorry, I already went over it." We have to find a different way to present the same information until they do understand. If this means dropping one of our favorite units of study because we can't connect it to the state standards, then so be it. We'll find a better unit.
- Collaborate regularly with colleagues. Collective wisdom solves most problems. Whenever professionals get together, there is a rich exchange of ideas. Without such dialogue, we become territorial, isolated, and, eventually, ineffective. We need insight and support from each other.
- Seek and use available resources. Good middle school teachers are versatile. Whether it means writing for free materials, applying for grants, seeking assistance from curriculum experts in the school district or the state, or relying on the expertise of parents and other people from the community, we must learn to ask for help.

- Give students time to learn the format and substance of the state exams. Learning is contextual. If we want students to perform well when they are asked to respond to writing prompts or analyze the steps of a scientific investigation, we must build their confidence and skills through regular practice.
- Give formative feedback. Students should never be surprised by their grades or their scores on state assessments. We must learn to think like coaches, showing students the goal, giving them opportunities to practice, and letting them know how far they've progressed.
- Embrace the premise that high standards produce good teaching and learning. Research and anecdotal experience both show that clearly defined, grade-appropriate standards that are addressed consistently from teacher to teacher improve student achievement. We can't ask for a better endorsement than that.

When we meet or hear about successful adults who acknowledge having been undisciplined or unwilling students, we usually ask what turned them around. As author and speaker Rabbi Harold Kushner reminds us, these people often reply, "There was this teacher . . ." (Scherer 1998/1999). I want to be that kind of educator, someone who is challenging, responsive, innovative, and highly effective. To do so, I must meet high standards and be accountable to my students and my profession. I'm betting that you want to rise to the challenge, too. So the next time you hear someone complaining about academic standards and educational accountability, join me in saying enthusiastically, "No problem. I'm a middle school teacher. I'll do whatever it takes to make my classroom an exciting place to learn and a place where all students achieve."

7 | Differentiated Instruction— Fitting the Lesson to the Learner

Thirteen years ago, a Cambodian family fleeing its war-torn country hid from soldiers in a rice paddy. Held just above the surface of the water, the baby began to cry. Frightened family members pleaded with the mother to hold the child underwater, thereby suffocating him and silencing his screams. She refused and held her son closer. Just as some of the cousins prepared to drown the child themselves, the soldiers moved away, leaving the baby alive but surrounded by contempt.

Two years ago, that young boy entered my English class. He had been kicked out of his home, he was living in a concrete tunnel, and he had joined a violent gang. I was supposed to teach him the importance of noun-verb agreement.

In addition to students whose lives are in turmoil and whose major purpose each day is staying alive, I have students whose intellectual development is as varied as their hair color. Some of my seventh graders read and write on a second-grade level, some read and write as well as college students, and the rest fall somewhere between those two extremes. Many of my students need concrete experiences with each topic, and some draw coherent abstract analogies with complex concepts. What's a sworn heterogeneous grouper to do?

"I differentiate instruction in order to meet the diverse needs of my students." It's nice to make such a claim, but close examination of my own lessons proves otherwise. With one hundred forty students, I often take the path of least resistance; I think that if I just say the information three different ways during the class period, then meet with those struggling few who might show up after school for additional help, I will meet everyone's need. In reality, I'm not always teaching the most effective lessons for the diverse students in my classes. It pains me to admit this, but it's true. Every day, I vow to do better, and each year in the classroom brings me closer to my goal. But boy, does it take work!

Assessing the intellectual growth of young adolescents is comparable to assessing toddlers as they learn to walk. Some will develop earlier and some later. Some will learn to walk with only a few mistakes, while others will make many more errors. And some will have visible disabilities, while other handicaps will be much more difficult to see. Similarly, children develop academically at different rates and in different ways. To assume that all middle school students will reach the same intellectual stages at the same time and to teach them as if they were one child instead of many would be just as wrong and ineffective as expecting all babies to start walking in the same month. In her book *How to Differentiate Instruction in Mixed-Ability Classrooms,* Carol Ann Tomlinson reminds us that "one-size-fits-all instruction will inevitably sag or pinch" students of the same age, just as same-size clothes would. (Gifted education usually uses the term *differentiation,* whereas special education uses the term *modification.* Tomlinson addresses both concepts in her work. For the purposes of this book, I will stick to *differentiation,* but many of the recommended classroom adjustments will benefit learners across the spectrum.)

This makes me wonder how many students passed through my classes over the years and never connected with the information and skills because I taught them all the same way. After nineteen years in this profession, I would like to think that I have figured out how to reach all my students. I haven't, but I'm working on it. I'm taking courses, researching varied strategies, and trying out new ideas in the classroom. And in the process, I have become a believer in differentiated instruction for both struggling and advanced learners.

What does that mean in actual practice? Teachers looking for the one right way to differentiate instruction will be disappointed. It doesn't exist. The quick definition is that differentiation means we do whatever it takes to meet students' learning needs, and that will vary from classroom to classroom. We can clarify the concept, however, by using some universally accepted criteria. The following examples will give us a good place to begin the conversation. As you read through these examples, ask yourself which ones demonstrate differentiated instruction, and which do not:

- In a heterogeneous classroom, the teacher asks the advanced readers to turn in two book reports but asks the students who are reading on grade level to complete only one. The gifted math students get an additional page of complex problems to solve in addition to the regular assignment for other students.
- A math teacher shows the whole class how to write large numbers in scientific notation and how to translate numbers in scientific notation back to standard form. Near the end of the lesson, he asks students to rewrite the given distances between earth and the other planets in the solar system in scientific notation and to rewrite the distance between earth and Alpha Centauri, the next closest star to the sun, from the given scientific notation form to standard form. Based on the responses, the teacher assigns students to one of two activities, one more open-ended and one more structured. In the first, students evaluate the merits

of writing in scientific notation form, providing three examples of their uses and advantages. The students also must describe three large-number situations in which scientific notation would be cumbersome to use, explaining why. In the structured activity, the teacher leads the students through a think-aloud in which someone determines the scientific notation for several large numbers and describes how to return those numbers to standard form. Next, the teacher asks these students to make a scientific notation recipe in which they must list the specific sequence for translating numbers, then practice using the recipe. Those who demonstrate mastery of content in a post-activity assessment move to an independent project using scientific notation, while those who have not demonstrated mastery move to an alternative project that reviews the important tenets of scientific notation.

- During a lesson on extinction, a science teacher asks one group of students to investigate changes that may have caused dinosaurs to disappear. Another group compares the dinosaurs' extinction to the endangered status of animals dependent on today's rain forests. (Tomlinson 1999, 47)

- When showing a filmstrip, a teacher asks some students to take notes on what they consider the most important points. She gives another group of students a list of questions to answer using information from the filmstrip, and asks a third group to fill in the correct words on a graphic organizer. A fourth group uses a photocopy of the filmstrip narration and highlights the answers to questions revealed in the filmstrip.

- Before beginning a research project on the Civil War, students review background material from videos, slide shows, field trips, class presentations/discussions, books, and guest speakers. The teacher asks the students to focus on one topic. After showing them how to narrow topics ("Civil War" becomes "Battles of the Civil War," which becomes "Gettysburg," which becomes "Strategies Used in the Battle of Gettysburg"), the teacher asks the students to brainstorm twenty questions about their topic. With the teacher or a peer, the students then narrow the questions to three that they consider most important and interesting, and use those questions to conduct further research.

- All students listen to the same guest lecturer and take notes in the same style modeled by the teacher. For homework, students choose one of the five options for reflecting on the speaker's message *based on their learning profile or skill* with the particular topic. They can write a poem, write and perform a skit, create a mind map of content, share the content with mom or dad and get their responses to it, or list the speaker's main points and categorize them according to similar attributes.

The first example does not demonstrate differentiation. All the others do.

As with many popular phrases in education, people have various interpretations of what differentiated instruction means in practice. Although some teachers never change their techniques from day to day, others flit from one method to another without a deep understanding of the meaning or appropriateness of each technique in different settings. Keep the previous examples in mind as we examine some of the essential features of differentiated instruction.

Essential Features of Differentiated Instruction

Early and Frequent Evaluations of Students' Understanding

We can use formal testing, quick pre-unit quizzes, class discussions, interviews, informal questioning, exit cards, work samples, student surveys, simulations, videotape, parent surveys, and personal observations to evaluate students' understanding. We should never change our instructional approaches in a vacuum. We must find out what and how our students need to learn.

Adjusting the Complexity or Range of Assignments

If I ask a group of students to include a detailed explanation of the respiratory system in their Hyperstudio projects and another group to include all five body systems in their projects, I'm really not adjusting the complexity of the assignment, just the amount of work for which each group is responsible. Requiring gifted students to complete more of the same type of problem that they have already mastered is a recipe for boredom or rebellion. Rather, after determining that the students understand the basic concepts, we should give them opportunities to apply their knowledge in varied settings (remember Bloom's taxonomy) or encourage them to research related topics. We also should not give fewer problems to struggling students because we consider them less capable. Some of these students might need to continue practicing until the concepts stick, or we might need to teach the topic in a different way if they didn't understand it the first time. Differentiated instruction means we match the challenge to the student, finding varied ways to help each child stretch intellectually. Keep in mind that true differentiation has three dimensions: the instruction varies depending on the student's readiness for learning, the student's learning style, and the student's interest in the topic.

In sixth grade, part of our history curriculum was to study the ancient civilization of the Romans. The easiest thing to do would be to tell us to read the chapter in the textbook and answer the questions at the end, but our teacher decided to be different and told each table group to take a different part of the chapter and present the information in a song. We were given a week to prepare. Our teacher was astounded by the effort we put into the project. I guess it paid off, because I can still remember the lyrics to the songs, even the ones I didn't sing. Besides, I aced the test.

■ Lisa, seventh grade

It's also important to examine the reasons for our assignments. What do we want students to gain from the experience? Would it be better to do the first three problems in each section or do all the problems in a few sections? What will indicate mastery?

Orchestrating the Learning Experience

In classrooms where everyone always completes the same assignments, the teacher is probably meeting the needs of only about one-fourth of the students. This is fertile ground for inattention and stalled achievement. When we walk into a classroom and see good differentiated instruction, we might perceive chaos when, in fact, the teacher has her finger on the pulse of every student. The learning just happens to be busy and loud.

Don't assume, however, that a loud classroom with students working on different activities is the only indicator of a differentiated classroom. Sometimes, the learning is quiet and subtle. Three students could be taking notes from a textbook using three different methods. Three other students could be scanning the same material targeted at three different reading levels.

There are times when all students should be doing the same thing. Sometimes direct instruction to the whole class is the most efficient and effective way to communicate ideas. Differentiation in these cases will come in the way students respond to or apply the information.

Varying Instructional Approaches over Time

I would become insane if I tried to meet every student's needs with every lesson. Instead, I use different activities over the course of a week or unit to tap each student's potential.

Differentiating Content and Skills, Process and Products

As we plan a lesson or unit, we should think, What is the essential and enduring knowledge my students need to know? What's nice to know, but not essential? What's fluff and should be eliminated from my lessons? How will I find out what students already know about the topic? Will any students need special instruction? What will I accept as proof that my students have mastered the material? In what order will we do everything, and why have I chosen that order?

Notice the sequence of planning. Before we consider any set of lessons, we first consider our objectives, the needs of our students, and the final outcome that would measure how effective we were in achieving those goals. The actual learning experience is the last thing we should design.

I have had the opportunity to travel to many middle schools during the past few years, and in each school I've seen excellent examples of differentiated instruction. Based on those observations, experiments in my own practice, and my readings and research, I've come up with some characteristics of successful instructors of mixed-ability classes. Not every good teacher shares these attributes any more than every student learns the same way. But the following sections can help you understand the skills that are necessary for effective differentiated instruction.

Characteristics of Successful Teachers of Differentiated Instruction

Risk Taking

People with this characteristic try anything that might work regardless of their comfort with the activity. Imagine a nondramatic and poetry-phobic math teacher asking students to write and perform poetry about concepts they have learned. The teacher doesn't remember any poetic devices from her own English classes, nor does she have a background in public speaking. She does understand, however, that writing and performing poetry on a particular topic for a particular audience enables some learners to know the material intimately and internalize it better than by completing a slew of practice problems. So, she takes a chance. The students become experts on the topics of their poems.

Taking instructional and professional risks in middle school teaching doesn't mean placing ourselves, our students, or our learning goals in jeopardy just to make our classrooms more exciting. What it means is that we should not be afraid to innovate, experiment, confront, dump "sacred" lessons, or reach out to others in an effort to improve our practice. We don't need to be haphazard or reckless; we can base our decisions on good pedagogy and an understanding of young adolescents.

Working in today's middle schools is one of the most exciting and rewarding jobs on the planet. Early adolescence is the birthplace of tomorrow's passions, inventions, and careers. Futurists tell us that current middle school students might live to be one hundred and twenty years old. This means that your students could live in three different centuries!

Business leaders estimate that 80 percent of all the jobs our students will perform haven't been invented yet, so our students have to be ready for anything. Employers want to

Some teachers that I used to have thought that the students would make fun of them if they tried new things. But the fact of the matter is, that if they remember it and it has a positive impact and they laugh, they will be sure to remember it on, like, a test. So going out on the limb just to teach your students really helps them remember the materials you taught them, and lets them know that you do care if they understand or not.

■ Ankur, eighth grade

hire people who can learn on the job, solve problems, anticipate needs, collaborate with others, think independently, and behave ethically. They're seeking individuals with a solid core of knowledge and a strong work ethic. To prepare our students for the future, we must think beyond yesterday and today, and that means taking risks.

One way to do this is to teach what is important, not just what is outlined in the curriculum. If the novel your department has determined every child shall read is not appropriate for a small group of students, let these youngsters read something else from the same genre. You know Carl will have a problem with percentages taught as the next step after decimals, as the curriculum indicates, so you teach him the same concept through a unit on fractions. In each instance, students' needs prompt instructional decisions. Curriculum and sequence are guidelines, not blueprints.

Most states have implemented academic standards and accountability tests, and we have to pay attention to them. But the state trusts us to think independently and to make tough professional decisions when necessary. As long as we can clearly demonstrate a student's need for alternative approaches or curriculum, and can show the positive results that occur as a result of those choices, we will find support.

Taking risks also means letting go of comfortable ways. We can ask questions for which we do not know the answers. I'm guilty sometimes of teaching to elicit particular responses from my students. When this happens, I'm not open to alternative answers. Pushing students toward an intended outcome can be valuable, but we also need to be open to insights and connections that we haven't previously considered. As teachers, all of us should release the reins once in a while and go where our students or the open inquiry take us.

Let students occasionally teach the day's lesson. If a student can help another understand a concept, he has learned the content well himself. Research shows that students retain information from their peers at higher rates than from their teachers, so give them opportunities to debate, participate in Socratic seminars, and coach their classmates. You won't always be able to control the outcome, but that's okay. Learning shouldn't be predictable.

One of my teaching heroes is Nancy Boush, a colleague from my time at Freedom Hill Elementary School in Vienna, Virginia. She told me that she always changed at least 50 percent of a lesson every time she taught it. Otherwise, she said, she'd go crazy, and so would her students. A variation of this strategy is to list the objectives for our lessons and come up with three new ways for students to experience the content and demonstrate their understanding. We can take a lesson we've taught the same way for three or four years, file it away, and start afresh. Or we can ask a colleague how he teaches it. Trying something new can show us how to do it better.

I learned early on that trial-and-error provides a clear path to competence. When I was a young adolescent, my dad used to check the outside of my pants after a day spent skiing. He told me that if my pants were dry, suggesting that I hadn't taken any spills in the snow, I wasn't advancing my skills. His words echoed in my ears on the fifteenth face plant of the day on the icy double diamond. More times than I can count, I ruefully shouted, "I'm learning!" straight into the thick snow pack smashed against my face.

I believe we need to give ourselves permission to make similar mistakes in the classroom. This is particularly true when we're starting out in teaching. Without failure, we will never improve. And without experiencing the frustrations of learning, we will have a difficult time empathizing with and guiding our students during their struggles. Through personal examples we can show our students that it's not only *okay* to fail but *enriching* because failure helps us grow in ways that consistent success never can. In stressing the inevitability of failure, we can also teach students how to profit from their mistakes, expand their understanding, lose gracefully, and develop an ethic of lifelong learning.

Empathetic

Such teachers understand what it's like to be a student in their classrooms. They often sit with students when coaching them or planning lessons. They take their own tests. They consider their own experiences as students in middle school. They listen closely to students' concerns, and they respond to what they hear and understand. They try to experience the lessons from the perspective of learning-disabled students, too. (Richard Lavoie is a master at providing such experiences for teachers. I highly recommend his video *F.A.T. City Workshop*. When I watched it and felt the creeping panic of not knowing the information he was presenting in the simulation, I changed my practices dramatically.)

Organized

Teachers who are organized spend a great deal of time thinking and planning before their students walk through the classroom door. They place plastic containers or boxes in their rooms, each serving a useful purpose. They rotate assignment deadlines for different class periods to avoid being swamped with grading duties. They orchestrate traffic patterns in the room. They plan for transitions between topics and activities to minimize time delays. They have considered and prepared for disruptions and breaks in the pace of the class.

Wait a minute, you say, no amount of planning and organization can eliminate the kinks that occur in a typical day in middle school. You're right.

You can't plan for an emotional meltdown in a seventh grader, for a serious lack of coherence in your fifth-period class's oral responses, and for the group of eighth graders who still don't understand the project design after the third explanation. But as Louis Pasteur said, "Chance favors the prepared mind." The more we plan and organize our lessons, the more likely we will be able to respond well to each new challenge. Organization helps us be more creative, flexible, impulsive, and confident.

Comfortable with Authentic Learning Experiences and Applications

Teachers who successfully differentiate make sure their assessments measure what students have learned. For example, if a teacher uses a verification lab, in which students follow a given procedure to arrive at a known answer, then she doesn't ask students to conduct an inquiry lab for the final assessment. Inquiry labs require students to design their own methods of investigation to answer their own questions. Assessing students through a technique with which they are unfamiliar is not a valid evaluation of their skills.

Flexible

If it's not working, then drop it and do something else. Successful middle school teachers respond to teachable moments instead of staying glued to the lesson plan. They seize every opportunity to make an analogy or create a vivid expression of the concepts they are trying to convey.

Tenacious

These teachers persevere, and they find ways to instill that doggedness in their students. They teach coping skills, such as breaking things down into smaller units. In addition, they "teach up," in the words of Carol Ann Tomlinson. They set rigorous goals and show students how to reach them. They know that hard work is motivating as long as students consider it important.

For example, when I'm teaching students to write persuasive essays, I post four strong examples and ask students to work together to identify the factors that made those essays so powerful. In a discussion, we jointly come up with a rubric that includes those factors, then evaluate other excellent persuasive essays according to our criteria to see if we need to revise our thinking. Afterward, students write their own essays according to the criteria, peer-critique them, then revise.

Fleet of Foot

Teachers who use differentiated instruction effectively take whatever steps are necessary to make ideas clear to their students. They photocopy handouts in large sizes for visually impaired students, put books on tape for learning-disabled students, and make large matrices to keep track of student achievement.

Resourceful

Such teachers have an ever-growing repertoire of instructional strategies. They are aware of the differences in learners, and they know how to engage them. They never stop looking for new ideas, and they welcome the advice of seasoned veterans as well as novice teachers.

Able to Collaborate

These teachers know that they make better decisions in collaboration with others than they would if they acted alone. They see accomplished education professionals as colleagues, not threats.

Having a Good Sense of Humor

Successful teachers of mixed-ability classes can laugh at themselves and the content, seeing the silly and the sophisticated in their middle school classrooms. Their students feel good about being in the classroom and are more inclined to listen to the substance of the teacher's message.

Designing Differentiated Lessons

It's easiest for me to teach by talking to students and writing ideas on the chalkboard. I can do it enthusiastically, using great analogies and stories to illuminate content. If all my students learned successfully this way, I'd never have to plan another lesson. They don't all learn the way I like to teach, of course, so I have to use varied techniques. This means not only being aware of alternative designs but actually using them.

I have a friend who is dyslexic, and struggles with reading books unless they are books on tape, and most reference books are not. She does not learn with lecturing, either, because she can get things mixed up easily. It is effective if, on a project, students are given a choice to do either fine or performing arts. It enables them to work in groups or alone, and to use the multiple intelligence areas that they are good at. I like how our middle school has an emphasis on working together and is referred to as a family a lot. It makes people more able to accept disabilities of others. In my elementary school, there were kids who were in L.D. They were always picked on and had a hard time. In this school, I find that they are all treated like normal by most of the teachers and students.

■ Lindsay, seventh grade

My sixth-grade chorus teacher was really nice. She had a great sense of humor and was willing to compromise. When I missed my audition, she added a part for me and some other kids. And during play practice we all laughed. When I need help, one of my teachers just gives me problems to sort out, nothing else!

■ Bethany, seventh grade

There are many good frameworks that can accommodate the needs of mixed-ability classes. A sample differentiated instruction lesson follows, and a second sample can be found in Appendix I. They are examples of a tiered lesson that includes differentiated instruction based on students' learning profiles (determined through multiple intelligences analysis earlier in the school year) and readiness skills (determined by a preassessment). Keep in mind that you can modify these groups as needed; I shuffle students around when my observations of their in-class performance and my analysis of their work samples suggest that they are ready for different challenges. I recently put the following lesson to the test when Carol Ann Tomlinson and the Association for Supervision and Curriculum Development videotaped a week's worth of my classes for a series on effective differentiated instruction. (See Appendix J for a suggested planning sequence for lesson design.)

Plan for Differentiated Instruction Lesson on Writer's Voice

I.   Inviting and thinking activities
   A.   Distribute and dramatically interpret literary selections with a strong writer's voice (good choices include Lewis Thomas, Mark Twain, Carl Sagan, and Dudley Randall).
   B.   Ask, What do all of these pieces have in common? Record characteristics on the chalkboard.
   C.   Distribute and dramatically interpret letter from Abraham Lincoln to Mrs. Bixby (who lost five sons during the Civil War). Ask, Does this piece have the same criteria listed earlier? Discuss. Revise criteria for strong writer's voice. Students record notes in English notebook.
   D.   Ask, What do we know about the writer that comes through his words? Brainstorm. Students record notes in English notebook and title the page "Writer's Voice."

II. Setting context for the lesson
   A.   Essential understanding: "Voice is the writer revealed." Make statement, briefly discuss, and ask students to write in response for two to four minutes.

III. Presenting the agenda or itinerary
   A.   Post on the chalkboard in restaurant menu style:
      •   Appetizers—Introductory activities.
      •   Entrées—Establish writer's voice journal. Break into groups for further study.
      •   Desserts—3-2-1 Summary.

IV. Applying learning models/experiences that best fit students' and lesson's needs
   A.   Establish writer's voice journal for three weeks. Assignment: Write in it every day for three weeks for at least ten minutes.

Remind students that the best thinking comes after fifteen to twenty minutes. Tell them to write quickly and honestly, no self-editing along the way, so as to liberate their writing voices. Ask them to write about an event that happened within the previous twenty-four hours and their response to it. Place each day's writing on a different page for a total of at least twenty-one pages. Conduct checkpoints each week.

   B. Move students into tiered study groups (and into new seats) based on pre-unit assessment on writer's voice.

   C. Advanced group tasks. Identify the tools for writer's voice; analyze voice. Look at the samples from today's reading. Identify the specific tools that writers use to express their voice. Assignment: Choose a well-known celebrity and write a narrative or speech that allows that person's personality to come through. Explain how you tailored the piece to fit the person. (Students should complete this writing assignment independently, share their writing with partners for critique later in the week, revise the piece based on input, then share with the whole class.)

   D. Introductory group tasks. Define writer's voice, play with voice, begin to identify the tools. Discuss what we've already learned about voice today. Assignment: Choose an event and describe it from three different points of view (three different inanimate objects in the scene). (Group students in two's and three's because they feel safer to generate ideas.) Suggested events: preparing a pizza, changing a tire, playing a basketball game, attending a rock concert, visiting the dentist. Students should explain what they changed to represent the "personality" and point of view of each item. Record all responses in writing.

V. Distributing and explaining essential understandings for the unit (whole-class activity)

   A. Voice is the writer revealed.

   B. There are specific tools to create voice, including word choice, audience awareness, sentence structures, punctuation, tone, and knowledge of topic.

   C. Voice takes time to develop.

   D. Writers can have strong voices.

   E. Students are writers.

VI. Distributing and explaining assessments

   A. Students will select a piece of literature and successfully write or perform it using two significantly different voices that accurately reflect the personalities of the authors and their intended audiences.

B.   Students will accurately describe the tools writers use to create strong voice, and they will provide an example of each tool.

C.   Students will accurately describe the writer's voice in a selected literary piece.

D.   Students will rewrite a literary piece that has little or no voice.

E.   Students will write a literary piece with a strong voice and explain how they accomplished it.

VII. End of lesson summary/closure (3-2-1 Style)

A.   Three things you have learned about voice and its creation.

B.   Two comments about your own writer's voice.

C.   One question you have about writer's voice or the unit ahead.

VIII. Advance look at the next lesson

A.   Read short excerpt from James Gunn's short story "The Boy with Five Fingers." Ask students to comment on the effect of sentence length on the writer's voice. (Tomorrow's lesson will focus on using sentence variety as a tool for effective writer's voice.)

In his book *Super Teaching,* Eric Jensen states, "Seventy-five percent of teachers are sequential, analytic presenters [whereas] 70 percent of all their students do not learn that way" (25). He reminds teachers to provide variety and choice in lessons so students will encounter one of their strengths at least half the time.

If our goal is getting students to the point of mastering, not just covering, the content, we owe it to them to provide highly effective practice. Does this mean we throw out all the traditional methods of teaching? No. We should use many methods in balance.

Traditional, direct instruction can be effective, depending on the learner. But understanding why and when to use it is critical. Let's examine two common instructional methods—traditional and constructivist—to see why good differentiation depends on our ability to use various approaches wisely.

> We always did a lot of fun projects and models in sixth grade. I remember when we were studying Greece, I made a balsa Greek warship, and also did a game show. Those were really cool, but I am disappointed that we have not had any cool projects like that in seventh.
>
> ■ Scotter, seventh grade

In traditional classrooms, curriculum is presented part to the whole, with an emphasis on basic skills. In constructivist classrooms, curriculum is presented whole to the part, with an emphasis on the big concepts. The difference is in the lesson's goals. For example, constructivist teachers don't seek to declare a student a reader because he can decode words. They assess students as they read a variety of materials for a variety of purposes.

In traditional classrooms, teachers tend to adhere to a fixed curriculum. In constructivist classrooms, the curriculum is a background for promoting student inquiries. In the latter case, I might initially teach the process of photosynthesis but let my students' questions guide follow-up inquiries:

Are plants the only living creatures that produce their
own food?

How does the energy in photosynthesis transfer to animals that eat the plants?

What would have to change for animals to be able to
conduct photosynthesis on their own? How would
this affect the web of life?

> In science, our teacher had us make a cartoon of the parts of a cell. This really helped me because I learn better from drawing or doing activities than filling out a worksheet or doing work in a book. I had no trouble remembering each part and its job when I took the test.
> ■ Jessica, seventh grade

Note that constructivist methods are not just for extension or enrichment activities. They are particularly effective in
helping students comprehend basic facts as well.

Traditional teaching tends to rely heavily on textbooks and workbooks.
Constructivist teaching seeks to use primary sources and manipulative materials that let students "hold" the concepts in their hands. Most textbooks not
only state the content but explain what it means. When we use primary
sources, students have to find the meaning for themselves. For example, I
could describe communist societies, such as the former Soviet Union, then
describe democratic/capitalist societies, such as the United States. Afterward,
I could give my students a test to see if they understood the difference
between the two forms of government. But if I wanted to let my students construct their own meanings, I could present excerpts from each country's constitution with the identifying names removed. Working in small groups, students could determine the country in which they would most like to live,
using evidence from the constitutions to explain their reasoning. Every time
I use this exercise, my students always choose communism. It sounds like
paradise to them. When I reveal the societies that each constitution represents, the students are shocked. This leads to fascinating discussions about
the ideals and realities of both systems. (I'm indebted to Dr. Josiah Tlou, one
of my professors at Virginia Tech University, for the genesis of this lesson.)

In math, instead of proving the Pythagorean Theorem to students, we
could give them three plastic squares and ask them to work in groups to
come up with a relationship among the squares that leads to A squared plus B
squared equals C squared. Brooks and Brooks remind us that Ptolemy's views
of the solar system were considered "right" for the time period, but in light of
Copernicus's views, they were found to be faulty. In middle schools today,
what do we fail to uncover in our messages about what's "right" and what's
"wrong"?

Traditional teachers tend to look for correct answers to see if students
have learned the required material. Constructivist teachers seek to hear students' perspectives, both to assess their understanding and to determine the
next step in the learning process. Ah, I think, Manuel said the correct
answer, so he must understand the concept. Or does he? To make sure, I ask
him to explain how he arrived at his answer and to compare those steps to

the example we did together. I ask him to point out any differences in the sequences that he can find. In addition, he must determine a second way to solve the problem in case he has to explain the concept to someone who didn't grasp it through the first example. I also look at Manuel's work to see whether he can compute the concept, and I use those observations to determine what I need to review or teach next.

Constructivist teachers seek to

- Encourage and accept student autonomy and initiative
- Ask open-ended questions
- Determine student understanding before sharing their own interpretations
- Provide time for students to construct metaphors and incorporate inquiry methods
- Make assessment an extension of instruction

Admittedly, constructivist approaches are time-consuming; it's easier to lecture. But our quick "guess what the teacher wants" activities will not prepare students to be intelligent thinkers capable of using information beyond our classrooms. Instruction with lecture as the dominant method appeals to only about one fourth of our students, leaving three-fourths out in the cold. Out of the many instructional methods available, lecturing moves the smallest amount of material to long-term memory and relies on symbolic and abstract thinking when the majority of middle-grade students still think concretely.

Since I've said all this about lecturing, you would think that I wouldn't use it in my classroom, but I do. I know that some students respond well to lectures, and if I truly want to provide different ways for students to succeed, lecturing must be one of my strategies. In a typical class period, I might lecture for fifteen minutes, use a constructivist or summarization activity, return to a short lecture, and conclude with another activity that gets students moving and thinking. Lecturing should be just one of many choices, not the only one.

Constructivist teaching can be scary. Students' explorations threaten the status quo. To some of us, this will sound exciting. To others, it might seem like a recipe for classroom chaos. But when we examine successful constructivist classrooms, we see evidence not of anarchy but of active learning, which should be a cause for celebration instead of alarm. In deciding whether to follow the path of constructivism, consider the words of broadcaster Fred Friendly: "Our job is not

> Lecturing about facts and talking about information is not a good way of teaching because it does not put the students' brains to work. The students aren't analyzing any information by sitting and listening to the teacher pointlessly emitting facts. They are merely just hearing facts. In order for information to be truly absorbed, it must be presented in a way that will be interesting to the students and will force them to use their brains to think of new ideas and conclusions.
>
> Data can bounce off the students' skulls like a bird running into a window. I think a teacher's goal should be to aim for having the students understand the material, not to aim for having the students listen to the teacher present it to them.
>
> ■ Ben, eighth grade

to make up anybody's mind, but to open minds and to make the agony of the decision making so intense you can escape only by thinking."

Traditional and constructivist are only two of the many different learning models we should consider in our practice. Accomplished middle-level teachers seek and use these models to better understand their students and make effective instructional decisions based on that knowledge. Some of the best models include the Myers-Briggs personality indicators (see Keirsey 1998), McCarthy's 4-MAT System, Gregorc's scale and teaching model, and Harrison and Bramson's styles of thinking.

No chapter on differentiation would be complete without a discussion of Howard Gardner's multiple intelligences theory and its middle school applications. When it was first published in the 1980s, his theory illuminated something we knew intuitively but had not been able to structure or express. "It's not how smart you are, it's how you are smart," Gardner said. He defined intelligence as "the capacity to solve problems or to fashion products that are valued in one or more cultural settings." "Bobby Fischer might inherently have had the potential to be a great chess player," Gardner wrote, "but if he had lived in a culture without chess, that potential would never have been manifested, let alone actualized. Intelligence is always an interaction between biological proclivities and opportunities for learning in a particular cultural context." Gardner received a MacArthur Prize in 1981.

General intelligence, according to Gardner, is divided into eight different and equally important parts:

- Linguistic. The ability to think about and use language to express complex meanings. Examples: poets, teachers, writers, public speakers, and journalists.
- Logical/Mathematical. The ability to calculate, hypothesize, quantify, and use symbolic and sequential reasoning skills as well as inductive and deductive thinking patterns. Examples: scientists, mathematicians, and detectives.
- Bodily/Kinesthetic. The ability to manipulate objects and use a variety of physical skills. Good mind-body coordination. Examples: athletes, dancers, surgeons, and carpenters.
- Visual/Spatial. The ability to think in multiple dimensions and use spatial reasoning and graphic and artistic skills. Examples: sailors, pilots, sculptors, painters, and architects.
- Musical. The ability to recognize, create, and reproduce music. Can easily determine the pitch, rhythm, timbre, and tone of music. People with this intelligence like learning with songs, patterns, and rhythm. Examples: composers, musicians, singers, and conductors.
- Interpersonal. The ability to understand and interact with others well. Uses verbal and nonverbal communications, is sensitive to the moods of

others, and can accept multiple perspectives. Examples: teachers, social workers, actors, and politicians.

- Intrapersonal. The ability to understand one's own thoughts and feelings and to use that knowledge to plan one's life. Very intuitive and reflective. Examples: psychologists, spiritual leaders, and counselors.
- Naturalist. The ability to tell the differences among living things and be sensitive to the natural world. Recognizes patterns in society and in nature, likes to categorize things. Examples: naturalists, collectors, campers, researchers, botanists, and zoologists.

Gardner is considering adding a ninth intelligence:

- Existentialist. People with this ability often ask the big questions of life, such as Why are we here? and What is our purpose in the world? They focus on humanity's existence. Example: philosophers.

Every person has a dynamic mix of all these intelligences, which are autonomous and at varying stages of development. Each person's intellectual package is unique. Commonly, one intelligence enhances another, for example, a mathematically inclined student who is also a gifted musician. Gardner says it is extremely rare to find a person with one purely dominant intelligence.

Each of these intelligences can be nurtured and strengthened. Unfortunately, schools don't always do this because teachers focus primarily on the logical and linguistic learning styles. But when we use authentic assessments that tap into the multiple intelligences of our students, we gain a better measurement of what they know and can do. If I allow students to respond in more than one way, I will get a more valid indication of all students' comprehension. Some students' understanding may not show up fully through writing, for example, but I will see it reflected in their art or their dramatic interpretations.

Appreciating the theory of multiple intelligences equalizes access to learning. Each year, I teach Gardner's theory to my students. Afterward, they become more tolerant and encouraging of one another. Just because David can't write well doesn't mean his PowerPoint presentation will demonstrate less than full mastery of the material. My students also seem more willing to try new things after they have analyzed their own learning strengths. Because they see themselves as having more than one intelligence and being capable in many areas, they are not as afraid to struggle in situations that call for the use of one of their minor intelligences. In addition, I let students negotiate their final assessments on some units, and most of the time they create far more rigorous projects and products than I would have required.

There are many good resources on multiple intelligences. Among the best I've read and used: Thomas Armstrong's *Multiple Intelligences in the Classroom,*

Howard Gardner's *Frames of Mind: A Theory of Multiple Intelligences,* and David Lazear's *Seven Ways of Teaching: The Artistry of Teaching with Multiple Intelligences.*

Putting Theory into Action

For each lesson, we should consider which model of instruction is appropriate, given the content and the needs of our students. We also should have a framework for managing the instruction. For example, we might opt to have a central activity that everyone is working on while we pull groups of students out for mini-lessons. When students finish those short lessons, they return to the main activity, and we can work with another small group. Carol Ann Tomlinson calls the whole-class activities to which students return anchor activities; such activities hold the weight of our topic while students float through various extensions and reinforcements. Four students don't seem to understand the science terms? Create a small group that you can work with while everyone else writes a persuasive essay on an environmental issue. Another group needs to redo the lab? Two students have been out with the flu and need to catch up? The anchor activity method is an effective way to deal with all these needs in one class period (see Appendix K).

Another model of differentiated instruction incorporates learning centers through which students can rotate at their own pace. I know this sounds like elementary school, but it's very useful in middle school classrooms as well. At each center, make sure to include substantive material to learn, clear directions, ample supplies, and a product that demonstrates mastery of the material. I strongly suggest laminating materials to increase their durability. Don't forget to appeal to different strengths at each center. In other words, don't ask students to read and summarize an article at every center. Make some of the tasks physical, some linguistic, some artistic, some visual, some reflective, some analytical, some open-ended, and some structured. When I create centers, I usually keep them up for several days to a week so everyone has time to move through them. My role is to move from center to center, refocusing students as necessary and monitoring their understanding.

Tomlinson says that good differentiated instruction also has a nice ebb and flow (see Appendix L). During the course of a unit, the teacher uses large-group activities such as class discussions, sharing information, creating rubrics, and setting goals. Alternating with these experiences, however, are activities that ask students to work alone or in small groups.

Build student autonomy. Teach students how to get help when you're teaching someone else. Give them as much

> I find it nice to be able to talk a lot, because in some classes you can't talk very much. In civics, at least lately, we've done some debates. I like that because I've got a lot of issues that I feel very strongly about and I have to talk about them or I get really frustrated.
> ■ Preston, eighth grade

responsibility for their learning as possible. Let them maintain records, stock supplies, coach others, find materials, check homework, and greet visitors. It might take time to teach these habits, but it will pay off later when you are able to reach more students while encouraging their overall independence.

Pay attention to student attention. Many young adolescents find it hard to concentrate on any topic or task for more than fifteen minutes. If you want to maximize the focus on your lesson, consider starting with a lecture, followed by a summarization technique, followed by a think-pair-share, and back to the lecture again.

Make sure to include regular moments of celebration in your classes. Students need affirmations of their progress; these provide perspective and hope. Help students to make calendars of completion and to refer to them often. For long-term projects, the calendars detail what should be done each week (or each day) in order to get to the final due date. After providing such a calendar for one project, ask students to design their own calendars on subsequent projects and share them in class for critique and approval.

Go for the big ideas with some students. Sweating complete mastery of every detail and procedure with students who aren't cognitively ready for them is a waste of time. Think of the curriculum as a spiral. Push as far as is reasonable, then move on. You can return to that topic later. However, some students will not need the normal unit sequence and content. They already know what you're going to teach, so after assessing their skills, let them move on to more advanced material.

Gifted and Talented Students

I teach students identified as gifted and talented, students identified as learning-disabled, and students identified as being in regular education. Parents often ask what I do differently with my gifted and talented students.

No matter what the ability level, I teach the essential and enduring knowledge first. The same standards of learning for the Commonwealth of Virginia hold true for all. Gifted students cover more material during the course of the year, whether by moving more rapidly, exploring concepts in greater depth, or researching a broader field of study.

For gifted students, I emphasize higher-order thinking skills, such as analysis, synthesis, evaluation, application, and justifying answers, as standard operating procedure, not something newly introduced. I invite tangential thinking and nontraditional grammar, sentence structure, vocabulary, and voice. I place additional emphasis on word morphology, editing and revising, desktop publishing, public speaking, multimedia skills, and all aspects of scholarly research. They use textbooks and novels as resources, not as the entire curriculum. They use primary sources more heavily. Gifted students know that enrichment does not equal fluff. All activities are academically substantive.

Everyone with whom I've spoken or whose work I've read, both math specialists and middle school reform experts, have cautioned against heterogeneous grouping in math classes. It seems to be the one subject where such grouping negatively affects student understanding and performance, especially in fifty-minute classes. As a former middle school math teacher, I have to agree. Although many inclusive math activities can meet the needs of students with varying abilities, a strictly heterogeneous math class is rarely effective. This is not to say that heterogeneous grouping and all the accompanying strategies *cannot* work in a middle school math class, especially with block scheduling, but it's certainly more difficult.

Taking Their Temperature

Responding well to a range of abilities in a regular middle school classroom is not easy, but it's possible. It requires serious reflection on our practice, and if you're like me, some important changes. Yet despite all these preparations sometimes we fail. The student from Cambodia mentioned in the opening paragraphs of this chapter turned out to be quite witty, even charismatic with classmates and staff. He tested in the above-average intelligence range, too. Unfortunately, we couldn't get him to stay with us after school to fill in his academic gaps. He fell further and further behind.

The gang lure was strong. When he entered high school, he had several weapons altercations with the local police and, the last I heard, was attending an alternative school in our district. I am filled with sorrow for him, but in the end school wasn't appealing enough. When I asked him once why he hung out with a nineteen-year-old gang member, he said, "Because he has a car, man," and smiled.

"That's it?" I asked. He nodded enthusiastically.

"Isn't that like you, a thirteen-year-old, hanging out with a seven-year-old? Doesn't that seem strange to you?"

"Not to me, man."

I asked him if he knew of any gang members older than twenty-one. He couldn't think of any. "Does that bother you?" I asked.

"No way, Wormeli," he said. "I'll go out full."

My heart fell. He already had settled for death at a young age. I pleaded with his peers to step in and help. They couldn't. His grades plummeted. We turned things over to the social worker and truant officer. It was one of the hardest things I ever did as a teacher, to let go. To this day, I look for him whenever I drive by gang hangouts, hoping to catch a glimpse of him—alive.

We don't succeed in reaching every student. We're only one of many influences in a child's life. And given how public schools are organized, with each teacher responsible for up to one hundred and fifty students at a time, it can be difficult to adjust our instruction for each one. Instead of causing us to give up or become indifferent to their varied learning needs, however, situations such as this one should serve to strengthen our resolve to work more closely with our colleagues and get the word out about the most effective strategies.

A teacher who uses differentiated instruction well is like a thermostat, someone who senses the rising and falling levels of intellectual achievement and emotional well-being of her students and adjusts accordingly. I can't say with certainty, but I believe that if more of the Cambodian student's teachers had given him varied opportunities to demonstrate his understanding, he might be in college today instead of on the streets. And I believe that if I had been more consistently successful at tapping this student's talents, I could have made a difference, too. It's easy to say that we can't provide individualized instruction for all the students we serve, so they should adapt to (or tolerate) our teaching styles and make the best of it. In my view, this is a cop-out. It is the statement of tired teachers who ought to move along and let others take their place.

I have implemented many mixed-ability practices in my classroom during the past few years. Several things are occurring as a result. I'm more focused on what's truly important in an overloaded curriculum, and I'm choosing the content and skills of my lessons with greater confidence. I have become more efficient out of necessity. Best of all, my students are comprehending more than they used to. Multiple pathways to the same high standard of performance do not weaken academic rigor: they strengthen it, taking students farther than they would have gone had the teacher not used differentiated instruction. It's a middle school challenge worth pursuing.

Effective Assessment

8

Danny, a student of mine, was a poor writer but an accomplished guitar player who performed regularly in a rock band. We were studying S. E. Hinton's novel *The Outsiders,* and I needed to assess what students understood about the book. Usually, I would ask them to write a summary and describe the theme and five major plot conflicts of whatever we were reading at the time. Although I realized from our conversations that Danny had read and understood the book, I knew that he would struggle to complete this particular writing assignment. I decided to find a different way to test his comprehension.

Danny eventually wrote an original score for the guitar, and he performed his piece for the class. At one point in the novel, a beloved character dies. When Danny finished his fast-paced electric guitar riff about the gang rumble that preceded the death, he struck a single, powerful note that seemed to hover in the air before fading away. Two classes of middle school students stared in silent awe, for Danny had almost magically conveyed the book's tragic climax. Through the lyrics, he also managed to describe the theme and five major conflicts in the story, using the proper literary terminology.

Danny probably would have received an F if I had asked him to write a summary of the plot, but I was not evaluating his summarization skills. I wanted to know if he understood the book. By offering a musical interpretation, he was able to demonstrate his knowledge convincingly. I gave him a well-deserved A. On another day, we tackled summarization. Appendix M shows sample rubrics and Socratic seminar questions for this unit.

Education researcher Jay McTighe says that assessment should promote learning, not just measure it. I think he's right. Assessment shouldn't only document the quality of a performance but also demonstrate a student's depth of understanding, which shows both the teacher and the student what they need to do next in the learning process.

Whether it's formal or informal, good assessment has clear characteristics. First, it is connected to the learning. Good assessment is never saved for the end of a unit but gives students feedback while they're learning. Track coaches don't wait until the meet is over to tell athletes what they did right or wrong. They assess progress routinely and offer strategies for improvement so the athletes can practice as much as possible before the big event. Depending on an athlete's performance during practice, the coach might adjust the training, just as a classroom teacher might change the lesson based on indicators of student comprehension.

Assess comes from the Latin word *assidere,* "to sit beside." I like the image that represents for teaching; we can consult with our students and use various assessments to diagnose their strengths and weaknesses. In the current climate of high-stakes testing and accountability, we must be careful to think of assessment as a tool for measuring progress along a continuum instead of as a single test score lifted from one day of the school year. Assessment should show us the big picture of a student's development over time as well as the incremental steps along the way.

When I observe or meet with students, I routinely jot notes on yellow sticky pads, indicating what concepts I need to teach or reteach. I know some teachers who carry clipboards containing charts of students' progress. Either way, we seek information about the skills or knowledge students have gained or missed. I use those notes to help me decide whether to alter my lessons or offer targeted intervention to a single student, a group of students, or the entire class. Sometimes I've thrown out the rest of the week's lessons because the feedback I received in Tuesday's classes indicated that students didn't understand the basic steps well enough to move ahead to more complex applications.

In "Practicing What We Preach in Designing Authentic Assessments," Grant Wiggins says teachers should focus on the outcomes or objectives of our lessons. He encourages us to think through statements such as, "The students really understand (the idea, issue, theory) when they can . . . provide credible theories, models, or interpretations to explain . . . avoid such common misunderstandings as . . . explain the value or importance of . . . critically question the commonly held view that . . .," and so forth. These are rigorous expectations. If my students can successfully perform these tasks, I know they have achieved at high levels.

I try to involve students in these ongoing assessments as much as possible. For example, students critique their classmates' essays using the same rubric that I will use when grading the final product. On an overhead projector, I show samples (past or present) of good writing and discuss the qualities that made them successful. Substitute a science experiment, solutions to a math problem, a comparison of political parties, or some other assignment, and you will see how the ensuing conversations can provide direction for every learner in the room. Another technique is to videotape students as they're presenting information, then review the videotape and offer constructive commentary, as a sports analyst might evaluate an athlete's performance.

The following sections describe the characteristics of good assessment.

Defining Clear Goals

Good assessment defines the goal at the beginning, not the end, of a unit. Students should know exactly what the objective is. In the real world, we usually know what success looks like. A plumber works to unclog the sink. A physician seeks treatments that will make the patient healthy. An auto mechanic knows that the customer wants the car to run well. If most adults know the expected outcome of their efforts at work, shouldn't students know, too? Why should a student ever have to ask, What's going to be on the test?

I know this will sound a bit radical, but I advocate giving students a copy of the test or expected performance when starting a new unit. Make the questions or standards difficult so students can't easily memorize the answers. The goal of learning should never be a mystery. As Jay McTighe says, "When students have opportunities to examine their work in light of known criteria and performance standards, they begin to shift their orientation from 'What did I get?' to 'Now I know what I need to do to improve'" (9).

I've seen a significant increase in subject mastery among students who received my assessments in advance compared to the students I taught years ago, when I still kept my test formats secret. My students used to say, "I didn't know you wanted that" or "You never told us it had to be in cursive" or "I thought one supporting detail was enough." Students with learning disabilities were overwhelmed by the need to study everything, so they studied nothing or the wrong things. Ambiguity bred stress in all students regardless of their academic skills. It also made the learning a teacher-driven process. I was the answer man, and I would bestow the mark of acceptance on selected individuals who were able to guess what I had in mind. Today, my students focus on key concepts and how to learn them instead of playing guessing games with me. The content and skills are the hub around which we revolve. I am the liberator, not the gatekeeper, and my students are achieving more as a result.

Rigorous and Motivating

Good assessment is rigorous and therefore motivating. Hard work inspires when it matters, which means it must be aimed at a specific audience that will respond to it, be useful to someone else, or be relevant to the student. Students' effort and skills increase dramatically when they know someone besides the teacher will read or respond to their work. They rise to the challenge, and they don't seem to mind subsequent coaching or revising.

> There are lot of things my teacher does that are very helpful. One thing is the way he gives us an advance look at the test to study off of. Sometimes when I am instructed to learn about a particular topic, I remember it better if there are specific things I need to know about. For example, if I needed to know about dinosaurs, it would be easier if I needed to know specific things like where they lived, what they ate, etc. An advance look at the test helps me because I can look at what I need to know, and I remember it.
>
> ■ Carrie, seventh grade

Good assessment also has depth. For example, when I use the computer software program SimCity, I don't ask students to play the game for the fun of it but to further their understanding of a topic. SimCity lets players build a city using finite resources, a growing population, and variables such as traffic jams, fires, and under-funded government departments. With a unit on communities or habitats, I would use the software to teach the basic elements of urban planning, then ask groups of students to plan an underwater city based on the principles they learned through SimCity. While they were designing the city, I would ask questions about factors such as oxygen supply, salinity, sea life, corrosion, pressure, diminished sunlight, underwater topography, hydroponics, and the three-dimensional nature of underwater transportation. Multiple-choice tests might be administratively easier to produce and score than these more elaborate assessments, but they won't give you as much information about what your students can do with what they've learned.

If you want to have rigorous and motivating assessments, let your students design the test or scoring rubric from time to time. They buy into the assessment when they write it, and they are often tougher on themselves than we would be. When my students create their own evaluations, they often have a keener understanding of their academic progress. Their insights amaze me. Students of all skill levels speak like seasoned professionals, using language appropriate to the assessment. These are some of their exact verbal and written statements: "I haven't found enough primary sources, only secondary." "My conclusion isn't an orderly summary of points made in the main body." "This doesn't really contrast the differences—it only shows I can draw well." "I need to label what I mean." "I've put so many funny lines in here, it's hard to see the mathematics I'm trying to explain. The lines are distracting." By creating and applying the assessment tool, they learn how to use it to hold themselves to high standards.

To encourage students to try different evaluation formats, we can provide three or four samples and ask them to brainstorm at least ten others. So for a demonstration of the differences between plant and animal cells, I might show the class a comic strip that includes superhero plant and animal cells, a clay sculpture, a poem, and a video of a mime act. Then I would ask the class to list the common characteristics of the products and the qualities that made them outstanding. After some probing questions and a discussion, we would revise the list until we could agree on a few important characteristics that would constitute our standard of excellence. At this point, I would bring out another product that I consider outstanding and apply the new rubric to it. If it works, we move on. If it doesn't, we revise our thinking and rewrite the rubric.

As often as I think of it, I throw out a few questions that I can expect students to ask later in the process, such as, What if the product gets high scores in organization and mechanics but really doesn't say much? What if it demonstrates full knowledge of the concept but is sloppily done? What if they do more than is required and some of the required items aren't as well done? By learning how to evaluate the sample products, construct the standard for assessing future products, and evaluate the rubric, the students know what I expect them to learn and how I will grade their performance.

The following list shows how you can give students choices in a culminating activity and appeal to different learning styles. The assessment reflects a unit of study based on Irene Hunt's novel *No Promises in the Wind*. Although some of the projects require students to collaborate, most can be done individually.

Collaborative Activities (Choose One)

1. Decorate a school doorway to represent the character from the book. Reflect four of the character's personality traits as well as how the character matured over the course of the story. Include excerpts from the book as evidence.
2. Reenact three important scenes for the character on a video. Submit the script, shoot the video, and show it to the class. Explain in class why the selected scenes were important to the character's development.

Individual Activities

3. Tell a story in detail about an experience that represented a defining moment for you (a time you learned a lot about yourself, your family, your friends, or life). Then write an essay about what this experience meant to you. How did it change you? What did you learn? How does it influence the way you approach life today?
4. Compose a folk song or rap about Josh, Howie, Joey, the mother, the father, Lonny, Emily, life on the road, the Depression, or the whole story itself.
5. Write and illustrate a poetry collection that expresses the personality and experiences of a particular character from the book.
6. Write a sequel to the story, keeping to the time period, the characters' personalities, and the author's style.
7. Draw three "unique perspective" illustrations—three moments from the experiences of one character in the story—using single-point perspective drawing.
8. Write the musical score of a character's growth (this must be performed live or on tape).
9. Design and create art (a drawing, a painting, or a sculpture) that expresses three things: the atmosphere of the Great Depression, two or more moments from the story, and the personal growth experienced by a character (new realizations, maturity).
10. Write an informational report about the music of the Depression that describes the wide variety of musical types, popular songs, and major

artists from the period. You will be expected to play a Depression-era song or a piece of music on an instrument of your choice or to offer a recorded sampling of music or songs, explaining their backgrounds (what they are about, who wrote them, why they wrote them, how they came to be).

11. Prepare a report on what our nation or community does to aid homeless people. Include at least two interviews with county leaders or professionals who work with the homeless as well as a book (or pamphlet) among your sources. Your report may be oral (with handouts) or written.

Focusing on Essential Knowledge

Good assessment focuses on essential and enduring knowledge. The first thing we should think about before teaching any unit is what we want our students to learn. We can factor in our state or district standards, our life experiences, our students' backgrounds and interests, our ongoing professional training—whatever context we decide to include, we should do more than stick to "I've always done it this way" objectives. Honest reflection gives us the impetus to eliminate activities that serve no real purpose. We should identify the major objectives, design an effective evaluation (formative, summative, varied, and frequent), then create the specific lessons that will help our students reach those goals.

Using Multiple Disciplines

Good assessment involves multiple disciplines. Life is not arranged in compartments or separate subjects. The president of a company doesn't say to an employee, "You will do one hour of history work, one hour of science, and one hour of math before lunch." I think we often compartmentalize in middle schools because we're more comfortable with familiar problems than we are with new solutions. But our world is changing, and we must change with it.

Consider today's factory workers. For many positions, they must know to how to communicate, understand basic computer technology, solve problems, allocate resources, manage other people and materials, and work efficiently. My cousin John runs a graphic design business in New Mexico. His assignments range from designing museum exhibits and T-shirts to restaurant menus and movie posters. To complete one brochure, he might have to research the culture, history, customs, and physical environment of a Native American tribe. He also must study the latest graphic art techniques and computer technology, and know how to communicate successfully in both oral and written forms to serve his customers.

Students need to have experiences that require a similar integration of skills. When studying Huntington's disease, for example, they can look at their family trees, examine mortality statistics, and research the biology of the disease. Students can use mathematics to prove a point in a persuasive essay. The brain seeks connections like this.

Subject integration can increase complexity and student motivation, and this applies to assessment as well as instruction. For many years, I've asked students to research and portray ancient cultures such as the Babylonians, the Assyrians, the Anasazi, the Mayans, and the Phoenicians in a United Nations–style debate on modern world issues. Students set up booths of cultural artifacts; other classes visit the exhibits, ask questions, sample items, and listen to the debates. Using their knowledge of ancient cultures, students tackle compelling questions such as, Should rap music lyrics be censored? Should the world have one language instead of many? Is formal schooling useful? What are the qualities of a good leader?

I also like to use the format from Steve Allen's *Meeting of Minds* television series, asking students to portray historical figures and debate modern world issues (see Appendix N). Another teacher I know put a different spin on this activity by asking students to portray endangered animals in a debate about environmental issues.

When assessing students' performances, I evaluate the accuracy of their portrayals, including the facts that they threaded through their conversations and whether they made reasonable predictions about how the person (or animal) would respond to a given issue. Each student has supporters who can offer advice about what to say in the debates. Students evaluate the historical accuracy of each speaker and team. They also must prepare a mini-report of what they've found out about the culture or person and present that to the class.

On other occasions, I have asked students to write sonnets reflecting their knowledge of human blood properties for a unit on health. With the model of Shakespeare's "Sonnet 18," which begins "Shall I compare thee to a summer's day?" students compare the four basic parts of blood (red cells, white cells, plasma, and platelets). Red cells are small, round, doughnut shapes that arc indented in the middle and have no nucleus in the mature state. White cells are large blobs that do have a nucleus in the mature state. I still remember the first two lines of one student's sonnet:

Shall I compare thee to a white corpuscle?
Thou art more pinched and have no brains!

Through this process, students learn how to synthesize information—a higher-order thinking skill and a habit of mind applicable to many disciplines.

Valid Indicator of Students' Knowledge

Good assessment is a valid indicator of what students know and are able to do. All assessments should provide a fair and accurate evaluation of the skills or knowledge we want students to gain. If I want to gauge whether my students can conduct research using primary and secondary sources, I wouldn't use a paper-and-pencil test that asks them to list certain library sources. Being able to identify the sources would not prove they can use them for research. Instead, I would expect students to demonstrate their knowledge of primary sources by presenting the results of their interviews with eyewitnesses to an event or by investigating artifacts from the period. Summaries of what others have reported will do for secondary sources.

Valid assessments give students a fair and equal chance to show what they know and can do. The best test of fairness is whether students are surprised by the format of the assessment. In other words, is the assessment congruent with the instruction that preceded it?

Source of Reliable Information

Good assessment produces consistently reliable information about student learning. To what extent will the assessment result in equivalent ratings by my colleagues and me? From time to time, members of my department gather to review essays or projects that students have completed to determine which ones deserve certain grades. We identify selected papers or projects that serve as a common frame of reference for the various levels of quality. When we return to our classrooms, we have a much better sense of how to provide uniform evaluations. This process is fairer for the student and easier on the teacher. Katie's essay on the Prohibition era might be the sixty-seventh essay I've graded this week, and I have another thirty-three to review. The demonstration papers and well-developed rubrics give me reference points that I can return to as often as necessary. Without those touchstones, my evaluation would be too subjective; I might read the essay and write the grade on the last page based on a gut reaction. Rubrics and periodic comparisons with colleagues help me stick to defined standards of quality.

Many middle schools have access to software programs that provide examples of student work; teachers can use these to assess and compare their opinions with experts'. New curriculum guides for teaching units in all subjects often come with sample student responses and how they might be evaluated. An even more authentic way to evaluate the reliability of the assessment is to save samples of student work from prior years (making sure to ask the students' permission first) and share the samples with your current students. Use this process when reviewing student work with your colleagues as well.

Using Various Formats

Good assessment includes a variety of formats, traditional and nontraditional, uniform and alternative. Researching alternative assessments has opened my eyes to the many ways students can express their knowledge. Some good alternatives to traditional tests or writing assignments include

- Pop-up or alphabet books
- Restaurant menus
- Journal or diary entries
- Radio plays
- Video productions
- Debates
- Interviews with experts
- Annotated catalogs of artifacts
- Historical fiction or science fiction stories
- Games and puzzles
- Museum guides
- News or feature articles
- Time lines or murals
- Speeches or oral presentations
- Advertisements
- Almanacs
- Musical compositions

Before you judge these as too soft or simplistic, consider what students have to do to create them. They must have accurate and complete information and present it with style and an awareness of the audience. To manipulate information in this manner requires mastery.

As a high school sophomore, I once gave a presentation about how cells die by conducting a funeral for a dead cell. In the middle of my biology class, I walked down the center aisle wearing a black graduation robe and carrying a tiny white box that was no bigger than a sugar cube. While a boom box near the biohazard hood played a Bach fugue, a classmate distributed a folded funeral program that I had designed, listing the events and readings in the service, all of which were facts about how cells die. The titles of the musical selections described the process by which phagocytes engulf and absorb waste material and other foreign bodies in the bloodstream and tissues. When I arrived at the front of the room, I turned to the group and a classmate stopped the music. I began the service by telling the story of Joe Cell from his first mitosis to his dream of serving as a soldier in Mrs. Robinson's liver tissue. With extravagant melodrama, I described Joe's physiology and how he had bravely battled without complaint whatever the blood vessels brought to his tissue section for filtering. Pausing to regain my composure, I described how Joe had eventually succumbed to the phagocytes that engulfed his cell body. I called this production *Death of a Cellsman*. The funeral programs became study guides for students. My science teacher graded me on content, but I'm glad he let me decide how to present it. I could have written a summary of the facts and distributed them, but I don't think I would have learned as much. Almost a quarter century has passed since that time, and I still remember the facts from that lesson.

Every year, I teach students about the multiple intelligences theory, and I often invite them to negotiate an alternative project or performance instead of the unit test I have planned. I give students a list of examples of different projects so they can refer to it throughout the year. I don't always let them choose a project that appeals to their strongest intelligence; all of us need to develop or explore other sides of our personalities and preferences. Yet given enough choices, students learn not to fear assessments, and I don't have to pretend to be enthusiastic about grading dozens of identical tests.

Instead of taking a test on Latin root words a few years ago, two of my students created a huge board game. They included game cards, spinners, markers, a colorful and organized game board, elaborate rules, and compelling twists in the progression of the game. Players encountered every Latin root in the course of the game. I read the cards, board, and directions for accuracy, then verbally spot-checked the students. They knew everything.

Another time, a student created a detailed restaurant menu to demonstrate her understanding of grammar terms. In the menu, she wrote, "Antecedent apple pie—a dessert so good, it's best served *before* the meal." Next to the item, she included a price, and she listed more desserts that incorporated the terms we had studied. From her examples, I could see that she knew how to spell the terms as well as how to define them.

Students almost always comment on the extent to which this kind of evaluation helps them master difficult vocabulary and concepts. The best endorsement came from students who decided to make menus on their own to prepare for a test in another class. What a delicious outcome!

Easy to Grade

Good assessment is easy to grade. Complex assessments aren't difficult to track. There are many ways to incorporate varied assessments in our traditional grade book matrices. First, remember that not all work has to be graded. Some of it can be checked off when completed. Look at a representative subset of the assignment, not each problem or sentence on the page. Check math problems four, ten, and sixteen because each represents one type of calculation, instead of checking all twenty-five problems. Check the grammar in the third and sixth examples, and check the fourth through seventh images among the science sequences students drew.

One year, I conducted some unscientific research about this process. I wanted to see if the spot-checking style of reviewing homework resulted in inflated or deflated grades for students. I compared the patterns of satisfactory homework of students whose assignments I had graded comprehensively and students whose assignments got a more cursory review. The following quarter, both groups of students had the same percentages of satisfactory homework. *Completed* in this context meant that they had demonstrated proficiency. I conducted the informal study again the following year and got the same result. It was enough proof to allow me to ease up on comprehensive review, enjoy my family, and get enough sleep at night.

For most writing assignments, I suggest requiring students to keep their thoughts to one or two pages. Why should we be so strict about page limits? Doesn't this prevent students from developing skills and demonstrating what they know? Not necessarily. I can tell if a student has the right idea by reading one or two pages of his prose just as clearly as I can by reading eight or ten pages. Shorter lengths force students to be succinct in their thinking and precise with their language. The seventeenth-century philosopher and mathematician Blaise Pascal got it right when he said, "If I had had more time, I would have written a shorter letter." Trust me, writing short is tough. It's a skill I'm still trying to develop. How I would love to rid the world of such phrases as "advance forward," "meanwhile at the same time," and "visible to the eye."

About twice a year, I ask students to write longer papers, those that require in-depth research. But for routine assignments, the most important thing I can do for students is to offer timely and specific feedback to help them improve their writing. If I have to grade one hundred long-winded speeches over the weekend, I will probably procrastinate, make a few telephone calls, and think about mowing the lawn. But a short stack of writing samples doesn't fill me with dread. I can move through them quickly, jot comments in the margins, and return them to students within a few days. They, in turn, can use my suggestions to revise their writing while it's still fresh in their minds. By the way, I also had to let go of some of the six-week projects I had been assigning. Instead, I decided to break them into smaller papers focusing on narrower topics; students can keep these in their writing portfolios. I evaluate each paper individually, and the quick assessment helps students strengthen the rest of their work.

A few years ago, a colleague suggested that I label the columns in my grade book according to the content or skills I was teaching, not by the assignments. I did this until recently, when I switched to an electronic grade book. The figure shows an example of how you can organize assignments and align them with academic standards. The shaded squares represent the average of the four assignments included in that standard.

Standards	Compare and Contrast			Justifying Opinion; Drawing Conclusions			Analysis: Break Things into Components			Synthesis: Brought Together to Make Something New			
Assignments	Leaf identif. lab	Art collage		Collab. mystery game	Point of view: century		Chroma-tography experiment	Multistep math problem		Collab. project	Persuasive essay		
Students	Interpr. movement to music	Categoriz. game		Science experiment	Role-play skit		Story com-ponent	Painting of analysis		Jigsaw activity	Notes to draft activity		**Summary Score/ Grades**
Bethune, Mary McLeod	3	3		4	2		4	4		2	3		3/B
	4	3	3	2	3	3	4	4	4	2	2	2	
Cousteau, Jacques	2	2		1	2		4	4		1	1		2.5/C+
	2	2	2	2	3	2	4	4	4	2	3	2	
da Vinci, Leonardo	1	4		2	3		4	4		1	4		3/B
	1	4	3	4	1	3	1	4	3	2	1	2	
Ride, Sally	4	4		3	2		4	4		4	4		3.5/B+
	4	4	4	3	2	3	4	1	3	4	4	4	

As you can imagine, parents and administrators love this system. The focus is on the standards and the student's progress in relation to them: "Jacques is having difficulty drawing conclusions, Mrs. Cousteau, but he's doing fine with analysis. Here are two strategies I want to try with Jacques this week that will help him draw conclusions." Or, reporting to the principal, Dr. Goodboss, "I have nineteen students who've demonstrated consistently high proficiency in experimental design, while eleven others are performing below grade level. Two pullout mini-lessons I plan to do with those eleven are. . . ." If we approach parents and administrators in this way, they will have more confidence in our professional judgment and in our instructional vision.

One of the toughest assessment issues is how to account for effort in the classroom. Homework and effort never count for more than 10 percent of a student's final grade in my classes because I believe that the real proof of understanding comes from mastering difficult assignments and not from the tasks that students practice through homework. I do take some heat from students and parents because I don't award extra points for effort. Students sometimes complain, "But I worked so hard on that," and their parents will reveal how much they assisted with that effort when they say, "But we worked so hard on that." In such cases, I wonder whose work I'm grading.

Although good work habits usually lead to high achievement, they can't substitute for it. As a parent, I don't want my children's grades to be based on anything but their understanding and application of content and skills. As a teacher, I make the same distinctions. To do otherwise is to ignore the importance of academic integrity. In the real world, we might applaud people who work hard, but we reward those who accomplish their tasks. If the microwave oven doesn't heat foods properly, we're not going to overlook it because the factory assemblers worked overtime that day. If the carpet isn't laid properly, we don't pay the installer regardless of how many hours and in what kind of heat he had to work. Back in the classroom, we can encourage students to try hard, and we can coach them as they practice, but we should never give them a false sense of their competence when evaluating their final project or work product. It's fine to award points for smaller, specific skill assessments, but the evaluations that count the most should be those that push students toward complexity—assessments that integrate more than one subject and bring them closer to real-world applications.

If we count homework as an effort grade (S for satisfactory and N for needs improvement, for example) and a student never turns in homework yet earns A's on all tests and projects, should her grade be anything less than an A? No, because the homework didn't help that student. Homework should be instructional, a form of practice, not punishment. Failing a student for not turning in homework when she mastered all I had to teach is wrong. If my course is too easy for her, then I need to make it more challenging.

Assessing homework in light of students' out-of-school pressures also can be tricky. If our first task is to teach so students will learn, then punishing a student who cannot complete an assignment because of something beyond his control is wrong. We can't just shrug our shoulders. We should work with families to find more creative and satisfactory ways to complete the assignments. I have a thirteen-year-old student who recently emigrated from a Central American country and works four hours after school every day to support his family. Yes, I can tell him and his parents that it is illegal for him to work so many hours at his age. Yes, I can tell them that school is his job and should come first. But food, medicine, and shelter are more immediate needs for this family. Completing a worksheet on objective pronouns pales by comparison. If the student masters the material, why should I give him an F for failing to complete his homework? Many of our students have harsh lives. Our compassion and alternative assignments will mean more than the worksheet they failed to complete at home.

Assessment is one of the defining parts of our jobs as middle school teachers. And because it is so significant, it deserves constant reflection and renewal. Assessment doesn't have to be a pain. It shows students and the community how we use instruction and evaluation to promote learning. I do not want to be defined as someone who documents deficiencies. I want to be known as someone who teaches middle school students well. Good assessment practices enable me to do that.

9 Planning for Block Scheduling

I had been teaching for several years before I figured out that what my students *learned* from the curriculum mattered more than what I had *covered* in class. Yet stuck with fifty-minute class periods, I whipped through the curriculum like a cowboy rounding up the herd. I accepted minimalist thinking: first, do no harm; get to the next point. Teaching with depth and understanding were luxuries I thought I could not afford.

Enter block scheduling. Longer class periods gave me the opportunity to step out of the darkness, as Plato described in "Cave Allegory," to the bright illumination of meaning and mastery. I now have the time to teach the way I've always wanted, using the rhythm of my training and experience instead of only watching the face of the classroom clock.

The positive results of changing instructional practices in block classes are well documented. In "Finding Time to Learn," John O'Neil tells the story of Roger Schoenstein, a teacher in Colorado Springs, Colorado, who said he once covered eight Latin textbook chapters within the traditional fifty-minute class periods. With longer class periods, Schoenstein said, he couldn't complete as many chapters. Yet by varying activities to accommodate the additional time with students, Schoenstein found that his students scored 12 to 15 percent higher on vocabulary and translation tests than they had under the traditional class setup. "My kids encounter less Latin on the block schedule of longer class periods," he said, "but they take more of it with them when the class ends" (11).

Donald Hackmann reminds us that average students are invisible in traditional schedules. They need the increased teacher attention that the longer periods provide. He points out that high achievers are successful in either situation and that low-achieving students need support from innovative teaching practices, close teacher relationships, and extended time to learn—all of which the longer classes provide.

On a personal note, I have found that I accomplish much more with my students in longer class periods meeting fewer times per week than I do with shorter classes meeting five times per week. The transitions between classes—

getting students settled, distributing supplies, answering questions, and cleaning up materials—drain time on task. With block scheduling I can maintain the learning momentum and integrate more than one objective into my lessons. Block classes also are less stressful on my students and me. Because I see only half my students on a given day, I can give them more individual attention, and because they have fewer classes in a day, they don't have as many responsibilities to juggle.

There are many different block scheduling formats. One of the most popular involves scheduling core courses on alternate days, so that a student would have extended-period classes of math and science on Mondays and Wednesdays and classes of English and social studies on Tuesdays and Thursdays, with all the classes meeting during shorter periods on Fridays (see Appendix O). Robert Canady and Michael Rettig's book *Teaching in the Block* is a good source of information about formats. They remind us that students will remember best what they hear at the beginning and end of our lessons. So make sure to start each lesson with materials and methods that are both intellectually rigorous and engaging. Get students involved in substantive tasks as soon as they arrive. Save clerical matters for the middle of the lesson or while students are completing the first activity. Leave time at the end of each lesson for reflection, summary, or synthesis.

Extensive planning is essential for effective block schedule instruction. Let's take a look at Joe Goodteacher's thinking as he prepares for a new math lesson on determining sales tax and interest earned on a savings account. Note how he considers different factors than he would in a traditional class period. I've indicated his thoughts in italics and the actual lesson plans in regular text.

Lesson Objectives

Okay, I have eighty minutes to fill. No, wait a minute. That's not the way to look at it. I have eighty minutes with my students. How can I maximize learning with the time I have? What are my objectives? Go over the homework on percentages, do the section in the textbook on sales tax and interest, keep the kids on task. Wait, those aren't instructional objectives. Focus on instruction, not coverage. Okay, I'll go for mastery—what students know and are able to do. Let's try this.

Objectives: As a result of this extended-period lesson, students will be able to

- Successfully calculate the total cost of any item in the store by adding the state's sales tax and any discounts offered to the base price
- Successfully calculate the interest earned on a savings account, given an initial deposit, a set duration for the account, and the interest rate

- Successfully solve word problems requiring students to incorporate their knowledge of these two processes

Are these the right objectives for my students? These skills are required on the state assessments, they're in the district's program of studies, and I know that students struggle with them every year, so I believe they are valid. They're also real-life skills that students should be able to understand and use. Are the objectives too much? Too little? Just right? Quit the Goldilocks reverie, Joe, and ask yourself, At the end of the period, will I look back and think these were enough to show for eighty minutes' worth of instruction? Yes, I think I will. It's a good amount. I'll plan for all three objectives but be flexible if I have to use more than one period.

Assessment—Formative

Assessment already? How do I know how I'm going to test students if I haven't written the lesson plans yet? Back up a minute. I want to begin with the end in mind, and assessment is incorporated with instruction, not saved for the end. It comes in many forms, not just tests. Assessment is so important that I need to plan my instruction around it, not periodically stop teaching in order to assess. Okay, I have to evaluate students' progress along the way so I can give them regular feedback. What methods should I use?

- For several sample exercises, provide the final answers and ask students to describe the process orally, in writing, or by calculation. Monitor thinking and correct misconceptions as needed.
- When students are checking homework with classmates, move around the room to record evidence of solid reasoning and to note any problems, then report what you observed to the class.
- Ask students to do think-alouds of the problems on the overhead projector or chalkboard.
- Spend one-on-one time with [learning-disabled students] Carrie, David, Sam, and Alan to make sure they have all the information they need.
- Read and comment on students' learning logs.
- Schedule pop quizzes throughout the lesson and during the next week. Use different formats—calculations, vocabulary definitions, oral explanations, paragraph description of processes. Quick, ten minutes or less, graded by classmates, recorded, and returned to students. Reteach anything that still seems confusing to students.
- Play the review game Tic-Tac-Sales Tax, in which students play tic-tac-toe but earn X's and O's by determining the sales tax on items.

Assessment—Summative

Sales tax assessment: Visit a store and ask students to identify any three items that cost more than ten dollars each; one of the items must be on sale. For each item, students must factor in the listed price, the state sales tax, and any discounts offered. Students turn in their responses, then take their items to the checkout counter where the clerk will total the cost and give them a sales receipt (without being charged for them, of course). If the receipts match the estimations, students earn maximum points. If not, the students can identify their mistakes and try again.

What if I can't find a cooperative store manager to help with this assessment? What if I can't take students to a store?

Alternative assessment: Run a simulation in the classroom. Bring in a real cash register, use one from the school cafeteria, or use a calculator with a paper tape. Provide a selection of items with price tags and discounts attached and ask students to total the cost.

Interest earned assessment: Encourage students to open a savings account at a local bank, if they do not already have one. Ask them to work out the interest earned on the account at years one, five, ten, and fifteen, given the current interest rate. Then ask them to reduce the rate by one percentage point every five years and determine the new balance after the fifteenth year. If they already have savings accounts, ask them to make the same determinations for their own accounts.

This is authentic, but what about next week or next month—will they remember how to do it?

From time to time, repeat the five-minute warm-up activity involving sales tax and interest earned on accounts.

Now that I've figured out where we're heading, how do I guide students so they can accomplish these tasks?

Lesson Design

This is the first lesson of the unit. Yesterday we reviewed percentages and decimals. Today, I need to create some context for what students will be learning, but I need to engage them and present the big ideas within the first ten minutes. I could turn this into two shorter lessons and have two prime learning times, the first ten minutes of each lesson.

I need to view this as a workshop, not just a single class period, and consider the background knowledge and cognitive levels of my students. I'll use opening hooks to build their interest, describe how we'll use a variety of resources and media in the presentation, vary the pace and the activities, make the topic vivid and compelling, and schedule bathroom breaks.

Inviting Thinking Activity

I have to get them engaged within ninety seconds of entering the classroom. How could I do that and lead them into today's topic?

Provide five items from a store, with the price tags still attached. Ask students to determine the total cost of each item, including tax. Students can work in small groups. When each group indicates that it has the correct answer, I will show students the actual sales receipt. If the two figures match, I'll praise the students. If not, I'll ask them to try to figure out their mistake. If they correct their mistake and find the right total cost, they earn public recognition.

Yeah, this will work with some students, but not all. A few won't know how to do it. Others will find this too easy. What else can I do to engage them substantively?

Alternative 1: Ask students to record in their learning logs or on paper the answers to these questions: Why is the price at the cash register usually a bit higher than the price tag? Why do we tax products? How do we tax? What does interest on a savings account mean, and why do you think banks award interest?

Alternative 2: Explain to students that for every full week they come to school, they will earn one day of vacation. To clarify, if the last day of school is June 17 and they attend school every day for three weeks, their last day of school would be June 14. Ask students to determine the last day of school if they have perfect attendance. Explain that attendance is like putting money in the bank.

Take attendance while students are doing this so you don't delay the lesson.

Setting Context

How does today's learning fit with what they've learned so far, and how will it fit into the larger unit of study? I need to make students aware of the big picture. We've been studying percentages and their uses in life. Remember the constructivist example of putting together a bicycle for someone's birthday and discovering that you have one piece left over. You look back at the picture on the original package, understand the purpose of the little piece, and place it accordingly. The picture (context) created understanding and gave the piece meaning (Brooks and Brooks 1993). These eighty minutes allow me to create context. Students won't have to ask, Why do we have to learn this? Let me try this.

- Role play with students. Let a few "plants" in the audience come up and buy things with play money. The pretend cashier can say something like, "That will be $32.61 with tax." Pause the simulation and ask, "What does that mean?" Continue the simulation by asking the customer (student) to say she brought only enough money for the listed price and doesn't have enough to cover the tax.

- Share articles about states with high sales taxes and their impact on consumer buying habits.
- Explain that this is one of the many uses of percentages studied in math.
- Tell a story about a student who wants to buy a computer game system but has only $50 in a savings account started by his grandmother. At the current interest rate (provided to students), ask how long he would have to wait to buy a game system. (Bring in catalogs for students to choose the system they want.) Allow only a brief discussion—no chance for misconceptions to develop.

These activities will work. They create background and a bit of wonder. Besides, the activities are connected to students' lives. And the best part: we have time to complete the lesson.

Presenting Itinerary

This is a road map of our journey together today. I could literally draw it as a map that identifies different points of interest. I'll go back and write this after I've completed the section on learning experiences.

Post itinerary on newsprint or the chalkboard. Tell students how today's lesson will progress.

Learning Experiences

What model do I want to use, or should I use a hybrid of several models? I have to choose a model that best fits my students' needs and the goals of the lesson. I need to consider learning styles, content, existing skills, available resources, momentum and pacing, applications of learning, and the ability of students to construct meaning from the activities. Plus, I want to make sure the majority of the class focuses on deep learning, not tending to clerical or management tasks. Whew, I better just close up shop and move to a tropical island! This is overwhelming. Maybe I can do a few of these things today and a few tomorrow and the next day until they become second nature. I'll start with this.

1. Begin the setting context activities listed previously. Complete as many as necessary.
2. Divide the chalkboard into three sections. In each space, record three different items with their price tags, any discounts, and the state income tax:

- CD portable player, $69, discounted 10 percent, sales tax 5 percent
- Restaurant meal for three people, $22.45, coupon for four dollars off, sales tax 7 percent
- T-shirt with favorite musical group printed on it, $12.50, no discounts, sales tax 4.5 percent

Ask students to figure out the exact cost of each item. Provide time for them to try the problems by themselves and reflect in their learning logs. Circulate around the room but don't assist. Check for understanding.

3. Post correct solutions in a step-by-step sequence on the chalkboard. Make sure the calculations are correct but don't explain them.
4. Place students in groups and ask each group to analyze the successful procedures for determining costs. Next, create a set of directions for solving the problems, recording the procedures in the learning logs (or on paper).
5. After the groups have worked for a bit, ask them to report their findings. Create a master set of directions for solving the problems. Post the directions.

The students must be getting stressed with all this sitting. I need to move them around a bit. If I don't, they'll lose their focus. This is a good place to stop for a moment and catch our breath.

[Stretch Break]

Learning is contextual. I don't want students to be able to do these calculations only in this location. I need to mix things up. I'll ask two students at each table to move to the next table in a clockwise fashion.

6. Summarization 1: Each partner can stand up for one minute and cite everything she knows about the procedures. When the second person speaks, he first summarizes everything said by the first partner, then adds at least two things not mentioned.
7. Change course. Check last night's homework. Post the answers on the overhead projector and ask students to check their answers, identifying any they don't understand or with which they disagree. Students then share with their groups and either explain the solutions to struggling students or provide evidence that the answer is wrong. Circulate, correct misconceptions if not caught by classmates, and record completed homework on the chart on your clipboard. Afterward, ask each group to offer one problem that warrants explanation for the whole class.
8. Return to the lesson of the day, which requires application of last night's homework. Give students another sales tax problem and its final numerical answer (not the calculations or the procedures). Ask students to apply the steps exactly as determined earlier and see if they can find the given answer.

9. Ask students whether the directions need revising, given our new experience.

10. Ask students to analyze three sample sales tax problems and their solutions, finding the mistakes. Provide public recognition for groups that find all the errors.

11. Open the catalogs again and ask students to choose any five items they would like to purchase, recording the name of each item and its stated cost on paper. Provide the sales tax and ask them to correctly determine the total cost for each item.

12. Collect papers and redistribute them so students can check a classmate's calculations and procedures against the set of directions accepted earlier. Return papers to each student with comments in the margins.

13. If time permits, repeat the procedure with each item being discounted at a different amount.

14. Assign homework: In the next week, students must go with their parents to a store and determine the exact cost of all items purchased before taking them to the cash register. Students record their calculations on the chart provided, give it to mom or dad, then get a copy of the receipt so they can compare it to their estimations. Students then must write a brief description of the process, explaining why they did or did not calculate correctly. The reflection, the original chart, and the sales receipt should be stapled and turned in together. Provide forms for all this information. Make sure parents sign the forms.

15. Summarization 2: On index cards or in their learning logs, students list three discoveries about figuring sales tax, two questions they still have about using percentages (if they don't have questions, they can cite two strategies for learning that worked well for them today), and one idea for teaching this concept in a way that might have helped them learn it better.

Extensions

- State five ways we use percentages.
- State two reasons we should understand how to calculate sales tax.
- State two reasons we should eliminate (or keep) state sales taxes.
- Compare sales tax calculations to grammar rules: How are they the same?

Shoot. I still haven't addressed the second or third objectives about interest earned on savings accounts and word problems. Let me go back and predict approximate times for each step and see if the lessons will fit what I've already planned.

It doesn't look like they will fit. How did I ever teach this in my fifty-minute classes? Okay, let me go back and see if I really need all these steps. Yes, I think I do, but some of the more advanced students might be able to skip some steps. I'll keep this plan in its sequence for most of my classes, but I'll write the next lesson for earning interest on savings accounts as a short add-on, in case I can use it with some students.

Looking Ahead to Tomorrow's Lesson

This is an advanced organizer for those who need it. I want to make it enticing, so I might end the class by asking, Should the government collect sales taxes on Internet purchases? Find out tomorrow.

This time, I'll discuss with students how their knowledge of sales tax calculations will help them calculate interest earned on a savings account. Ask them if they can predict the highest interest someone can earn on a basic savings account. Ask what they would earn in five years if they invested one hundred dollars at that higher rate.

Reviewing the Lesson for Sound Extended-Period Practices

Okay, now let me go through each step and list the supplies I will need, then check them off as I prepare each one. Set up the desks in clusters. Whoops, did I check to see if I had something for different learning modalities? Yes, some visual, some oral, some auditory. What about physical activities? Well, that's okay; I can do something with movement later in the week. Make a note of it. What about accounting for their different learning styles? Yes, graphics on the itinerary and step-by-step directions, some lecture, some interpersonal and some intrapersonal activities, a lot of mathematical-logical, some verbal experiences. See if I can work in some different experiences later in the week. For my students with learning disabilities—Carrie, David, Sam, and Alan—do I need to change the content, the process of understanding that content, or the products (assessments) by which they demonstrate mastery of that content? Consider each student in turn and make notations about how to adjust the activities.

Subject integration? Yes, some real applications and some writing in their learning logs. I could identify examples of percentages used in science and art, too. Ask the science and art teachers about this. Go back and check to make sure I'm teaching for understanding, not just to do a favorite activity. I hate it when middle schools do culminating activities like Ancient Greece festivals and all the students learn is how to keep their togas tied.

Did I really have closure with this lesson? Yes, I have two summarizations along the way and the advanced look at tomorrow reviews today's learning.

Have I planned for transitions? Yes, there is very little downtime. Momentum seems appropriate—a good balance of individual versus group work, doing versus listening, minimum interruptions to thinking. The place I inserted time to check last night's homework seems to be a natural break, not forced. The majority of the time seems to be in direct instruction, not dealing with clerical matters. I could verify this by videotaping this lesson and watching it later. Checking papers can be an excellent instructional assessment tool, though, depending on how I do it, so I can't always say it's purely clerical. The lesson looks good on paper right now, but when it plays out, will it be effective?

Does Joe Goodteacher do this sort of analysis for every lesson? No. He was correct when he mentioned that this process will become second nature after a while. But when teachers first learn how to change instructional practice for extended-period classes, they often need to carefully map it out like a workshop. It takes a few sessions of carefully mapping out each step before it becomes natural. A suggested sequence for planning lessons for extended-period classes follows.

Planning Sequence for Extended-Period Classes

1. Imagine you are preparing to conduct a useful and enjoyable workshop on a topic.
2. Identify your objectives. What are the essential content and skills you want your students to master?
3. Identify your formative and summative assessments. How will you provide multiple and useful assessment along the way and at the unit's end? How can you alter the lessons should the assessment indicate the need to do so?
4. Identify/design the learning activities and experiences that will support your objectives.
5. For students with special needs, determine what adaptations they will need to achieve the objectives.
6. Ask a colleague to review your plan and make suggestions.
7. Run a mental tape of each step in the lesson sequence. Check the lesson(s) against the established criteria for success for extended-period lessons. Make revisions as necessary.
8. Obtain/create necessary materials.
9. Enjoy the lesson.
10. Evaluate and revise for the next group.

Additional Considerations

With extended-length classes, we can use instructional practices proven successful by the latest brain research, as Joe Goodteacher did. Teaching for transfer is one way. Provide opportunities for students to use new skills or concepts in progressively farther distances from the situation in which they were introduced to show whether they have retained the information and can use it. For instance, when using direct instruction to teach students how to divide fractions, we probably would ask them to practice several problems in very controlled situations so we could limit the number of variables. Later, we might ask them to apply their new understanding to fraction word problems, critique other students' problem-solving sequences, then apply their skills by using fraction division to build scale models of local playgrounds.

Joe Goodteacher's initial struggle with objectives was an important part of planning for block schedule classes because it helped him clarify what was most important and guided all his subsequent decisions. He knew the target of his teaching and his students' learning.

Saphier and Gower (1997) identify five levels of instructional objectives: coverage, activity, involvement, mastery, and generic thinking skill. Each has a progressively stronger emphasis on student learning.

Consider how you would answer the question, What are your objectives for today's lesson? If the answer is, I'm going to *cover* the energy cycle today, you're saying that you're going to expose students to the idea, you'll mention it. Nothing in your objective indicates what students will actually learn or gain as a result of your lesson.

Activity objectives such as, Students will accurately label drawings of the energy cycle, and *involvement* objectives such as, Students will form groups and interview an ecologist on the effects of pollution on the energy cycle, do not address what students will know or be able to do as a result of your lesson. *Mastery* objectives achieve that focus on the essential and enduring knowledge of the subject: As a result of today's lesson, students will know and be able to explain five points of the energy cycle, including producers, first-order consumers, second-order consumers, scavengers, and decomposers. They will know and be able to express how each point contributes to the continuation of the cycle. Students will be able to determine what role an organism plays in the energy cycle by virtue of what it eats and what eats the organism.

Joe Goodteacher also mentioned subject integration in his planning. Extended-period classes give us more opportunities to connect with other courses. For example, writing and producing a class newspaper or literary magazine could incorporate the content for a particular course as well as writing skills. The classroom becomes a production office. Integrated learning results in real learning because it is an application of knowledge and is authentic. In block classes, subject integration is no longer just an extra activity, it's standard procedure.

We can use graphic organizers in both short and long class periods very effectively. When students focus on how information is organized or presented, they internalize the information. Given the time provided in the longer class periods, students can learn a variety of graphic organizer styles, then choose which are most appropriate for subsequent units. Discussions about content—which fact relates to another and why, whether something is inductive or deductive—help middle school students clarify their thinking. *Organizing Thinking: Graphic Organizers* by Sandra Parks and Howard Black is a great resource for this.

In extended-period classes, we also have the luxury of increasing wait times, which adds to the quality of student responses. Teaching young adolescents how to ponder, reflect, analyze, and revise their thinking is difficult in our fast-paced world. Overloaded fifty-minute periods don't help. I often wonder what we're missing by moving through the school day so quickly. How much more clearly would students think if they had time to contemplate? One strategy that can help is the think-pair-share technique. Students think individually (using art, writing, or just sitting quietly) about a topic or issue, share their ideas with a partner, then offer two or three salient points to the class. Or try carousel brainstorming. Display posters with words and topics about the day's lessons around the room. Students move to each poster and record their responses to whatever is written on the poster. This stimulates their thinking by helping them focus on the major points of the lesson.

Longer periods also allow us to change the person doing the teaching. We can invite students, parents, community leaders, and colleagues to lead our classes occasionally. Here's one idea that works well: co-presenting. Education consultant Gayla Moilanen taught me several highly effective co-presenting techniques a few years ago. One strategy calls for the first person to present for a few minutes, then a second person to debrief the class. In another situation, the first person explains one side of an issue and the second person explains the other side. Presenters can go back and forth presenting information, or they can act like human videotapes. In the human videotape, one person presents material and in the midst of it, the other person pulls out a remote control, presses a button, and calls out "Pause" or "Stop." The first person freezes while the second person debriefs, summarizes, points out critical attributes, or perhaps "rewinds the tape" to make sure students understood the point. After a few minutes, the second person once again presses the remote control and calls out "Play," and the first person continues the presentation. Another way to maximize this technique is to "fast-forward" to the point at which the speaker concludes her presentation. The remote control specialist can say to the students, "Okay, that's where we're heading. Now let's rewind the tape and see how we got there." This is analogous to the principle "Begin with the end in mind."

Some teachers might consider these attempts to slow the lesson and focus on comprehension as opportunities for misbehavior. What about classroom discipline, they ask? Won't longer periods provide more time for students to become disruptive? In my experience, students will use the time properly if they are engaged, appropriately challenged, and able to move around frequently. They need direction. They want to feel connected to ideas and to other people. They learn best with adequate time and nurturing, not with superficial coverage and short class periods. Most discipline problems in schools occur at class transitions. Longer classes mean fewer classes per day and fewer transitions. Principals whom I've consulted across the country say they have had fewer discipline referrals after their schools moved to block scheduling.

One additional concern is what to do when students are absent from school. If you're using a block schedule that alternates classes every other day, absent students might have a tougher time making up missed assignments. Every school has its own way of handling this concern. Here are some I've gleaned from colleagues:

- Assign study buddies or homework pals for every student in every period. Make sure each person has two different homework pals and their phone numbers in case one is not a careful listener or was absent, too.
- Use an Internet homework posting service. I use schoolnotes.com. See Chapter 15 on connecting with parents for strategies and how to access such sites easily.
- Teachers stay after school two or three days a week to work with students who've missed lessons that week.
- Reserve one day a week for a traditional schedule—no block classes. All classes meet.
- Teachers review material from the previous class at some point in the next class.

If you're still skeptical about using block scheduling, try it. There's enough valid research, personal testimony, and physical evidence of superior student achievement to warrant experimentation. Roger Schoenstein initially protested the block schedule switch at Wasson High School in Colorado Springs but later changed his mind. He said that after his school began using block scheduling, students' attendance, grades, and college admissions all increased. Today, Schoenstein presents information in multiple ways, conducts lively debates, and lets students work together and write extensively, all in one period. Before, he would present the material and say to his students, "We'll practice it tomorrow."

The professional development that teachers receive when switching to block scheduling might be the most important factor in its success or failure. If the training is plentiful, interactive, and ongoing, extended-period classes work beautifully. If not, students and teachers will learn to endure, not benefit from, the extra time.

Teachers who have participated in professional development in which they learn to change their instructional practices find new perspectives. School is no longer an arbitrary conveyor belt that moves students through the day. Curriculum and learning drive the schedule, not the reverse. Teachers become aware of differences among their students and how to best engage those learners. They have renewed interest in varied models of instruction and assessment. They claim that they would never return to the inflexibility and ineffectiveness of shorter periods.

Teachers who successfully use block schedules develop a "lab school" mentality, as if they were connected to a local university and working with professors and student teachers on a regular basis. Conversations focus on teaching practice, not gripe sessions about parents, co-workers, and administrators. Faculty members develop camaraderie and accountability to one another. In such schools teachers see themselves as not only able, but inclined, to improve their practices. They accept Piaget's observation that the best methods are the most difficult ones.

When I think about the freedom and effective strategies that longer class periods permit, I wonder why I didn't switch to longer class periods long ago. When I teach in a school that does not have longer class periods, I feel like the kid with his face pressed against the candy shop window, salivating at what could be.

I never really considered models of instruction before I taught in extended-period classes. I just did what felt right professionally, often piecing together various models or using one to the exclusion of others. Teaching on a block schedule reminds me of what inspired me during my undergraduate training. In shorter classes, we tend to use direct instruction and more traditional models. In extended periods, we have time to choose the best methods, not just the quickest or easiest ones.

Switching to longer class periods? Count yourself lucky. Nervous about doing so? Count yourself among the many. William Blake, in *The Marriage of Heaven and Hell,* reminds us, "The hours of folly are measured by the clock, but of wisdom no clock can measure." With an armful of innovative teaching strategies, a classroom full of eager students, and a risk taker's passion, we will see a longer class period as an opportunity, not something to fear or avoid. Take the challenge and teach the way you've always wanted to—now that you've got the time.

10 Writing in the Content Areas

Abraham Lincoln was the President during the Civil War. He had to deal with the issue of slavery. Also, the Civil War had killed many men and women. Lincoln had to worry about the deserters of the Civil War, too. George Bush was the President during the Persian Gulf War. He had to send troops to a foreign country to fight for what Americans thought was right. Bush also had to have a plan of attack. He too had to worry about casualties. Bush had the knowledge of past presidents who served terms during wars to help him make decisions. Lincoln and Bush experienced similar problems and had tough decisions to make about war during their presidency.

When Ryan, a seventh grader, wrote this essay comparing presidential decision making in the Civil War and in the Persian Gulf War, he became a teacher conveying what he knew about the topic to an audience. He had to research the subject, organize his information, and choose a format that would enable him to communicate his message. In the process, he gained valuable experience using correct grammar and writing mechanics and interpreting historical facts.

As standards-based education becomes the norm in many states, teachers of every discipline are being asked to incorporate writing into their regular assignments and assessments. It's a worthy goal but not always easy to accomplish if your training as a writing instructor and your own experience as a writer are limited.

I'm teaching English this year, but I previously taught math, science, history, and physical education. In each subject, writing helped my students learn both content and self-expression, whether they were describing an improper algorithm, analyzing their lab results, comparing political themes, or explaining the benefits of cardiovascular exercise. In *Writing to Learn* William Zinsser says that writing can make other subject disciplines accessible for students: "I've found that ideas were never so specialized that I couldn't grasp them by writing about them or by editing someone else's writing about them" (11).

If you're just starting to focus on writing, seek out an English teacher on your team or grade level for advice. Create a lesson together. Your colleague will help you understand some of the writing mechanics to emphasize, and you can help her focus on the important subject content. Better yet, take the state standards for each of your areas and look for natural connections between your two subjects. Think of the various forms of writing that your students could use to demonstrate their knowledge at the end of the lesson. Here's an example from Kelly, a seventh grader:

> In this diagram, everything is in balance. Just like if a writer uses all three parts of Aristotle's Rhetorical Triangle, their writing or essay will be totally in balance. The three parts are ethos (ethical appeal), pathos (emotional appeal), and logos (logical appeal). If you remove one of the parts of the triangle from the diagram, all of a sudden it becomes lopsided.
>
> If you take out one of the parts of the triangle while writing an essay and are only left with two, the essay will be lopsided. If you remove another part of the triangle from the diagram it tilts even more and almost falls over. If you only write with one appeal, then your essay will be about to fall apart because you do not have enough of any of the others. Therefore, in order to write a balanced essay, you have to include all three parts of the triangle.

Components of a Writer-Friendly Classroom

Time

What factors contribute to a writer-friendly classroom? The first is time. For most people, their best thinking occurs after they have been writing for at least fifteen or twenty minutes. It might seem difficult to devote adequate time to writing in a typical fifty-minute class period—extended-period classes in block schedules have the advantage—but you still can find space in shorter periods. Five to ten minutes are good for brainstorming and categorizing. Longer writing can be assigned for overnight homework.

If you have to choose between spending time writing and spending time covering new material, however, err on the side of writing. Students are thinking deeply about content as they write, which means they will retain more of what they're learning. Cutting short the writing process so you can cram in another lecture on industrialization won't lead to higher achievement. The careful thought processes involved in writing about industrialization usually will. When students write regularly, they develop a writer's sense of exploration and analysis. They look forward to using their writing as a tool for understanding new material. As one of my seventh graders, Miguel, said when we were discussing his confusion about something I had just taught, "Maybe when I write about it, I'll get it."

One day after hearing Dr. Clyde Roper, a guest speaker, talk about the giant squid not sinking or floating but hovering comfortably without much exertion a mile below the ocean's surface, a student, Amy, became curious. In the midst of a busy lesson later that day, she asked me how the giant squid could hover. I explained that the squid maintain neutral buoyancy in the water.

"What is neutral buoyancy?" she asked.

"It means they can float while completely still, not floating to the surface or sinking to the bottom, without moving their arms."

She asked me how the principle works. I directed her to a Web site and asked her to summarize what she found. In her learning log she wrote the following:

> It's all because of the stuff that's in kitchen floor cleaner. The giant squid is full of ammonia, I mean ammonium ions. I'm not sure what ions are, but the Web site said they were lighter than water. I guess if you have just the right amount of these ammonium ions, it could keep you from sinking. I wonder if a giant squid sometimes gets too many ammonium ions and floats to the surface. Where do the ions come from?

In this example, Amy uses personal inquiry and summary writing to explore her ideas about a topic. She doesn't have everything correct (ammonia is different from ammonium ions), but she has a basic understanding and the desire to find out more. In next year's science class, she will learn about ions and make solid connections. I told her Dr. Roper once ate a piece of giant squid and had to spit it out before swallowing—it tasted too much like ammonia.

Choice

As much as I like poetry, I can't assume that requiring all students to write a poem or even a rap song about a topic will help them understand it. Young adolescents, like adults, write best when they're interested in the topic or in the specific form of writing they're attempting. So even when I'm emphasizing a general event or a format that everyone must learn, I try to give my students choices within those defined objectives. For example, when I ask students to write a pretend diary entry from a person who lived during Reconstruction, I invite them to choose from a list of people representing different roles in society. The students get the same benefit from the assignment whether they are writing as a freed slave, a despondent Southern colonel, a homeless eight-year-old boy sleeping under a bench at a train depot, an ex–Northern soldier returning to his job in the city, or the mother of four sons killed in the Civil War. Depending on the choice, each student will view the culture of the time from a different perspective, but all the students will learn about this important period in our nation's history. I can assess students' comprehension of the content by requiring them to include reflections on certain events in their diary.

> I like to read about wars, even though I'm not sure why. Maybe it is because I have never lived through a war that affected me as much as World Wars affected others. I did not know what an evacuee was until I read this book. None of my family members had to actually fight in the Gulf War, and I didn't have to move because of the war.

Let's apply choice to another subject—math. You might want your students to learn more about a famous mathematician or an important mathematical discovery. Instead of requiring all students to learn about the same person or event, let them select from a list you have compiled, or let them choose different writing formats. Some students might choose to prepare a traditional report, some might decide to compare two mathematical discoveries, and some might choose to write an ode to a famous mathematician. In each case, your students will learn something they can share.

Structure

All of us can remember assignments in which our first response was, I don't know how to start. We needed something to help us focus our thoughts. Good writing rarely follows when a teacher says to students, "Write something." Most middle school students do not have enough experience to choose appropriate writing formats to meet the specific objectives we want them to achieve. Sometimes all they need is a hook, such as a good action verb in the writing prompt. For example, instead of "Explain photosynthesis" try "Compare photosynthesis to a computer." Instead of "Tell the story of the *Lusitania's* sinking," ask students to argue against the government's theory of how the *Lusitania* sank. Students can rank the causes of the Civil War in order of their impact on the nonfarming citizens of the Confederacy. They can blend two theories into one, and they can critique political actions instead of simply reporting about them.

Sometimes we get in a rut and use the same writing prompts over and over again. If your ideas seem stale, try these action words to spur creativity: analyze, summarize, construct, decide between, why did, argue for, contrast, identify, classify, evaluate, interpret, interview, expand, find support for, predict, paraphrase, show, simplify, deduce, infer, outline, formulate, revise, invent, imagine, devise, compose, recommend, justify, choose, assess, and create.

Structure comes in many forms: analogies, written interviews, fill-in-the-blank paragraphs, mind maps, five-paragraph essays, and more. Here's a list of different ways to incorporate writing into subject areas:

Writing Formats

Correspondence	Museum maps/tour guides	Oral histories
Almanacs	Magazines	Radio plays
Newspapers	Scripts	Historical fiction
Commercials	Picture books	Journals/diaries
Science fiction	Mystery stories	Romances
Poetry	Autobiographies	Animal stories
How-to books	Biographies	Alphabet books
Pop-up books	Field guides	Mini-textbooks
Friendly letters	Bulletin boards	Choose-your-own adventures
Time lines	Murals	Coloring books
Calendars	Annotated catalogs	Travel brochures
Manuals	Games	Recipes
Personal narratives	Folktales/myths	Information reports
Persuasive essays	Book/movie reviews	Wills
Contracts	Weather forecasts	Wanted posters
Resumes	Satires/spoofs	Speeches
Songs/raps	CD covers	Soap operas
Slogans	Sermons	Sequels/prequels
Schedules	Lab instructions	Protest letters
Postcards	Pamphlets	Flipbooks
Odes	Requiems	Rebuttals
Play programs	Travel posters	Movie posters
Thank-you notes	Interviews	Telegrams
Sports accounts	Scary stories	Quizzes/tests
Rubrics	Surveys	Monologues
Jokes/riddles	Menus	Job applications
Indexes	Headlines	Grocery lists
Graffiti	Comic strips	Constitutions
Contracts	Conversations	Spreadsheets
Definitions	Epilogues	Evaluations
Fortunes	Comparisons	Character sketches
Certificates	Cereal boxes	Captions
Bumper stickers	Advice columns	Epithets
Codes	Observations	Musical scores
True-or-false books	Cookbooks	Wedding vows
Metaphors	Inauguration speeches	Annotated family trees

Sometimes students are more inspired to explore content and communicate their understanding through alternative writing samples. It's relatively easy to provide options for writing while at the same time ensuring meaningful incorporation of research.

Structure doesn't just refer to writing format. It also refers to the classroom protocols for writing. For example, you might want students to keep their drafts in folders labeled "Works in Progress" and to place these on a certain shelf in your classroom. Perhaps you would like students to keep learning logs in which they complete summaries after each lesson. You might define a procedure for requesting peer critiques from classmates or designate an editor's corner in your classroom where students can go when they're helping each other with writing. Providing both written and environmental structures for students can help them become accustomed to writing as a normal part of learning.

Response

Response is the fourth component of a writer-friendly classroom. In other words, writers need an audience (readers) for their work. Nothing motivates students to write well more than knowing that their work will be received by a real person. That person shouldn't always be you, the teacher. Students in other classes, business professionals, parents, grandparents, magazine/newspaper editors, politicians, celebrities—all these people can read and respond to a student's writing. Don't hesitate to ask them.

> I think it is a great way of reviewing and studying for a test if you write a quiz for another person and then take theirs. It is true that you remember something more if you write it. You need to know the answer to the questions you write so you can check them and even if you don't, you would have to look it up. Taking another quiz would prepare you for some of the types of questions that would be on the test and if there's an essay it would give you practice in writing one.
>
> ■ Kaitlin, seventh grade

The Writing Process

Writing is a process that we must teach our students to follow until they can do it intuitively. We can't just assume that if we give them data, they will be able to turn out a product based on it. I've known teachers who announced a writing assignment on Monday, told students that it was due on Friday, and never said anything else about it other than to remind students about the deadline. That approach does nothing to help students learn how to write or how to improve their writing. As teachers, we have a responsibility to use writing as an instructional tool, providing opportunities for students to craft sentences while they're summarizing the philosophical teachings of Socrates, making sense of algebra, or analyzing the conflicts that led to World War I.

The full writing process looks like this:

1. The teacher provides a prewriting exercise, something that matters, sets context, or stimulates thought.
2. Students brainstorm/web/map ideas.
3. Students write initial drafts according to the chosen format.

4. Students revise drafts after conferring with others and obtaining more information if necessary.
5. Students edit their final drafts.
6. Students write the final version.
7. Students share the writing in some way.

Use this list as a guideline, not as a hard-and-fast formula. Some students won't need to follow all these steps; some will need every one. I include the full list here because not every teacher was trained to be a writing instructor, although most of us today are expected to teach writing to some extent. Remember to keep the goal of your lesson in mind when determining which steps to include and which skills to emphasize.

Let's examine some steps of the process more fully.

Prewriting

The prewriting experience might consist of reading a passage from a textbook or novel, viewing a two-minute video clip, conducting a class discussion, or touring a museum. It could be a one-minute demonstration or a thirty-minute debate.

Brainstorming and Initial Draft

A brainstorming session usually lasts from two to ten minutes before we ask students to begin writing. The draft itself can take ten to twenty minutes, or it can be completed overnight or later in the week. If students are generating writing for a learning log response, they won't need as much time, and they might be able to skip step 2 altogether.

Revising

Revising refers to adding, deleting, and moving around ideas, sentences, and paragraphs; changing the tone; addressing a different audience; or making any number of changes that will improve the writing.

Editing

Editing, the stage when students deal with issues such as noun-verb agreement, punctuation, spelling, word choice, organization, and capitalization. Focusing too much on grammar and mechanics before this stage decreases its effectiveness as a teaching strategy. A colleague once told me that revising writing was like changing the architect's plans for a house and editing was like painting the walls once the house was built. When the goal is clarifying students' thinking, we want to focus on the ideas and connections they are making, not just on whether they have indented all their paragraphs and placed periods at the end of each sentence. Some teachers fall into the same trap as much of the public does, equating good spelling and punctuation with good thinking. Final versions of writing should be evaluated for good grammar, but we should care about the content as well.

As I wrote these pages, I looked back through the rough copy and found many mistakes—misplaced commas; run-on sentences; fragments; misspellings; verbs that don't agree in number ("There is other reasons"); using the wrong *there, their, or they're*; and using the wrong tense. I don't mean to minimize the importance of these mechanics, only to put them in their proper place in the writing process. Later, when I'm editing my work, I'll attend to the "pretty stuff," but I won't let these errors inhibit me from thinking through all the information I want to convey. Consider what educator Marjorie Frank says in her wonderful book *If You're Trying to Teach Kids How to Write, You've Gotta Have This Book!*: "If a student knows that her writing will be evaluated with heavy emphasis on mechanics and spelling, she will use only words she's sure she can spell, keep sentences simple to avoid making mistakes, avoid any unusual punctuation situations, stick to ordinary structures, all of which adds up to no risk, no stretching, little growth, and even less excitement or discovery."

Developing the habits of good writing helps students learn grammar. For example, Karla, a seventh grader, asked me to proofread her essay about Homestead Act settlers. She wrote, "Fortitude gives them their success. The government was also generous." Our conversation went like this:

"Was it mainly fortitude, or government generosity, or both?" I asked her.

"Both," Karla replied.

"Equally?"

"Yeah."

"Are fortitude and government generosity equally important the way they are written here?" I asked.

"I thought so, but maybe not," Karla said. I kept quiet.

"Maybe I could put them in the same sentence," she said.

I nodded. "That government generosity statement seems tacked on to the bigger idea of the settlers' fortitude. If you think they're equal in importance, then combine them. If they're not, leave them separate," I said.

Karla then wrote, "Fortitude and government generosity gives them their success."

"Read it aloud. Are they equal in importance now?" I asked.

Karla read the new sentence aloud and said, "Yes, but it doesn't sound right."

"How so?"

"There's two ideas in front of 'gives,'" she said.

"So?"

Karla thought a moment, then read it aloud again with a change: "Fortitude and government generosity give them their success."

"Why did you change the 'give'?" I asked.

"Because you change the ending of the action word when you have more than one subject. It just didn't sound right the way it was."

"Good. You matched the verb to the number of its subjects. How about when it happened?" I continued. "Is the Homestead Act happening right now?"

Karla smiled. "No."

"So what does that mean about the action word?"

"'Give' should be 'gave,'" she replied.

"Check the rest of the essay to make sure everything happened in the past, okay?" She nodded.

I continued, "Karla, what two ideas did you remind yourself about today?"

"Match the action word with the number of subjects and match it with when it happened, too," she said.

"You're referring to verbs that agree in number and verbs that agree in tense," I explained.

"Yeah, those two as well," she said, grinning.

I smiled, too, and bit my tongue to keep from explaining that fortitude and government generosity don't give things to people. They are causes. That verb would have to be changed, but I decided to discuss this problem during another editing session. Too many zingers at one time might muddle the learning.

Writing Anxiety

Every writer experiences some anxiety before putting pen to paper or fingers to keyboard. Here are a few ideas to help your budding writers move past this stage. First, consider letting them write under a pseudonym that is known only to you. Doing so might release some of their deeper thinking because they will be free to explore ideas without fear of rejection. Second, consider starting small by requiring only a few sentences or lines. When students don't have to worry about filling up the page or writing a certain number of words, they can concentrate on their ideas. Third, ask them to describe their ideas orally. When they have finished, ask them to write what they've said, as if continuing the conversation. The goal here is to show them how to move their ideas from thought to paper. Finally, consider providing a forum for student writing, such as a wall display, a class newspaper, letters to an editor, submissions to local magazines, a class speech, or something for the school library.

Make a point to share samples of excellent writing, and let students follow those models if they wish. This might be one of the most overlooked steps in the writing process. Sometimes we become so focused on getting everyone to complete the required number of essays for their portfolios or on teaching persuasive and narrative articles by the end of the first semester that we neglect to show and discuss the standards we want students to reach. William Zinsser reminds us, "Writing is learned by imitation. I learned to write mainly by reading writers who were doing the kind of writing I wanted to do and by trying to figure out how they did it. . . . We eventually move beyond our models, we take what we need and then we shed those skins and become who we are supposed to become." It helps to provide frequent examples of writing by professionals in our subject areas: scientists, mathematicians, hairdressers, historians, artists, mechanics, police officers, daycare providers, store clerks, and so on.

You can teach and use the writing process in any subject, not just in language arts class. When writing becomes a regular tool for learning, students get accustomed to expressing their thoughts on paper, and they develop a clearer sense of subject integration. Consider the applications in math. Marco was a sixth grader in my class a few years ago. At one point in a math lesson on multiplying and dividing exponents, he asked, "Why does everything to the zeroeth power equal 1?"

I started to answer the question, then stopped myself and said, "Good question. Write about it to figure it out." I wasn't trying to deflect his inquiry, and Marco didn't groan that this was math class, not English class, so he shouldn't have to write about things. The atmosphere was right for using writing as a tool for learning because we wrote frequently in math class that year. Marco looked at the textbook samples, completed a few math problems I gave him that would push him in the right direction, then came up with this:

Anything to the zeroeth power equals 1. How does this work? Well, five divided by five is 1 and so is 137 divided by 137. Anything divided by itself is 1.

Next, you have to look at how to subtract exponent numbers. Five-squared divided by five-squared is really twenty-five divided by twenty-five, which is 1. When you divide numbers with little exponents above them, you subtract those little exponent numbers, as long as the big base number is the same. You couldn't do this with six-squared divided by five-squared.

So each number divided by itself equals 1, and when dividing numbers with exponents you just subtract the exponents. So five-squared divided by five-squared is really a five with a zero exponent because the exponents in the five-squared numbers are subtracted (2 minus 2 = 0). It's the same with any number. Five to the third power minus five to the third power is a five with a three-minus-three as an exponent. Three minus three is zero. It's really the base number divided by itself that equals 1. This would be 125 divided by 125, which is 1. Anything to the zeroeth power equals 1.

In this example, Marco uses writing to express his comprehension. He rambles a bit, but he gets the gist of it. When I asked him to explain exponents to a classmate using his written comments, Marco's confidence and coherence grew. Sorting his ideas on paper and searching for the right examples with which to explain the mathematical principle helped him understand it more deeply than if he had simply listened to my lecture and completed a few calculations in class.

No Separate Grades for Writing and Subject Content

When we provide separate grades, one for content and one for writing, we emphasize a duality that doesn't exist in the real world. Writing and thinking are entwined. One grade should indicate mastery of the material. As Zinsser says, "There's little point in having a teacher clean up the messy syntax in a chemistry paper if he can't also clean up the messy chemistry. The indivisibility of language is what gives writing its authority and its majesty. Lewis Thomas writes eloquently about cell biology because in his bones he is a cell biologist" (54).

I do try to provide feedback that is specific to the issues involved in writing. For example, I occasionally use an analytical rubric that includes two or three columns. One column might be labeled Organization and Ideas, and another Grammar and Conventions. Under each heading, I include a set of descriptors that flow from the criteria necessary for success. I give a student a score in each column, then average the scores for the final grade. Depending on the assignment, I might weigh one column's influence on the final grade more heavily than the other one. I don't want to do this too often on final papers, however, because I want students to see that sloppy writing yields sloppy thinking, or the corollary: good thinking yields good writing.

Text Structures

If you're a math teacher, do you speak math? If you're a science teacher, do you speak science? There is a way to use expository writing in each of our specialty areas. Each subject's text material has structures and syntax that are different from those in other subjects. For instance, science journals tend to have passages of facts that are observable or provable ("The anole crawled to the left side of the container and returned to the original green color. Its chest rose and fell rapidly."). The situation or problem is fully described without interpretation. Conjecture and inference are saved for later when the writer answers the question, What does it all mean? On the other hand, history textbooks and articles often follow a chronological sequence, reporting how things occurred in time, frequently with running commentary.

Many books and Web sites list the basic structures of information writing. Alice Foster, a reading specialist at Herndon Middle School in Herndon, Virginia, shared five of them with me a few years ago:

Structures of Text

- Enumeration. Listing information, facts, characteristics, and features. Signal words and phrases include *to begin with, second, then, most important, in fact, for example, few, several, numerous, first, next, finally, also, for instance, in addition, many.*
- Time Order. Putting facts, events, concepts into sequence using time references to order them. Signal words include *on* (date), *now, before, when, not long after, as, after, gradually.*
- Comparison. Explaining similarities (comparison) and differences (contrast). Signal words include *however, as well as, not only, but also, while, unless, yet, but, on the other hand, either/or, although, similarly, unlike.*
- Cause/Effect. Showing how things happen (effect) because of other things (cause). Signal words include *because, therefore, as a result, so that, accordingly, thus, since, consequently, this led to, nevertheless, if/then.*
- Problem/Solution. Shows the development of a problem and its solution. Signal words are the same as for Cause/Effect.

To help them learn these patterns, ask your students to design a graphic organizer that best represents the way information is grouped within each pattern. For example, a Venn diagram is perfect for comparison/contrast. After students learn the basic idea, let them practice writing about the subject using each of the patterns (see Appendix P).

Writing Activities

Teachers of all content areas can develop a large repertoire of strategies in which writing is used as a tool for reflection and intellectual pursuit. Following are some examples of writing activities that can be incorporated into any subject and some exercises adapted especially for certain subjects.

Double-Entry Journal

Some people call this an interactive journal or learning log. I first learned about it in Nancie Atwell's book *Coming to Know*. Here's the basic idea: students open their notebooks to the next available page. They record notes, observations, and other information on the left page, then make some sort of application of the information on the right. For example, while learning the difference between a parallel and series circuit design, students record the diagrams, experiment results, and comparison data on the left page. On the right page, they must list five household items that run on electrical circuits and explain which circuit design is used in them. I've used double-entry journals with my students for years with positive results. An added advantage is that students learn to use writing to clarify their thinking.

Sample Test

This activity enables students to monitor their understanding by designing a written test for the material they have just learned. You might want to brainstorm possible test formats, such as short essay, compare and contrast, and other forms of analysis. Students create the prompts as well as the answers. After they have finished, ask them to exchange papers, take a classmate's test, and critique it in a short analytical paragraph that they append to the test. For added fun, tell students that you will take the ten best questions and use them on a real test.

Relay Summary

Each member of a group writes a one-sentence summary of a topic and passes it along to another member, who adds a new fact to the summary. Provide enough time for each group to include several facts in the summary. This process requires students to assess their understanding about a topic: Has this fact been used? Is there another aspect of the topic that we haven't communicated? Does this statement say the same thing as another? Such reflection and interaction helps young adolescents process and remember information. At the conclusion of this activity, let each group read its summary aloud to the whole class, and let the other groups evaluate the summary for accuracy, clarity, and comprehensiveness.

Rap Song

Ask students to write a rap song incorporating accurate content from the lesson. The wordplay and rhythm serve as mnemonics for retaining the information. The most effective learning, however, occurs in the song's creation. Students have to manipulate the words into rhymes and beats that are accurate to the topic and subject. As they say the phrases over and over, they memorize the facts. In addition, when students can follow a beat, they can remember long passages that would rival Homer's *Iliad*. During the test, they can recall the words to the rap and the facts will pour forth. Here's what one student wrote about the alkali metals in the Periodic Table of Elements:

You know I don't lie, I said, al-ka-li.
You ask me why, here I say al-ka-li.
They're metal with the mettle, they go into action,
They're soft and white with volatile reaction.
You know I don't lie, I said, al-ka-li.
You ask me why, here I say al-ka-li.
Quick with temper, high velocity,
Watch the low melting and density.
They're al-ka-li, they're al-ka-li.
Like Hansel and Gretel, it's alkali metal,
Soft and white with a volatile reaction
Soft and white with a quick infraction
They're Hansel and Gretel, alkali metal,
1, 3, 11, 19, 37, 55, 87
Numbers to alkali heaven
They're al-ka-li, they're al-ka-li
They're brothers and sisters, be careful you see 'em:
There's lithium, sodium, potassium, rubidium, cesium, and francium.
Man, you've had enough of them.
Say, al-ka-li, give it a try,
Say al-al-ka-li, al-al-ka-li.

Filling Out Forms

Get blank copies of any form students will encounter outside school and ask them to fill out the forms using correct vocabulary terms that pertain to your lesson. Examples include a will, a checkbook, tax forms, employment applications, hotel registrations, loan applications, wedding applications, car registrations, medical insurance forms, accident reports, and time sheets.

One-Word Summary

Ask students to write one word that summarizes the lesson's topic, followed by two or three sentences that explain why they chose that word. These analyses help students isolate critical attributes of the event and label them appropriately. Examples: "The new government regulations for the meat-packing industry in the 1920s could be seen as an opportunity." "Picasso's work is actually an argument for . . ." "NASA's battle with Rockwell Industries over the warnings about frozen temperatures and the O-rings on the space shuttle were trench warfare."

Speech

Ask students to write and present a speech to a local association or a group of experts. Again, awareness of an audience requires students to write with clarity and purpose, two vital characteristics of writing that teach the author about this topic. Contact Toastmasters or a professional association in your subject area and ask about opportunities for your students to speak at the next meeting.

Web Site

Ask students to design their own Web site based on the topic. Students must present all information accurately on the site, and they must make it interactive so visitors can learn as well.

Coming to Know Math Through Writing

Many teachers consider mathematics the most difficult subject to connect with writing. I haven't found that to be true. The first time I asked my math students to write an analysis of a student's calculations of a multistep problem with fractions, I knew writing was going to be a major strategy in my math lessons. Students described the problem solver's thinking, mistakes, and successes, then offered advice on how to avoid those mistakes in the future. A regular diet of this analysis helped them critique their own work—great skills to have in mathematics. On another occasion, we used creative writing to learn geometric concepts. I asked students to produce a love story between two geometric shapes, each one pointing out unique characteristics of the other. We studied population trends, used scientific notation, described fractals and tesselation patterns, considered probability and statistics, and wrote about math discoveries that changed the world.

Almost any topic or skill in math can be linked to a writing assignment. Ask students to identify more than one way to determine the amount of paint needed to cover a ten-story building with certain dimensions and to write about the advantages and disadvantages of each approach. Let them draft a proposal to the city council for a bridge structure and explain why they believe it would be the sturdiest and most cost-efficient option. How about a speech advocating the value of math in today's society?

Math is a writing-friendly subject. Once you get started, it's easy to make connections. In addition to the general ideas just listed, try some of the following ideas to get the juices flowing. Ask students to write

- A paragraph about what the world would be like without numbers.
- A math newspaper or magazine with the latest from the world of math and your classroom. If you choose a newspaper, students can write for different sections, incorporating facts into each. Imagine the sad letter to advice columnist Jane Scalene, the play-by-play sports column about last night's slope and y-intercept game—was that rise-over-run a legal

move?—not to mention the front-page stories about the possible corruption of number theory by irrational numbers, or an editorial about the confusion over Celsius and Fahrenheit temperatures.

- A report on the geometry of a basketball court.
- A story about an underwater or lunar colony in which all architecture reflects three-dimensional solids. Students can write building descriptions, folktales, a constitution, and a travel brochure, all emphasizing math concepts in the colony.
- A summary of cash transactions for a business over ten years and advice for the business owner based on the data.
- Directions for solving a problem.
- A "Dear Abby" column for math-phobic students.
- An autobiography of a right angle.
- Jump rope rhymes.
- A diet for an overweight ton.
- A math dictionary.
- A consumer letter of complaint.
- A math autobiography (a student's experiences with math over time).

Coming to Know Art Through Writing

Many textbook series now include transparencies for overhead projectors and other handouts that show teachers how to use art as a teaching tool in multiple subjects. If the textbook you're using doesn't include some of these, ask a colleague in the art or English department what he has. On my treasure hunts with colleagues, I have turned up photographic slides of tesselations, fractals, and other patterns; sculptures of Greek and Roman politicians; bridges from around the world; and optical illusions, among others.

Whenever I use art in my classes, students demonstrate improved interest and understanding. For example, Claire Simanski, an art teacher at my former school, shared her collection of slides from Depression-era artists. She knew the background of the artists as well as the context in which the art was created. To expand on her presentation, I put together an evocative slide show for students who were reading Irene Hunt's *No Promises in the Wind*. Everything we had been reading became more vivid, including the plot and character motivation. Along the way, we learned a lot about the United States during the 1930s. A few years earlier, Claire had discussed with me the connections between fractal art, chaos theory, mathematics, and murder mysteries.

There are many other ways to integrate art and writing. Students can

- Write autobiographies to go with portraits.
- Sculpt with clay while using writing-process terms.

- Explain how the feelings evoked by a particular painting or photograph can be created through the written word.
- Answer the question, If a picture could talk, what would it say?
- Develop synthesis writings: What does blue sound like? Describe red through other senses and experiences not associated with what we can see.
- Explain what a particular piece of art tells us about a particular time period.
- Write an analysis of art focusing on lines, shapes, composition, texture, light, or color.

Coming to Know Science Through Writing

Science has many natural uses for writing, from lab reports to poetry. The blend of personal discovery and science that we might see in *National Geographic* or *Discover* magazines is achievable in our middle school classrooms. In addition to the ideas mentioned previously, try some of the following. Students can

- Write the life story of a scientist.
- Make a schedule.
- Make up a tongue twister.
- Write instructions.
- Write a consumer's guide.
- Write an origins myth.
- Create a calendar in which the picture for each month shows a particular aspect of a scientific topic.
- Write a science fiction story.
- Examine a common science misconception, how it is perpetuated, and what can be done to correct it.
- Explain why another student obtained certain lab results.
- Create a board game focusing on the basic steps of a science cycle or principle.
- Research and write a report about a scientific discovery that changed the world.

Coming to Know Social Studies Through Writing

Social studies lessons provide many natural connections to writing. In addition to those ideas already mentioned, consider asking students to write or create

- A tall tale about a current event.
- A prediction.
- A conversation between two famous people, using vocabulary from the era.
- A comparison of two different forms of government.
- A description of how a piece of literature changed an era.
- An analysis of a political cartoon.
- A biography of a famous person from history.
- Notes for a debate.
- A comic strip that retells a famous incident.
- A response to the question, If someone from the time period under review were around today, what would he or she say about such modern world issues as gun control, censorship, women's rights, public education, or global warming?
- A pledge/anthem/symbol/flag/constitution for a new country.
- A movie poster with eye-catching graphics, titles, sound-bite reviews from movie critics, and a list of the cast and crew responsible for the film about [fill in the appropriate word, such as *democracy*].

A New Way of Thinking About Writing

I can't say enough about writing as a teaching tool. Writing this book, I have learned many topics so well that I can call upon their basic ideas without hesitation. Writing about them has helped me understand their nuances and applications much more than if I had just discussed them and moved on to the next topic.

If you haven't incorporated writing into your assignments, consider doing so. Writing is a wonderful instructional and diagnostic tool. While you're at it, consider writing more yourself, for personal and professional purposes. As you do, notice how clear your thinking becomes, how fast the good instructional ideas flow, and how much new information you discover about the subjects you teach. Now imagine what writing can do for your students and their learning.

Teaming   11

M rs. Kapoor's eyes opened wide as she entered the room. She leaned over to Carol Burkowitz, the guidance counselor who was escorting her to the meeting.

"All these teachers are here to talk about my daughter, Umber?" she asked. "Is there something wrong?"

Burkowitz smiled. "No, it's not like that," she explained. "These are Umber's teachers. A couple of her other teachers are in class right now, but they've submitted observations to share with you. We thought you'd like to have perspectives from all of the adults who work with her throughout the day. It's a team for Umber."

The members of the Crusaders teaching team introduced themselves to Mrs. Kapoor, then invited her to sit with them at the round table in the center of the room. Burkowitz stated that the conference had been called by the parents to discuss Umber's difficulties in English and history classes, particularly with the extensive writing and reading required in those courses. Umber had been released from her English as a Second Language classes last year, but she was having trouble keeping up with the work and understanding all the material. Burkowitz explained that Mrs. Kapoor did not want Umber to be at the conference.

"She feels badly about her grades," Mrs. Kapoor said. "In Pakistan, Umber did very well, but her classes were in her native language. Thank goodness for science, math, and music. They are the reasons she comes to school in the morning."

Team members nodded, then shared their thoughts on Umber's successes and struggles. In science, she did well with the readings. They were separated into short sections, which meant she could respond to each section instead of trying to digest whole chapters. The history teacher offered to provide the same format in his class. In math, the teacher said, Umber responded well when directions, algorithms, and word problems were read aloud to her. As each of Umber's teachers spoke, the team recorder took notes in the team handbook and summarized the issues at the end of the session. After fifteen minutes, the team leader reviewed the list.

"There's a lot here," she said encouragingly. "Let's take four of what appear to be the most effective strategies for Umber and try them for the next four weeks. Given what we've heard, that includes extended deadlines, allowing her to listen to the history book and English novels on tape, breaking up readings into shorter sections and asking for responses to just those sections, and using the summarization techniques that Mr. Velasquez suggested every day after school. Will that work for everyone?"

Mrs. Kapoor and the teachers agreed to the strategies, and they were recorded in the team handbook. The teachers also recorded them in their own notebooks.

"Mrs. Kapoor, can you meet with the team again after four weeks to see whether these strategies worked for Umber?" Burkowitz asked her.

"Yes," she said. "And thank you, all of you, for your time and work with my daughter. She's really a very good girl."

Umber's science teacher smiled. "We know," she said. "We've seen her really shine. She's going to be very successful."

When students, parents, and teachers work together as a team, such happy endings to conferences and other interactions in our middle schools are not only possible but probable. Middle-level teams function like the pit crew for a race car driver. They provide support, offer encouragement, make mid-course adjustments, and perform as many different roles as necessary to keep the driver in the race. They provide academically and emotionally safe environments in which to explore and take risks.

Good teams also foster positive relationships between and among teachers, students, and parents. Middle schools can be large and intimidating places, and teams can make that space seem smaller and friendlier. A team gives students a good place to belong. As they sort through the conflicting messages in their lives and try out new hairstyles, history partners, and value systems, they need trusted adults to stand with them and offer maturity, wisdom, and compassion throughout the day.

A middle school team can teach students to be responsible learners by recognizing their developing maturity but also understanding the various pressures in their lives. Working as a team, teachers can decide through their collective observations that Martha would benefit from keeping her assignments in one notebook instead of several, that the Cornell note-taking system might help Lakiesha prepare for tests, and that Ryan's successful defense of his science experiment means he's ready to tackle public speaking in his English class. Within teams, teachers can alter a student's schedule to mitigate personal conflicts with peers or to maximize optimal learning time with difficult subjects, such as placing Adam in a morning math class instead of the one after lunch, where he doesn't concentrate as well. Team teachers can try a variety of approaches with a particular student (or with a group of students) because they work closely with each other and support each other throughout the day. In short, by working in teams, teachers have more chances to make quick, individualized, and consistent responses to students' needs.

Teaming can be done with two or more teachers but usually not more than five. In many schools, a team consists of the teachers who specialize in English, history, math, and science as well as a guidance counselor and one or more special education teachers. Specialists in foreign languages, physical education, music, the arts, gifted and talented education, speech pathology, or English as a Second Language can be consulting or full-fledged members of a team.

Subject Integration

Subject integration is one of the major benefits of teaming. Students can write coherent and objective lab reports in science class because they have learned about technical writing in another class. They can think abstractly in math class because of their work in art and music. They can comprehend a research article in social studies because they learned how to read for information in their English class. The real world is not compartmentalized, so giving students integrated learning experiences will prepare them to be successful when they leave school.

With subject integration, they can see that real jobs are seldom separated into pure disciplines. Take the auto mechanic, for example. She has to know math, calibrations, how to diagnose and solve problems, how to work with customers and suppliers, how to write and speak clearly, how to use computers and software applications, how to read and interpret state regulations, how to predict the number and kind of parts customers will need, and in many areas of the country, how to speak more than one language.

When teachers work as a team, they can coordinate their assignments to help students see the connections among topics and not get overwhelmed by the increased workload in middle school. Without that coordination, teachers can inadvertently set students up for failure. Consider the science teacher who asks students to read a chapter on genetics over the weekend and answer some questions at the end. On the same team, the history teacher requires students to watch a television special and summarize it for Monday's class. The English teacher asks students to begin the initial research for a fiction writing assignment, and the math teacher assigns a set of lengthy algorithms to memorize and apply to real-life scenarios she's designed. Having to complete all these disjointed assignments, students and their parents justifiably could throw up their hands in despair. Sometimes there's no way to avoid overlapping assignments. But by working together as a team, teachers can try to stagger deadlines and activities to improve the chances of success for students and each other. If a deadline for the major research paper is the same as the due date for the science fair project, students probably won't perform as well as they could in either subject alone. Thoughtful conversations and compromises on our teams can help us avoid such problems.

Instead of creating disjointed activities, we can serve our subjects and our students better by focusing on the larger skills and concepts we want students to attain, then trying to organize them so they make sense to students. Young adolescents learn better when they can progress logically from unit to unit and activity to activity. It's much easier to integrate two subjects than four. Try one, thoughtful integration the first semester and if it goes well, try a second following semester. Or try a three-subject integration.

Venn diagrams are great for brainstorming subject connections. Start by listing all the major concepts and skills you have to teach, then comparing lists with your colleagues. Look for those "Aha!" moments or lucky links among ideas. Some common themes that you can build units around include independence, analysis, cause and effect, transition/metamorphosis/change, authority, self-sufficiency, and patterns. Identify the basic concepts within each theme. For example, when we examine the theme of *change,* we find several things to be true.

- Change requires flexibility.
- Change is constant and inevitable.
- Change causes conflict.
- Change is necessary for growth.

Don't force the connections by making silly projects out of weak interdisciplinary links. Subject integration works well when it clearly helps students understand *who* and *why* and *how.* Focus on the substance of your subjects and see if there's a logical tie-in with what one of your colleagues is teaching.

Core Values

Good teams understand the dynamics of growth, and just as in any union, they know that it takes commitment and flexibility from all the partners to maintain a positive relationship. To begin with, teams must ask themselves some tough questions, including, What are our core values? How will we deal with conflicts? How can we nurture each other?

In their book *How to Bring Vision to School Improvement Through Core Outcomes, Commitments, and Beliefs,* Jon Saphier and John D'Auria explain that a core value permeates the team, driving its decisions. It elicits strong reactions when any part of it is violated. It's the last thing the team will give up. Saphier and D'Auria describe three kinds of core values: outcomes for students, commitments about how to operate as adults, and beliefs about conditions for learning. Here are a few samples of core values we identified at Rachel Carson Middle School:

- All students belong to all of us.
- All students and staff are leaders.
- All students and staff can learn.
- All students and staff should have equal access and opportunity to quality education.
- All students and staff shall learn in a safe, nurturing environment.
- All students and staff must merit trust and honor.
- We are here to nurture one another's success.
- Conflict is opportunity, and we work toward resolution.
- Positive risk taking is highly valued.
- Mistakes are opportunities to learn.

Notice that the first six statements refer to both students and staff—a healthy approach. Examining core beliefs as teams and departments led to our school's strong mission statement

> Within a safe and nurturing community, the students, staff and parents of Rachel Carson Middle School seek to foster personal and academic excellence, treat one another with dignity, respect our environment, embrace diversity, and develop character that merits trust and honor. We encourage positive risk taking and perseverance in pursuit of our goals.

Core values help teachers gain a sense of balance and direction as a team. We make decisions more easily, without feeling territorial or betrayed, because we all agree on the big picture. Is it in the best interest of students— yes or no? If so, we adjust our agendas and find the necessary resources. If not, we search for better strategies. Determining core values as a team can create unparalleled collegiality. It's worth spending the time to develop those beliefs.

In *Camel-Makers: Building Effective Teacher Teams Together,* Daniel L. Kain writes,

> If you were to ask most team members why they were together, you'd get fuzzy answers like these: "Because teaming is the model for middle schools." "My principal put us in teams." "It's good for kids." "It's the latest thing." "It's the middle school philosophy."
>
> These aren't purposes. If anything, they're excuses, apologies, and accidents. A few team members might speak of issues like the increased

collegiality or support they receive, but again, this is probably a consequence of teaming rather than a purpose. (8)

Kain suggests trying to define your purpose as a team by writing a team charter or creating a fictional advertisement for a new team member:

> This doesn't mean you're kicking out one of your friends. It's a way of getting at what's important. Take a large sheet of paper and together construct an ad that indicates your team name, what you look for in team members, and most important, what your team is together to accomplish. (By the way, if you haven't got a team name, get one. It's clear from our experiences in sports and business that people can generate much more enthusiasm for an entity with an identity.) Through the act of putting your purpose into words, you can begin to build a commitment to this purpose. (9–10)

Successful teams have zero tolerance for put-downs or cheap shots about others' ideas. They make sure that each team member has a voice in the group's decisions by remembering that no subject is more important to the team than another. Middle school teachers can get passionate about issues, but good teams learn to suppress hidden agendas and the urge to preach or politicize.

Additionally, good teams celebrate achievements and mark their progress. They do this with silly awards, birthday cakes, humorous poetry written about a person, or crazy stunts such as asking all students to applaud while waving "Ms. Smith's Fan Club" signs. Here are some ideas for making all the adults and children on the team feel valued:

- Create a team Wall of Fame. Post photographs of the students of the month, attach newspaper articles about members of the team, mention citations and awards they have won, or display the outstanding projects, essays, and art they have completed.
- Design a team banner together or create a special team greeting.
- Write and perform a videotaped segment that explains the team's practices and successes to show prospective students and parents and interested members of the community.

Middle school teams often begin with polite yet guarded relationships. After a few months, they might encounter a few conflicts or some stagnation. The goal is to arrive at what one in-service training leader I know calls mature closeness. At this stage, teams become more open, resourceful, supportive, and effective. In *Camel-Makers,* Kain calls this sequence "forming, storming, norming, and performing."

After establishing purposes and policies, teams still will encounter problems: the team leader who doesn't delegate, teachers of elective courses who feel left out, unnecessary competition among teams, colleagues who resist or ignore the changes you've agreed upon. If any of these apply to your team, try to talk directly to the person with whom you have a conflict instead of discussing your concerns with someone else. Don't let issues fester. Put them on the table as soon as possible. If the issue elicits too much resentment, it may leave wounds that will never fully close.

Sometimes we need formal strategies for dealing with a student or a team member. One I recommend is a Teacher Assistance Team. Brenda Quanstrom, the former coordinator for middle schools in my district, gave me a great list of questions to use with Teacher Assistance Teams:

- Ask the referring teacher to describe the concern.
- Ask, What kinds of things have you tried in dealing with the problem?
- Ask, What kinds of things would serve to motivate the student?
- Ask the teacher to define specifically what she wants the student to be able to do.
- Ask the group, Does everyone understand the teacher's concern?
- Ask the team members, Does this student act like this in your class? If so, what have you tried? Does anyone have any other ideas for solving this problem from research, books, graduate courses, and so on?
- Add any ideas of your own last. Begin by saying, "Once I read" or "Once I heard of" or "Once I tried"—never start with "You could."
- Turn to the referring teacher and ask, Of all the ideas you have heard, what do you think might work with this student? What kind of support would you need in order to try this? From whom?
- Ask the team, Would each of you be willing to consistently reinforce this action plan?
- Ask the referring teacher, When would you like to evaluate the results of this action plan?

If you substitute *team* for *student,* the process becomes a strategy for solving team issues as well.

Finally, try to be proactive with your team relationships. Talk about potentially difficult situations before they happen and examine your responses. The conversation is more important than the solution. Consider using some of these situations as the basis for stimulating discussions:

- One member of your team is constantly assigning too much homework, and parents regularly complain. When responding to the problem, the teacher says he is toughening students for high school, and if he decreased the homework, he wouldn't finish covering the required curriculum. How should you respond?
- Each day in the staff lunchroom, a colleague complains about a school program, a committee decision, or a staff member who is not present.

This teacher doesn't serve on any committees after school because she commutes an hour from home each day and must pick up her children at the day-care center before it closes. How should you respond?

- A colleague on your team frequently overreacts and yells at his students. It's upsetting to you and your students. Your colleague also assigns four worksheets a day, and one project and test each week. You disagree with the yelling and the assignments. Your students come to you with complaints about this teacher. You've discussed your discomfort with such practices in general during team meetings, but your colleague hasn't taken the hint. How should you respond?

- A colleague has taught the same way for more than twenty years. You've been assigned to work with her on a new team. When you suggest some different strategies, she says, "If it ain't broke, don't fix it." How should you respond?

By discussing some of these potential problems in the abstract, you can recognize and resolve them more easily if they become a reality for your team. Successful collaborations depend on group harmony, as demonstrated by teachers who have won the Disney American Teacher Awards. Andrew Lucia, Vonneke Miller, and Brenda Goldstein, a team of science teachers from Peterson Middle School in Sunnyvale, California, won the top honor in the 1999 Disney team competition. One of their trademarks, according to an interview by Bob Deitel in the February 2000 issue of *Middle Ground* magazine, is brutal honesty about successes and failures.

> If one teacher seems misguided, boring, or lazy, he or she must go on a figurative "hot seat" and answer to the other two. As Miller explained, "We have to be accountable and we trust one another to know that the only thing we care about is doing the right thing for the kids. We expect each of us to grow every day and be better than we were the day before. The only way that I can think to express this is that the power of the team makes the program stronger, and that's why we're able to achieve so much."

Successful Team Teaching Interactions

If you're going to function well as a team, you and your colleagues must be able to meet on a regular basis. Common planning time is essential. In a longitudinal study of Michigan middle schools that participated in the Kellogg Foundation's Middle Start Initiative, researchers at the Center for Prevention Research and Development at the University of Illinois reported in *Middle School Teaming Facts* that classroom instruction rarely changed without common planning time for teachers. The report also found that students considered at risk of failure were most likely to benefit from a teaching team's coordinated focus—a sign that teaming can help reduce the effects of social inequity in schools.

But as anyone who has ever sat in an unproductive meeting knows, time is wasted if you don't use it well. It's important to set a substantive agenda and stick to it. Let all the participants know the topics in advance so they will be prepared and attentive. Try not to let the urgent overtake the important. Resist the impulse to take one more phone call or to check your e-mail before the meeting. Honor the times you've set aside as a group.

Having said that, it's not necessary to meet every day of the week. Try assigning topics for different days. For example: Monday—meet only if needed; Tuesday—team calendar, paperwork, and administrative deadlines; Wednesday—curriculum and integration planning; Thursday—discuss students; Friday—meet as needed. Rotating the regular meeting place by moving to different classrooms can help everyone see what's going on in other subjects.

I know it's easier to recommend these things than to do them. Admittedly, we don't always achieve those goals on my team. We sometimes get bogged down with details that might be handled better if two of us discussed the issue outside of the group. Instead, we might miss the chance to respond to the three students in danger of failing for the school year or overlook curriculum tie-ins for upcoming units. But agreeing on an agenda and honoring certain meeting protocols enable us to focus successfully more often than not.

Strong middle school teams constantly evolve. They don't stop developing after the first or second year because they recognize that reaching peak performance will take time. A geese analogy is appropriate here. When geese fly in formation, they travel about 70 percent faster than when they fly alone. Geese share leadership. When the lead goose becomes tired, it rotates back into the V and another flies forward to become the leader. Geese also keep company with those that fall behind. When a sick or weak goose drops out of flight formation, another one will fly beside it for protection. A similar respect and responsibility for students and teachers defines successful middle school teams. Reaching the end of the journey is nice, but it's not nearly as satisfying and meaningful as the trip we take together.

A true teacher advisory experience from May 1997. Throughout the week, the weather forecast for Friday had been rain showers. On the morning of our planned hike, however, the weather report indicated that thunderstorms probably wouldn't arrive before evening. After a quick conference with my principal, I decided to go ahead with the trip. Two hours later, our group of thirty-seven middle school students and eight adult chaperones arrived at the base of Old Rag Mountain in Shenandoah National Park, paid our permit fee, discussed hiking etiquette, and began our ascent.

Although the day was overcast and slightly cool, we quickly became warm from the exertion and shed layers of clothing at each rest stop. The first hour was an ascending back-and-forth traverse through dense forest. At the entrance to a large boulder field, about one hour into the hike, we shared a snack before starting the steepest portion of the climb. Along the way, we peered over sloping ledges and saw birds riding thermal columns of air below us. The scenery was majestic, and students paused frequently to comment on the beauty all around them. We lowered ourselves into well-marked crevices and hoisted each other up boat-sized boulders, along ridges and pathways, through a staircase, a cave, along ravines, and up rocky pathways until we were within two minutes of the summit. Then we heard the first sound of thunder from the mountain ridge on the other side of the valley. We had planned to eat lunch on top of the mountain but decided it would be safer to take some quick photographs on top before returning to a protected lower level in case the storm moved our way.

Within minutes, however, we were caught in a swirl of wind and sleet. We hurried from the summit to the side of the mountain and began our descent. Before we had gone very far, a curtain of freezing rain slammed into us like an ocean wave crashing across the deck of a tilting ship. Our voices were garbled by the torrent as we made our way down, taking small steps and sliding on our bottoms when it was too tricky to walk. Soon the open-faced boulders were coated with ice. Cold and soaked, we gathered under an overhang to let the thunder pass. The noise and freezing temperatures frightened several students, so their classmates comforted them by putting their arms around them.

After twenty minutes, we decided that it would be best to move the students down to the cave through which we had passed earlier. It would be dry inside, and the cave had three openings in case one was closed by the storm. We moved out of the relative calm of the overhang into the most difficult portion of our trip—a half mile of pathways, boulders, crevices, and mountain shrubs. We were at the shoulder of the mountain, at three thousand feet, and the high ridge was about twenty feet wide and steep at the sides.

We moved into the maelstrom. Once again, the wind whipped our voices away and swirled our ponchos until they were perpendicular to our bodies. The freezing rain pelted our bare arms and soaked our remaining clothing. The adults shuttled small groups of students down ledges and across the ridge to a windbreak between boulders. We told students to hold on to each other, take small steps, and stay low. Miraculously, everyone moved as indicated and we reached the cave on the far side.

Inside, we cared for those who were frightened and cold. We unpacked the dry sweaters and shirts some had brought and shared them with the coldest among us. The entire group huddled together, the shivering ones in the center to get the most from our collective body heat. One of our chaperones, a paramedic, assured those claiming to have hypothermia that they would be fine as soon as we moved below the wind line.

As we waited in the cave, the sleet turned to rain, then faded to drizzle. We decided to make our move. We climbed from the cave to the crevice, across the wide surfaces of multiple boulders, and down into the forested area. Each new gust of wind frightened some members of the group, but they persevered.

Once we were in the forest, our muscles warmed with the increased pace. It became easier to talk and laugh. Our heart rates slowed and some students tried to sing and tell jokes. When we reached the parking lot at the base of the mountain, we hurried into the warm and inviting bus.

As the sun broke through and illuminated the mountains and fields around us, a student leaned over to me. "So this is what you mean when you taught us about irony," he said with a grin.

It's the evening now. We've arrived safely back at school and the students have gone home to their families. I am warm, in dry clothing, having finished a twenty-minute shower, a hot meal, and a bedtime story with my own children. My muscles are sore but my mind races, recalling the amazing events of the day.

Student after student took those who were nearly paralyzed by fear and held them close. They took each other's hands and said, "Follow me. I won't leave you here alone. You're going to be okay." Cold and wet students gave their last dry sweaters and shirts to those who were colder and wetter. Boys who wouldn't dream of letting anyone touch them in the classroom comforted each other by wrapping their arms around each other's shoulders. Some students took leadership roles, pulled classmates through the tough parts, and offered words of encouragement to every person, regardless of popularity back at school. The adult chaperones commented afterward that they had never seen such unity.

On the bus afterward, we asked the students, "How many of you saw a side of someone today that you've never seen in the school building?" Every hand rose. "How many liked what you saw—it was a positive side?" Every hand stayed up. "Despite the struggles and the cold, how many of you are glad you came today?" Only two students pulled down their hands, saying they were still cold.

Some students seated near me said, "You know, this was a lot like Inner Quest [referring to a problem-solving Ropes Initiatives Course]. Except Inner Quest is fake. This was real. In order to survive, we had to work together. Everything we did mattered." Several students said they were surprised at how brave and selfless some of their classmates had been. One student leaned over to me and said, "They ought to make a movie about this."

They won't easily forget the trip, nor will I. Although I regret having inadvertently placed my students in such a dangerous position, I am grateful for having been on the mountain with them. And I am thankful that I discovered another reason why full-day advisory experiences are so valuable in the middle grades.

Since the early 1980s, many middle schools have scheduled structured teacher advisory programs. The most common schedule seems to be two or three times a week for twenty minutes. Ideally, every advisory group should have one staff member and twelve to fifteen students.

According to National Middle School Association's *Research Summary #9,* an advisory program is when one adult interacts with a small group of students on a regular basis to "provide a caring environment for academic guidance and support, everyday administrative details, recognition, and activities to promote citizenship." Such groups should "ensure that each student is known well at school by at least one adult who is that youngster's advocate." The summary says advisories give students a safe place to explore academic and personal interests while building strong relationships with trusted adults.

Although advisory programs can be extremely beneficial, the traditional structure does not work for every teacher or every student. Some teachers can't find good lessons that fit the limited time periods, so we wing it or resent having to plan one more lesson. But change is in the wind. An increasing number of middle schools are moving away from short, daily advisory periods in favor of weekly advisories supplemented by three to six full-day experiences spread throughout the year.

Education professors Tom Gatewood, Ed Brazee, and Vera Blake recently completed the first phase of a study of full-day advisories in Bermuda middle schools. In a 1998 interview Gatewood said teachers, administrators, parents, and students gave the full-day experiences "a thumbs up over the old way of doing teacher advisories." He describes the Bermuda approach:

> Nothing else happens those days. Each advisor plans activities for the group. The advisory group first provides service to the school or to the community, then does some fun things. The goal is to choose activities that help students interact. Some groups start the day with breakfast. Some advisors have kids over to their houses for breakfast. Some groups go to beaches, clean them up, play, and gather data for a science class. Some go to a museum in the morning and play games together in the afternoon. . . .
>
> The advisors really, really got to know the kids well. It was highly effective, with interesting and engaging activities. The basic outcome was that everyone found it a great success. Almost to a person, if you asked what was the best thing about the year, it was advisory days. It's one of the few places I've run into where people are really excited about advisory.

In Gatewood's view, the best advisory programs include these components:

- Full-day experiences.
- Monthly advisory lunches where students eat with their advisor in small groups. "Kids love these things," says Gatewood. "They really mobbed it."
- Individual interviews with every student so the adolescents and adults get to know each other more intimately. These meetings can occur before or after school or during lunch, three or four times a year for each student.

In my experience, full-day advisory sessions can be great equalizers. Students who might not shine academically earn respect for their physical prowess, leadership skills, or organizational skills, and students who never struggle in the classroom become more compassionate when they have to lean on others for support outdoors.

Here are some students' reflections from our hair-raising trip to Shenandoah National Park:

> I learned that I had great determination and that you think your body has natural limits, but if you are determined you can overcome the limit.

> Many of my teammates' performance and actions were so different than the way they were in school. Many of the troublemaker kids turned out to be really adventurous and nice. I got to see a side of them that I have never seen before.

I learned that I really enjoy helping others and being a leader.

I learned I can do anything if I push myself.

It made me feel good and strong and capable of doing things that I'm a little scared of. Yes, I would do it again and again. I learned I was tougher than I thought I was.

When planning an advisory day, try to include enjoyable activities that provide service to the community; involve physical movements, the more strenuous the better; and require both reflection and interaction. Some ideas in each of those categories:

Service Activities
- Rake leaves.
- Pick up trash along a creek or scenic route.
- Build park benches or picnic tables.
- Wash cars for a charitable cause.
- Paint playground equipment or signs.
- Maintain or build hiking tails and pathways.
- Create books on tape for needy children.
- Serve as traffic guards at a charitable walkathon.
- Tutor children in elementary school.
- Create a community service video.

Physical Activities
- A festival of games
- Clowning
- A musical performance
- A ropes course
- Roller skating, bowling, skiing, or camping

Reflections
- Discussion with a guest speaker
- Journal writing
- Puppet show
- Conversations about related themes such as aging, racism, child raising, consumerism, conflict, politics, drug abuse, censorship of rock music lyrics, loneliness and solitude, self-esteem, fear, friendship, growing up, stress, peer pressure, parents, self-expression, honesty, dealing with difficult people, and making decisions

Social Activities
- Tour the city on a bus or subway.
- Have an ice cream sundae party (everyone brings a favorite topping).
- Attend a concert or a play together.
- Play board games.
- Build and fly kites.
- Take field trips to a hospital, a jail, a courtroom, a television station, a government office, a newspaper, a homeless shelter, a factory, or a nursing home.

The knowledge gained through these extended advisory activities can help young adolescents learn more about themselves and each other than almost any other experience in the middle grades. Powerful connections occur when we work and play together. Confusing ideas become clear. We are motivated to solve complicated problems and achieve excellence. During these times we ask, Why can't the real world be more like this? The truth is, with full-day advisories, it can.

13   Outdoor Adventures

I will never forget the time I went on a night hike as part of a sixth-grade field trip. Five grown wolves passed between my classmate and me as we sat seventy feet apart on a high cliff trail in California's Santa Cruz Mountains. One moment I saw the dark profiles of evergreens and my friend against a large star field, and the next moment wolves stood on the soft ground between us. The pack paused for a moment, sniffing the night wind. Wolves in the valley below howled up the mountainside, and the ones near us returned the call. We waited, breathing almost without oxygen, pleading with the disobedient drums of our hearts. The pack finally moved down into the brush and I exhaled, exhausted yet exhilarated.

I also will never forget the time my Boy Scout troop arrived after dark at a camp site in Northern California and awoke to discover that it was a nudist beach. "Look out to sea, boys!" the adult leaders called to us as we hiked later that day. Yeah, right. We enjoyed plenty of subject integration on that trip—ecosystems, cultural anthropology, and human growth and development, among others.

With outdoor experiences, there's always something new to learn. For me, any outdoor activity that requires some exertion and some interaction between nature and humans is worthwhile. But the most meaningful activities ask students to reach a difficult goal.

There are two dimensions to substantive outdoor experiences. The first is the focus on our physical, emotional, and intellectual selves. John L. Crompton and Christine Sellar, in their review of the literature, found that outdoor experiences gave students greater peer acceptance and more control of their lives, thereby creating greater confidence and self-esteem.

Personal autonomy also increases. Without being told to do so, students on camping trips make their beds, clean up their messes, cook their meals, and complete routine activities more independently than before. In addition, parents note that after their children return from these trips, they seem to have new appreciation for the simple things of life: carpeted rooms, space, and a refrigerator full of food.

Gender equity is an added benefit. Katherine Martin reports that having outdoor experiences with children "creates a legacy." She cites one author talking about outdoor experiences: "Being exposed to these things as a young girl, she's learning to go beyond the role traditionally established for women. She'll have an image of herself as strong and fast at the same time that she's playing with her dolls."

McBride and McBride report that most boys do not learn how to nurture children. Outdoor experiences, particularly those involving overnight stays in the wilderness, teach boys the basic skills of caring for themselves and others. These skills go beyond dispensing first aid, tying knots, and assisting someone on a difficult trail. The boys also learn how to encourage and be tender with others. I don't want to oversimplify things, but I can't help imagining the difference extended days of camping together or rappelling cliffs together might have made to the boys who are responsible for so much of the bloodshed in our nation's schools during the last decade.

Outdoor experiences help students see the adults in their lives as more than authority figures. Parents and teachers become more human, more approachable. One time when I took my students through a ropes course designed to build teamwork, I dove Superman-style from a small rain-swept platform sixty-five feet in the air. My grip on the rope's slick wrist straps broke and I fell from the platform like a sack of potatoes. My descent yanked to a stop when I reached the end of my belay line and folded involuntarily around the cinched webbing strapped to my waist. I had started my leap with "Geroni . . . ," then finished with ". . . mo!" when my body recovered its downward momentum and slid down the 350-foot zip wire to the awaiting students below. Amid the collective gasps from these students, I smiled and added with complete embarrassment, "I'm such an idiot."

In spite of my regrettable immaturity that day, something good happened. A nervous and rather large student who had declined to participate in the zip wire experience watched as the system supported my six-foot-three, two-hundred-and-ten-pound body in free fall. He decided that it was safe enough for him, and he maneuvered across the access rope and slid down the zip wire. He smiled triumphantly as his classmates helped unhook him in the receiving area.

There are plenty of other not-so-heart-pounding opportunities in the outdoors that help middle school students see teachers as fellow travelers in life's journey. Imagine a teacher and eight students lying on their backs on the top of a grassy hill scanning the vast Milky Way on a clear night. With each new shooting star, new questions and theories arise: Why do we kill people to teach other people not to kill people? Do a President's activities in his private life affect his ability to be a good President? What if I'm a clone and I don't know it? Why does school teach us conformity and to think for ourselves at the same time? Are we alone in the universe? Why can't my parents get along? What if I don't want to go to college? Am I normal?

Or, consider the powerful insights and connections from these outdoor experiences that I observed or in which I participated:

- The teacher's face contorts with anxiety and his hands shake as he gets ready to fall from a tree stump into the waiting arms of his students. Their encouraging words help; the teacher learns to trust the collective strength of the class, and the students know it.
- The teacher and students are thigh-deep in pond muck, shrieking in delight at the newest creatures found in the marsh.
- Students develop new respect for the teacher who gently plucks off the large and squishy banana slugs that have crawled onto everyone's sleeping bags during the night.
- On a hot, humid day climbing through dusty boulders and steep trails on the shoulder of a jagged mountain, a student bandages the back of a teacher's elbow where he scratched it guiding another student through a crevice.
- Students shout with joy after successfully navigating a complex compass course over rough terrain, using skills taught by their math teacher two hours before.

I have experienced all these moments and more with my middle school students in the outdoors. These are the times in which I feel most alive as a teacher and am able to do what middle school students want most from adults: listen, coach, share challenges, demonstrate and applaud strong character, take them seriously, and embrace their potential. Each time I venture forth, I discover additional proof that learning doesn't have to happen in a classroom.

Taking Students on an Overnight Camping Trip

Administrators approved your trip, and you're ready to create a wonderful outdoor experience for your students. While there are many ways to plan your adventure, try to choose activities tied to your curriculum objectives or your state and district academic standards. At the same time, don't overlook the importance of having fun and building friendships. For some of your students, especially recent immigrants, this might be a once-in-a-lifetime experience. Camping, making s'mores, catching fireflies, and telling stories around the fire seem to typify America.

Following are some activities my colleagues and I have used successfully through the years.

Math as a Tool to Study Nature, from Water Flow to Tree Grow

With mathematics and lots of water work, students will determine the average width, rate of flow, and depth of the creek. They also will examine the impact of the creek on the surrounding farms and forest, and build their own miniature rafts to use for timing purposes. Scientific, yet wet! Later, they will learn how to use protractors, geometry, and ratios, and find the height of various trees. Skills and concepts: math, art, hiking, measuring, ratios, angles, and geometry.

Get an adult who's creative, vigilant, and a good sport for this activity. An extra pair of shoes is necessary, too. Students get caught up in building mini-rafts to float down a measured stretch of water. This is a lot of fun—and it should stay that way—but the adult in charge will have to gather students at several points to conduct the measurements, calculate the math, and reflect on the results. Designate one person to record data on previously made charts. To measure the creek's width, send along a hundred-foot rope marked off in one-foot sections. Tie each end to a five-foot pole. When it's time to measure, one student can hold one of the poles while the other student crosses the creek or moves downstream with the second pole and unravels the rope. Send along a yardstick for creek depth as well. Record data for three different measurements of stream width, depth, and rate of flow to calculate the average. Discuss why it's necessary to take those measurements and who might need to know them, such as farmers and environmentalists. Students love this activity, particularly if they can return a little early to change their clothes and post the results of their work for others to read. Ask the group to present its findings and reflections to the camp administrative staff to draw more attention to their work.

Sketching

This is a great way to take a break, get a closer look at nature, and learn about forest cycles. Skills and concepts: forest succession, leaf identification, drawing/sketching skills, and observation.

Students often crave a quieter activity during the busy camp day. Whoever leads this activity should bring some sample ideas for drawing logs, trees, leaves, landscapes, shadows, and animals, such as those found in *Learn to Draw* books in local hobby shops. Bring a few copies of these books, if your budget allows. A few ideas about perspective drawing also help. Provide all supplies—sketch pads, pencils, and erasers—so students can get to their drawings right away. Before class, locate an interesting area, perhaps one with a grotto of trees or an unusual tree, some overturned logs, a water source, or an interesting play of light. After teaching students a few sketching techniques, challenge them to capture a moment in time on paper. Suggest that students complete one sketch with fine detail of the surface of a log, leaf, or lichen, then pull back and complete a larger perspective sketch. Sharing a few poems about nature can set a nice tone as well. Insist on silence for at least a short time. Every year, students and parent volunteers surprise me with their talented sketches. Spray the products with fixative so you can display them at camp.

Compass Conquests

Do your students know how to follow a course with a compass? Do they know which way is north? Are they willing to solve logic puzzles in nature? In this activity, they will get a new angle on fun as they become compass experts. They also will learn to read a topographic map and solve a riddle on the point-to-point compass course. Skills and concepts: problem solving, compass use, math, cooperation, and geography.

This one never fails to evoke "Aha!" moments from both students and adult leaders. Make sure to set up your beginner's course in advance—the day before is fine. You will need about a dozen compasses, clipboards with paper, a mallet for pounding stakes, a hundred-foot measuring tape, and a beginner's compass course package from the American Camping Association or the Silva Group. A large demonstration compass can help explain compass reading to the group. Students should work in pairs to complete the course.

Give your volunteers opportunities to learn how to use a compass and run the course. Students should feel confident after completing this activity. If time permits, let them set up their own compass course with specific readings, number of steps between each location, and some sort of treasure at the end. Make sure to provide certificates of achievement for those who successfully master the compass.

There are excellent Web sites that offer instructions for beginner compass reading and products and games to teach proper compass use:

http://www.acacamps.org (American Camping Association)
http://www.johnsonoutdoors.com/camping/silva/nav/pro.html (Johnson Outdoors)
http://www.flinders.com.au/silva.htm (Silva Group)
http://www.benmeadows.com (Ben Meadows Company)
http://www.megsinet.net/~gdt/Catalog.htm (Go Orienteering!)
http://www.uio.no/~kjetikj/compass/ ("How to Use a Compass" by Kjetil Kjernsmo)
http://www.geocities.com/Heartland/Pointe/9385/ (A fantastic site that details everything needed for a full orienteering experience for Girl Scouts, but applicable to all students of orienteering, male or female, youth or adult)

These books also are helpful: Björn Kjellström, *Be Expert with Map and Compass*; Steve Boga, *Orienteering*; and Cliff Jacobson, *Basic Essentials, Map and Compass*.

Geology Hike

With a geologist, groups of students can explore the fossil history and geology of the area, and conduct an archeological "dig" with real fossils they can take home. Skills and concepts: geology, fossil study, history, and lots of digging.

I have a friend who is a geologist. He takes the group hiking to a local quarry or along areas of geologic interest, then returns to an area located several hundred feet from camp in which we secretly buried real fossils. Students set up grids with mini-stakes and twine across the patch of ground we have indicated. They then sift through the soil and find our buried fossils and identify them with posters obtained from the U.S. Geologic Survey in Reston, Virginia. They draw and chart the locations of each fossil using inch-square grid paper. We provide glass cases with sides that magnify the contents, and students take home their identified fossils. In some years, when we were short of fossils, we let students display their discoveries for the camp, but they could not take them home.

One year, one of my student's parents donated fossils, and we buried the artifacts as usual. When students dug up the artifacts, they couldn't identify them. Luckily, we had brought books about fossils from around the world that we had planned to use for a later discussion. Reading the books, students discovered that their fossils originated in the Middle East—Pakistan, Turkey, and other areas near the Fertile Crescent. Students concocted wild theories of mutant plate tectonics and volcanic eruptions until we told them that the fossils were donated by a family recently relocated from that region of the world. With a nervous laugh, I speculated about the dinner table conversations when students returned from camp: "Mom, did you know that Virginia was once part of Pakistan?"

Creek Study and Stream Quality Indicators

Investigate the quality of streams, including temperature, velocity, clarity, odor, and oxygen content, as well as the bugs and plants that inhabit the water. Help your students learn about water contamination, both good and bad, and catch creek critters and plants that they can later identify. Sneakers required. A fun and wet course! Skills and concepts: observation, identification of plants/animals, critical thinking, pollution, and animal habitats.

If you plan to use the water flow activity described earlier in the chapter, don't use this one, too; the ensuing conversations will be too similar. Make sure you have a vigilant adult watching out for students' safety and for science connections. Don't forget to bring a kit of litmus papers to test for acidity if you do not plan to use the acid rain study described later.

The Creek Study is perfect for write-ups for camp newsletters. Bring Tree Finder and Flower Finder books, along with guides to aquatic and forest animals. Prepare questions for reflection, and ask students to record their responses before starting an open discussion. Take a camera.

Surviving with Nature

Teach students—or let them teach others—how to build a debris hut, find water sources, blaze a trail, tie knots, start a safe campfire, and increase the likelihood of being found if you are lost. Skills and concepts: minimal-impact camping, water sources, problem solving, fire building, knot tying, trail blazing, and survival skills.

Before we started using outdoor learning experiences on my middle school team, I never would have believed that for so many students it would be their first camping experience. Many did not know how to build an outdoor fire, pitch a tent, apply first aid, tie knots, or identify poisonous plants. I spent my boyhood days hiking in the nearby mountains and backpacking with the Boy Scouts, so it hadn't occurred to me that other youngsters had missed out on these character-building experiences. This activity is designed to set free the hidden Huckleberry Finn in every student. Needless to say, it's among the most popular courses with students.

Ask a camp staff member or an experienced camper to lead this activity. A Scout handbook or other outdoor survival guide can provide good content ideas. If you don't plan to offer the problem-solving activity described in the next section, use this one instead. For example, if there are bears in your area, discuss how bears can get into campers' food supplies and what students can do to prevent the pillage, such as hanging food on a branch at least eight feet from the ground and eight feet from the nearest tree trunk.

Don't tell students how to put up the tent; let them figure it out for themselves. Explain the main ingredients of a good fire, then let them design and debate the proper arrangements of kindling and logs to create a robust fire. After teaching them various knots, ask them to discuss which knots work best in different situations, such as a knot that holds fast but releases quickly when needed and a knot used to attach two ropes to each other. Practice identifying poison ivy/sumac/oak in all their forms—vine, leaves, and berries.

Outdoor Problem Solving

Activities include physical problems to solve (walking a forest trail blindfolded, tying and untying certain knots, building a campfire, setting up a tent), savvy camper situations (how to store food for the night while camping, where to build a fire or pitch a tent), and examining ethical issues in ecology. Skills and concepts: problem solving, task analysis, and coping devices.

The same comments as for the Surviving with Nature activity apply here. The difference is that the conversations are pushed toward larger ethical issues such as deforestation, strip-mining, endangered species habitats, genetically engineered crops, and humanity's impact on nature. Students love the competitive nature of this activity, and they like having the opportunity to discuss serious issues with no easy answers.

Creature Features

Let students build new creatures using items they collect from the forest floor. Ask them to design the new creatures' habitats. Skills and concepts: art, creativity, habitat study, and writing.

Bring some of those inexpensive glue guns you see in art and hobby stores; middle school students can use them well. Start the session by discussing the elements needed for a thriving habitat. Take photographs of all the creatures, if possible, then return any items still in their natural state (not covered in paint or glue) to the forest where you found them. Make sure to provide display areas for the creatures and the write-ups about their habitats.

Pond Study

Show students how to identify small water organisms they can view under a microscope, and use these as the basis for a discussion on pond ecology. Wade, collect critters with nets and seines, and observe adaptations for feeding and protection. Skills and concepts: observation, ecosystems, microorganisms, microscopes, environmental protection, insects and pond animals.

Many camps have these supplies on-site. In case they don't, ask around for secondhand microscopes, magnifying glasses, specimen bottles, netting, coffee cans with both ends removed, and pond critter identification books. Provide drawings of insects and animals that students might find in the camp pond, and ask them to check off the creatures as they find them. To make magnifying glasses, cover one end of the coffee cans with clear cellophane wrapping and place some water in the concave sag of the plastic.

Although we spend a lot of time up to our knees in muck and water at the pond's edge, we always start and finish the activity by discussing the pond's ecosystems. Make sure you have a few extra adult chaperones whenever you work near water. Finally, watch out for geese and ducks. They nest near ponds. If some of your students inadvertently disturb the birds' nests, they might cause the geese to go on a rampage, honking and pecking savagely.

Outdoor Writing

Find a great spot and let the creative juices flow! No limitations on imagination or paper or style. Encourage students to write poems, adventures, mysteries, plays, and dramas with the wilderness as a theme. Finished work taken to final draft form can be included in their classroom portfolios. Skills and concepts: creativity, writing (drafting), and observation.

Just as with the outdoor sketching activity, you will want to provide all the supplies for this one; writing paper, clipboards, and plenty of pencils or pens. Scout the grounds for an area in which everyone can sit away from each other but within view. As you begin, spend time with students brainstorming possibilities. Allow enough time for these three writing process components: prewriting (ten minutes), drafting (forty-five minutes), and sharing (twenty minutes). Prewriting and sharing can be done in the group, but drafting would be better completed in a quiet area of the forest where students can spread out. Give each student a copy of the writing ideas, if that would be helpful, or read the list orally and discuss the possibilities. This is your turn to light the fires of their imaginations. Encourage the creative process. You can ask questions that help their ideas, but try not to squelch their own creativity by giving them your ideas. One of the best ways to provide a good atmosphere for writing is to participate in this activity yourself. Give it a try.

Writing Ideas
- Focus on describing an object or a relationship in the forest. Describe this in great detail, using comparisons (similes, metaphors, personification).
- A tree finally lets you see inside . . . .
- List twenty-five uses for a stick or a mushroom.
- Write a story about the arrival of a new animal to the forest.
- Write a poem or story about how the forest is different at night than during the day.
- Write a children's story about the forest and its inhabitants.
- Write a love story about a bush and a mushroom, lichen and a stick, a leaf and a piece of moss, or a fallen log and a termite inside.
- Rewrite any existing children's tale from the point of view of one of the animals.
- Interview a tree.
- Write an ode to something in the forest.
- Write a dinner invitation from a wolf to a rabbit.
- Write a poem describing the sound of sunshine.
- Write about waking up in the morning on the forest floor in your sleeping bag.
- You are alone in the woods. Through the trees, you hear voices spoken in a different language. The voices pull at your curiosity.

- You and a friend are playing or hiking, and one of you gets hurt. Describe your adventure.
- While in the forest, you encounter a bear, a mountain lion, a skunk, a snake.
- One of the forest animals or plants starts talking with you. Record the conversation.
- The forest has an important message for people: . . .
- You crash in the forest and must survive alone. Describe your first few days.
- Travel in time, forward or backward and describe how the forest changes.
- Write a letter to someone about your camp experiences.
- Write a letter to the President or to members of Congress, trying to persuade them to declare a new national holiday related to trees or animals.
- Write a series of forest, tree, or animal jokes and riddles.
- Write a story entitled "The Camping Trip I'll Never Forget."
- Create the perfect picnic menu for ants.

Simulations: *Oh Deer, It's the Grizzly Bear Forest*

In these two simulation games from Project WILD, students portray different animals coping with a variety of habitat factors such as short food supply, winter storms, housing developments, and more. In Oh Deer! students will race each other as they compete in herds for food, shelter, and water. A progression chart of the herd's population increase and decrease will be maintained over a pretend ten-year period. Students will graph the results. In Grizzly Bear Forest, students portray grizzly bears as they forage for a limited food supply. Skills and concepts: math, running, graphing, problem solving, reasoning, appreciation of the balance of nature, and cycle of energy: producer/consumer/decomposer/producer.

These activities, which provide clear examples of turning abstract concepts into physical experiences, and vice versa, require a large area that is protected from wind and human disturbances. You will find the description of both activities in the Project WILD activity book.

Sample Questions After the Bear Activity
How many pounds of food did you (as a bear) collect?
How many pounds of food did the group collect?
If black bears need eighty pounds of food to survive, how many bears
   would have survived?
What would happen to the other bears if there were not enough food to
   sustain them?
How many pounds of food did the blind bear collect? Will the blind
   bear survive?

Did the mother bear feed her cubs first or herself? Why?
What does "the carrying capacity of a habitat" mean?

Take photographs during this activity. You will get wonderful candid shots of learning in action. Make sure to display the results.

Acid Rain Study

Student teams will hike to different water supplies on the camp property, test the water acidity levels using litmus paper and color charts, then prepare a report to the camp administration. Students will learn the effects of acid rain on both nature and human developments. They will understand the basics of alkalinity and acidity, and explore different ways to reduce acid rain. Skills and concepts: acids and bases, hiking, using color keys, the cause and effects of acid rain, presenting information clearly.

This activity works best if you set it up as an investigative journalism project. It's amazing to watch students walking long distances (such as between the camp pond, the creek, the water pump, the quarry, the bathroom, the kitchen sink, and the water spring) for a cause. This activity is as aerobic as it is academic. Make sure to discuss acid rain and its effects on wildlife and human habitats before you begin. Also, review alkalinity and acidity and how to test for each. If your middle school doesn't have the litmus paper test packets, try to borrow some from a local high school or order some through various science Web sites.

At the end, ask students to present their findings (including bar graphs and written summaries) to the camp administrative staff.

Freedom Trail

On this self-guided walk with a fictional slave who is trying to escape to freedom, students will listen to a written narrative and imagine the slave's actions and emotions.

The camp we have used in recent years set up a trail with markers indicating where certain events occurred during the Civil War. We also have stationed reenactors along the way to make the activity more realistic. If a camp near you doesn't offer these services, create them. Visit the intended trail several months ahead of time and identify locations along the way that would make good stations for trail hikers to stop and learn about the history of the area. Ask volunteers from area senior centers, churches, and historical societies to dress in appropriate costumes of identified characters and to surprise or greet the students as they move along the trail. Give all the characters prepared speeches that they can use to introduce themselves to the students and some additional background material in case the students ask questions.

When students have finished walking the trail, ask them to share what they have learned through artwork, journal writing, or some other product.

Civil War Reenactment

These soldiers don't know the Civil War ended. Step back into time and a Civil War camp site. Interview the fully costumed soldiers who have captured your group and taken you to their authentic Civil War soldier camp site. These professional reenactors begin and remain in character, sharing the history, struggle, character, and lifestyle of Civil War soldiers.

This is similar to the Freedom Trail, except your group is "captured" by Union or Confederate soldiers and taken to camp. Give students a few questions to begin the interview, but let their natural curiosity take over. Negotiate with the reenactors ahead of time about what they would feel comfortable talking about or demonstrating for the students.

Service Project

Each year we give something of ourselves back to the camp and to future campers. Our service projects have helped preserve the natural beauty of the area so others can enjoy it as well. Sometimes we build hogans (canvas-covered platforms) for summer campers. Other times we might plant trees, clear trails, build camp sites, or paint buildings. Skills and concepts: cooperation, giving, environmental awareness.

This activity elicits the most groans when announced but often inspires more pride and memories than any other. Students recall for younger siblings and friends years later that they built a particular trail, cleaned out the debris, pitched those tents, repainted that fence, planted those saplings, or built those steps to prevent soil erosion. The more labor-intensive the job, the stronger the memory. Add bad weather to the mix, and you maximize the personal growth and feelings of accomplishment. Call the camp staff a few weeks ahead of time and ask about activities that you can do with your students. Bring extra work gloves, shovels, or other tools needed for the job.

Sample Reasoning for a Letter to Parents

Successful outdoor experiences build from parent support. To justify the days spent away from the classroom, spend time beforehand sharing the trip's curricular connections with parents. Here are some examples of letters to parents that set a constructive tone:

> We are very excited this year to offer an interdisciplinary environmental education experience for the students on the Champions Team of Anywhere

Middle School. This program gives your child's teachers the chance to meet individual needs, apply school subjects in the field, and challenge students in ways not possible in the regular classroom. Such experiences lead to significant maturation and renewed academic motivation for middle school students.

Or

Research and experience consistently demonstrate the positive effects of extended residential experiences in the outdoors for middle school students. Our team is providing a program in which our parents, teachers, and students will live in small cabins for three days while engaging in a program of academic discovery and application, personal growth, independence, and problem solving. Such experiences create confidence and motivation, which translate into increased academic achievement. They also promote the development of self-esteem, cooperation, and risk taking.

Addressing discipline:

We want this field trip experience to be successful for everyone. All students must conform to school standards of behavior and to special rules for safety and crowd control. We expect all children to listen carefully to all the instructions and to pursue activities as directed. While the "classroom" on this field trip will be newly defined, normal classroom behavior and manners still apply. Please check the regulations found in our school's Rights and Responsibilities handbook. Students will be expected to obey and respect all adults who accompany us on this trip. Students who cannot maintain appropriate behavior will be sent home.

Other Practicalities

- Ask students to label everything with their names. I mean *everything*.
- Don't let students call home from camp. Call for them, if absolutely necessary, and deliver messages. This also means persuading parents not to call their children, because it escalates homesickness.
- Don't allow candy, sweets, disc players, hairdryers, GameBoys, radios, and the associated trappings of a materialistic adolescent's life. Help them learn that they can survive without these things.
- Take the parents out for a precamp visit to walk the facilities, ask questions, and get the flavor of camp a week or two in advance, even earlier if you need to persuade some that the camp will be safe.
- Ask one or two adults on duty each night to stay up until everyone is asleep.

- Assign one adult to distribute medications and deal with injuries. Bring three first aid kits.
- Bring duct tape. You will need it.
- A few months before the date of your planned trip, survey the parents and ask about their outdoor skills. Identify others who might need training and provide it ahead of time. Also, check the camp for expertise. Camps often have staff naturalists who can lead the activity-period programs while your adult chaperones control the crowds.
- Teach camp ethics responsibility daily.
- Check on food allergies, special diet needs, or religious needs. Most camps will accommodate special requests.
- Purposefully plan for downtime. Bring some Frisbees, cards, and quiet activities, but also allow students to chat, write letters, and take naps during these times.
- Make sure the trip is affordable. Seek donations whenever possible. Encourage families and businesses to provide scholarships for those who can't afford the cost.
- Innovate. What can you teach that's better suited to the outdoors than the classroom?
- Let students take home souvenirs such as camp artwork, photographs, writings/journals, and awards.
- Provide substantial time and structure for reflection upon the campers' return to the regular classroom.
- Whoever is coordinating the camp should not be responsible for teaching any classes. Three or four adults should be free at all times to deal with discipline or emergencies.

If it rains, dance in it. Two of my trips have been complete washouts, with rain all day, every day. When students from those trips have visited me in later years, they don't remember the rain. They remember the activity periods, the campfire skits, the people they got to know, and the late-night talks in their tents and cabins.

14 Mentoring New Teachers

Uneven paper piles and week-old projects threaten to topple my stacked turn-in baskets. Reverse chalk imprints of "Identify the Verbs" from the blackboard are smudged across the back of my shirt, and cotton-mouth has set in for the afternoon. I pour myself some water and avoid looking in the direction of seven unwritten evaluations that were due yesterday. Into my classroom walks a new teacher.

"Can I talk to you for a moment?" she asks. Her question helps me escape the piling pressures on my desk. Relieved, I take a seat in one of the students' desks and switch to my role as a mentor teacher.

"What's on your mind?" I ask.

"I'm not teaching the way I really want to teach," she begins. "My last class has several really disruptive students. They monopolize all my time."

"Tell me about them," I encourage her.

She continues, "I'm doing more babysitting than teaching. It's not fair to the other students, or me. I know we're supposed to be understanding and encouraging of students at this age, but I'm running out of ideas. I dread that class when it comes each day."

"You're getting frustrated about the impact those students have on your teaching," I say, nodding in understanding. "Let's take a look at what you've tried so far and where we might go from there."

She begins to list the troubling behaviors and her responses to them. I listen, offer feedback, and together we list variations on the approaches she's already used and three new strategies she can try. We also discuss the most difficult students. She agrees to contact the other teachers on the team to see how the same students behave in their classes. She will try some of the strategies they suggest and meet with me in a week to reevaluate. I also propose to videotape her classes for two days and analyze them at our next meeting. By the time we finish talking, we both feel energized and enthusiastic.

Mentoring can be extremely helpful to new instructors as well as to the mentors themselves. In their Situational Leadership model, organizational behavior theorists Paul Hersey and Kenneth H. Blanchard have identified four basic interactions that define these relationships: *telling*—the mentor provides direction and monitors the new teacher's completion of tasks; *selling*—the mentor explains her decisions and seeks other suggestions from the new teacher; *collaborating*—the mentor and new teacher work together to complete goals; and *delegating*—the new teacher takes responsibility for decisions and actions, and the mentor withdraws as the new teacher develops more independence.

This sequence parallels a new teacher's growing confidence as an instructor. Education consultant Barry Sweeny said he has found that most new teachers initially take all negative experiences personally and feel an acute sense of failure. After a few weeks, however, they're usually ready to seek support and encouragement, becoming more realistic about their own abilities. Finally, they take risks to learn.

In the beginning, Sweeny says, first-time teachers often need to view their work through the lens of a more seasoned professional who can offer guidance and coaching. Later, the novices want the autonomy to use the suggestions or not. New teachers can ask themselves where they are in this sequence, whether they're ready to move to the next level, and what it will take to make the leap. Communicating goals, getting feedback from a mentor, reflecting, and clarifying decisions are very important to the new teacher's growth as a professional.

New teachers and struggling teachers ask great questions: Do you really believe all children can learn? Is it okay to have favorites? How do you get to all the standards in a year? How do you decide what will be on a test? Heterogeneous groups don't seem to work in my subject—what can I do? How do I know I'm doing well? How can I get it all done in less than fourteen hours a day? Do I let a kid who studied take a test again? Are you accountable for the performance of your students? By responding to these questions, mentors revisit the original reasons they entered teaching, and the two teachers develop a more collegial relationship.

Suggestions for Teachers Who Seek Mentoring

If you are a new or struggling teacher, here are some suggestions for strengthening your relationship with your mentor:

- Be flexible. Locked knees make you fall over, but bent knees keep you stable and ready to respond effectively. If your mentor suggests something, try it before deciding whether it's right for you. I have found that my teaching usually improves when others push me to try something different.
- Be honest. Work on real problems and you won't waste time playing games. Also, be an intelligent consumer. Let your mentor know if things aren't working. Both partners need to be committed to the relationship.

- Give yourself permission to fail your first year. I was a much better teacher the second year for having made the mistakes I did the first year. Your mentor can help you develop this perspective.

- Ask your mentor to meet with you regularly, at least once a week. You might think this time is unnecessary some weeks, but once the conversations start, you probably will find new approaches, solutions to unresolved issues, and emotional support. Regularity creates security; when you can count on a definite meeting time, you won't worry as much about the daily challenges.

- If the cynicism of some veteran teachers concerns you, discuss the issues with your mentor. New teachers need to learn how to think for themselves, and that means being able to respond to negative comments that drag you down. Your mentor can provide perspective or context as well as some reasoned responses.

- Thank your mentor once in a while. Spread good comments about her. As with a marriage, making your partner look good reflects well on both of you.

- Ask your mentor to help you identify the most critical concepts/terms/ideas in the units of study for which you're responsible. I remember feeling paralyzed with uncertainty when I was told to teach the major points in each chapter of the seventh-grade history textbook during my first year. I also taught novels in English that year, and I was supposed to teach the major themes and literary devices in each one. I feared that I would misinterpret something. What if I didn't teach what everyone else did? What if I didn't prepare my students well for the state tests? Such anxiety kept me awake at night. Ask your mentor for guidance, and don't be afraid to ask the same question five or six times. Mentors know how much you're juggling—they were once new, too.

- Ask your mentor about your school or school district's professional library. It should contain manuals and publications featuring strong instructional practices. You can review them with your mentor.

- Share good classroom experiences with your mentor, not just the problems.

- Ask your mentor to videotape you in the classroom. If he cannot do it personally, he can help you arrange a session with a media specialist or an off-duty staff member. Afterward, watch the tape privately, noting things you did well, practices you want to improve, and the impact on student learning. There's no evaluation here. If you feel comfortable, review the tape with your mentor. Let him know your concerns and goals before viewing. Stop the tape when necessary, rewind it, play it again, and explore alternative responses and strategies. Watching your teaching in action can bring an entirely new perspective to your work.

- Help your mentor or other teachers set up a Faculty Portfolio of Ideas. Such a portfolio consists of plastic crates or boxes located at each photo-copying machine. The containers hold folders for each course at your school. When staff members photocopy materials for use in their classes, ask them to make an additional copy and place it in the appropriate folder. The folders soon will bulge with tests, projects, vocabulary lists, chapter summaries, classroom policies, graphic organizers, unit plans, field trip forms, letters to parents, behavior contracts, bulletin board ideas, articles, diagrams, and other instructional samples. The collection becomes a great resource for everyone in the school building, but especially for inexperienced staff members who don't have file cabinets full of lesson plans. Teachers of elective classes can see what teachers in the core subjects are doing and vice versa, thereby fostering interdisciplinary connections. Different grade levels get a better sense of what students have experienced or will experience in the future. At the end of the year, bind the year's collection into one portfolio and store it in your school's professional library. Don't forget to seek permission from colleagues before using lessons from the next grade level. You wouldn't want to force someone to toss out a well-developed lesson just because you exposed students to the same routine a year earlier.

- Finally, consider joining professional associations and fraternal organizations. National Middle School Association is a great place to start. There are nearly seventy affiliate organizations in most U.S. states and Canadian provinces. These middle-level groups offer members professional development workshops, targeted publications, and other resources that are critically important to new and veteran teachers alike. Also, check out the associations that cater to your subject specialty, such as the National Science Teachers Association, the National Council of Teachers of Mathematics, and the National Council of Teachers of English. For cutting-edge curriculum resources suitable for any subject, don't overlook the Association for Supervision and Curriculum Development. Most of these groups have Web sites that you can browse for resources and membership information.

Suggestions for Mentors

If you are an experienced teacher who has been asked to mentor a new colleague, consider yourself lucky. You will benefit from the opportunity to coach, perhaps preventing the "sink or swim" isolation that so many new teachers experience. At the same time, mentoring will give you a chance to reflect on our profession, examining your practices with an eye to what's truly exceptional instead of merely routine. *Mentoring Beginning Teachers:*

Guiding, Reflecting, Coaching, by Jean Boreen and colleagues, has a wonderful chapter called "'What If?' Questions from Mentors" that can help you think through issues and problems. The book is practical, well organized, and full of ideas that demonstrate the latest thinking in teacher mentoring.

There are many ways to help inexperienced teachers or teachers new to your school feel confident and welcome in their new positions. New staff members usually must report to work a day or up to a week sooner than returning teachers. Although they probably will be busy with mandatory in-service training sessions, you might be able to schedule some time with them.

Remember that orientation doesn't have to end on the first day. Consider breaking up the sessions and scheduling them over the course of the first month of school (see Appendix Q). New staff members will be eager to get into their classrooms. Save anything that isn't absolutely necessary for three or four after-school meetings during the first month.

If you're working with a new teacher, try to stop by her classroom once a day and check to see if she needs anything. After the first week, you might not need to check with her so often. If both of you agree, consider meeting once a week for the first semester. As I said earlier, the reasons for meeting frequently might not seem obvious at first, but the regularity keeps problems from escalating. You make an opening suggestion such as, "Name one thing that worked well today" or "Tell me about one of your students." Listen carefully to the new teacher and offer commentary as necessary. The conversation probably will last ten minutes or less, but during that time you will have set the stage for an ongoing dialogue that should prove fruitful for both of you.

Other ideas for making the transition easier:

- Prepare and distribute a list of school procedures, if they are not clearly described in the teacher handbook. Include everything a teacher might need in the course of the first year: contacts for scheduling field trips, guidelines for using various machines in the building, and procedures for reserving audiovisual equipment. Sections explaining the school calendar, discipline policies, and any other school procedures would be helpful.
- Send reminders about deadlines imposed by school administrators. Explain the importance of having substitute teacher plans on file in the office. Identify what the new teacher will want to include in those plans.
- Explain school acronyms and jargon.
- Spend time explaining the unique characteristics of middle school learners. Explain the middle school concept and how it works in your building.
- Discuss effective assessment practices and homework guidelines. Be very accessible before the deadline for report cards.

- Explain the state or district academic standards and any required standardized tests. Discuss diversity concerns and how to address them. Review the school plan. Discuss the school's grading policies.
- School districts often have special services that new teachers need to know about, such as the print shop, the technology center, or the professional library. Consider taking the new teacher on a field trip to visit these sites and see what they have to offer.
- Explain successful activities for open house nights and conferences with parents. Show the new teacher how to "sell" his classroom as an exciting place to learn by preparing outlines of some of his best units and posting samples of students' work. Remind him to display representative teaching materials, provide an overview of the topics he plans to teach, and share a few personal interests, such as a favorite hobby or an unusual preteaching job.
- Hold a "new teacher shower" in which faculty members donate or purchase an item they consider essential for the classroom. Provide refreshments, and invite the entire faculty to attend.
- Provide a Teacher Survival Kit (see Appendix R). This can include a few mild gag gifts to remind new teachers to laugh and nurture one another. I often donate rubber bands, with a note reminding the new teachers to stretch, physically and mentally. Other colleagues sometimes contribute a small bottle of aspirin for the inevitable headaches, a small pack of bread crumbs to leave behind in case a new teacher gets lost, and a pack of adhesive strips to heal the blows to our egos. Middle school teaching is a tough job, but it can seem easier when a new teacher feels supported.
- Help first-year teachers identify extracurricular responsibilities that might overwhelm them at first. Watch for activity overload. Help them prioritize their time.
- Be an ambassador for new teachers with the rest of the faculty. Hook up people of similar interests. Organize some social gatherings.
- Point out professional development opportunities. Encourage new teachers to sign up for conferences and seminars. (See Appendix S for a sample survey to help new teachers identify their professional development needs.)
- Cover a new teacher's classes occasionally so she can view some of her colleagues in action.
- Share generously.

When editing my students' work, I see the strengths and weaknesses clearly. When editing my own writing, I'm practically blind. The tendency to use passive voice and repetitive phrases doesn't always leap out at me when I proofread. Fortunately, I found some mentors in my book editors, Holly Holland and

Philippa Stratton. I'm a better writer for having submitted my work to their scrutiny and then acting on their suggestions.

Mentoring teaching colleagues is similar. The relationships I've had with new teachers have been among the best of my career. From each partnership, I have learned something that I could use to improve my instructional practices. So if you're feeling overwhelmed or burned out, consider getting a mentor, whether formally or informally. And if you want to elevate the profession, sign up to mentor a new teacher. In either case, you will be better for the experience.

Parents as Partners in Twenty-First-Century Learning | 15

In early September, Mr. Morales called home from work to ask his son, Raul, if he needed any supplies for the new English/math project introduced that day in school. Raul was finishing the electronic flash cards posted by his science teacher for the week's study of microscope terms.

"Wow, Dad, how did you know about that?" Raul asked.

His father chuckled. "Your teacher and I have entered the twenty-first century," he said. "I knew about your project before you did. I've also seen a copy of the test you'll have on those vocabulary terms in science. You'll need to be able to point out every knob, stage, and lens on that microscope. By the way, you never showed me the interim report card I was supposed to sign. Pull it out for me by the time I get home, please."

Raul suddenly understood. "It was schoolnotes.com, wasn't it?"

"Yes," his father said. "See you at dinner. I'll pick up your mother on the way home."

Raul returned to his studies, knowing that he should have something to show his father by that evening.

Today's middle school classrooms can include students' parents in every step of the learning process. Current technology, innovation, and invitation can improve yesterday's approaches to parent communications. Online posting services are among the amazing tools that have become available in the past few years. Depending on the service, teachers can post daily, weekly, and monthly homework assignments, tests and quizzes, project directions, maps, samples of student work, vocabulary lists, reminders, research findings, book lists, recommended Web sites, and much more.

Let me add that while I use technology regularly to communicate with the parents of my students, I recognize that every family and every teacher does not have access to computers, electronic mail, or the Internet. Because of that and because I firmly believe in the personal touch, I also use more traditional ways to bring parents closer to the classroom. E-mail provides some great opportunities for parent-teacher sharing, but it won't substitute for those heart-to-heart conversations when Mr. Jones tells you that his daughter is being treated for depression or when you need to sit down with Jason and his parents to discuss the specific strategies that each of you will try to help him compensate for his auditory processing problems. Middle-level teachers should be prepared to handle multiple interactions with students' families. In this chapter, I offer suggestions for both technologically enhanced connections and those that require more interpersonal skills.

Have Computer, Will Travel

I've been using schoolnotes.com, a free service, for two years. It's better than the homework hot line phone-based systems I tried before. Fortunately, almost all my students have access to the Internet after school hours, whether at home, the local library, or the local recreation center, or through parents at work. I can make special arrangements for those who don't.

The advantages of online postings build each year. Parents can download the latest information from my class from their computers at home or at work. Parents know what their child knows. There is no "he said, she said" in the student/teacher/parent triad. All sides understand the expectations. The student realizes quickly that he can't get away with anything less than full accountability for the homework assignment. If parents need help understanding how to assist their children, they can access the information easily, twenty-four hours a day. The site includes a button to click, sending an e-mail message to the teacher, asking for clarification. Schoolnotes.com also lists suggested Web sites for student research. And don't forget those electronic flash cards.

Another benefit of having both parents and teachers use schoolnotes.com is that I'm getting almost all the homework turned in on time. Let me emphasize that: close to 100 percent of my middle school students do their homework, and a large part of that achievement stems from the online posting service. Students get triple-teamed by parents, teachers, and their own ability to access the information. Students who couldn't copy the vocabulary terms or the homework assignment from the chalkboard can retrieve them from schoolnotes.com. This process is particularly helpful for learning-disabled students, who need multiple strategies for success. Similarly, students who are sick or on vacation can find out what happened in class that day from anywhere in the world.

Electronic bulletin boards can help ease the tensions for parents who are exasperated by the daily struggle to figure out the teacher's expectations. Parents and students report that everyone's calmer and playing fewer games about finishing homework. Parents of children who haven't been responsible

> My teacher is good about answering students' questions after school. Students can e-mail him questions at his home and he almost always responds by 10 o'clock that night. Also, students can get information over the weekend when they won't see him for a few days. This is especially useful if students are uncertain about a homework assignment. This is also good so students can ask him questions before they have a chance to forget.
> ■ Jesse, seventh grade

about homework can print the daily postings and ask their children to show them a one-to-one correlation between the product in their hands and the posted directions from the teacher. There's little room for misinterpretation. The online postings also provide another way for teachers to affirm the moments of strong character, academic achievement, and leadership experienced in the classroom. Students look forward to these spontaneous recognitions.

To see how this process works, check out my homework site by going first to schoolnotes.com, choosing View Notes, typing in my zip code, 20171, then clicking on my name near the bottom of the list. Schoolnotes.com is free to both teachers and viewers.

Other recommended sites include the following:

Blackboard.com. You can create a Web site for your course with more details than you can on schoolnotes.com. For example, you can create and administer quizzes, calendars, and discussion boards.

MyClass.net. This is similar to blackboard.com in that you can create your own class Web site, post tests, and let students upload homework. You can also conduct class and parent discussions. The service is free, but it will post advertisements on your Web site.

Funbrain.com. This site includes education games for students and their parents, a lab to help teachers prepare quizzes, and a bulletin board for parents. It will automatically grade quizzes generated on the site and send teachers the scores by e-mail. You can access other teachers' quizzes as well. This site is free.

Schoolnotes.com offers the most opportunities at no cost, but the others might meet your needs better. Look for advertisements for online posting services in educational magazines and journals. Also, check Caroline McCullen's column, "The Electronic Thread," in *Middle Ground* magazine for other good Web sites for middle school classrooms.

Online posting services aren't the only way to communicate with mom and dad.

E-mail really works. I give out my home and school e-mail addresses to my students and their parents. In two minutes, I can alleviate several days' worth of anxiety or struggle. Students learn to conduct themselves with maturity and use "netiquette" when conversing with me, and parents don't feel as if they're alone when dealing with early adolescent angst. It makes the parents and the teacher truly a team, not us versus them.

Don't forget about the school's Web site. If it's well maintained, you should bookmark it as a good site for useful school information, including how to contact anyone on the staff and the latest links to state test scores, school policies, club sponsors, sports and academic competitions, and student work.

Reach Out and Touch

While technology connections work well with some school communities, they are not universally available or useful in others. Some of the low-tech standbys can inform and involve parents just as effectively. Find out which methods or combination of methods suit your students' families best. Consider adopting some of the following practices at your school.

Postcards

My colleagues and I preprint students' addresses on labels and buy several hundred blank postcards. During team meetings, we jot down a few positive things a child has achieved, sign the postcard, and stick the address label on it. After the meeting, we drop the postcards in the mailbox.

Parents in the Classroom

I invite parents to observe my classroom whenever they like. They might find it boring to sit through twelve PowerPoint presentations on a science fiction book, but that's the chance they take. I want parents in my classroom in order to show students that parents are part of their education. The parents also get a common frame of reference, and the students know this. Communications become easier. Parents should be in my classroom, advocating for their child and for good education. In nineteen years of teaching, I've never had a parent abuse the privilege or detract from the lesson. The opposite has occurred: their presence has helped to strengthen our relationships and to keep their children focused on school.

Parents can assist us in the classroom in other ways, too. They can co-present a topic, supervise breakout groups or learning centers, and tutor individual students. They can set up labs, care for plants and animals, and maintain portfolio records, among other things. Don't hesitate to ask for their help.

Home Visits

My colleagues and I routinely visit parents in their homes. It's very instructive to see how students interact with their parents. These maturing adolescents in the classroom become little children at home, with both parent and child enabling those roles. The yin and yang of children in transition is clear. When we combine the observations at home and school, we understand the whole child. In addition, parents often are more comfortable talking at home and are more willing to consider your concerns without feeling threatened and defensive. Besides, there's almost always food involved, which is enough motivation for me to stop by!

Quarterly Newsletters

We send quarterly newsletters with calendars, goals, major assignments, books to read, contact numbers, dates and supply lists for field trips, helpful study and parenting tips, school policies, and much more.

Teacher Report Card and Surveys

As I mentioned in an earlier chapter, I send home a teacher report card that my students developed. It includes a section for parents to write comments. In addition, my colleagues and I often ask parents to provide input about various topics through surveys. When we later follow up on their suggestions, it demonstrates that we heard them and responded accordingly. See Appendixes T–V for other forms that I have found useful when communicating with parents about their children.

Index Card Inquiries

At the beginning of each year, I ask parents to fill out an index card and answer this question: What do I need to know about your child to teach him/her better? I ask students to fill out one that states, What would you like me to know about you so that I can teach you better? I use the information they provide throughout the school year. In some years, I've repeated the activity in February.

The middle school years are a scary time to be a parent. The intimacy of elementary school relationships is replaced by the intimidation of large secondary school protocols. Young adolescents increasingly say "nothing" when asked to describe what happened in school that day. Parents and teachers need each other more than ever during this period. Parents are the experts on their children, and teachers are the experts on learning. Imagine the powerful possibilities when parents and teachers join forces to ensure that children succeed in school. United allies make for powerful achievement.

> Watching my son grow up is so bittersweet. My influence is waning fast, my conversations with him increasingly—I don't know—inconclusive! I compare my interactions with my thirteen-year-old to my interactions with my seven-year-old. With my younger son, I dominate his entire horizon; with Matt, I'm mostly just blocking his view of the TV set.
>
> Is this his elaborate form of self-protection? Is he insulating himself from my "I-know-I-shouldn't-but-I-do half-hearted responses because I'm too busy thinking about something else" rejections? It's easy to imagine the worst, to view this egocentrically, and think this is about me. It's not, I know. But still it's important to me to want to be a central part of his life. So, I flip-flop between casual, superficial stuff and wanting to talk about "big stuff."

The former has become easier and more comfortable while the latter has become more strident and ineffective.

I can tell by a glance how receptive he might be to my attempts to pull him back into my world. If I time it right, I can catch him open-minded early on a Sunday morning with the offer of a trip to McDonald's. Sometimes, we get into serious discussions then, but always he draws the invisible bounds around his world, and cordons off certain things he reserves for himself, for his own identity.

I've come to learn, as I'm sure millions of parents have before me, that his world and mine no longer overlap the way they once did, and that it's okay. I've come to learn that Matt having his own world, distinct from mine, is a critical part of his development as a person. Invading it is not okay. As a parent, I have an obligation to protect him even when it is the last thing in the world he thinks he may need. But in order to protect him, I have to know what's going on in his world. No wonder parents fill their kids' schedules with sports and music lessons and camp! It's totally about trying to control their world, to shape it in a certain direction one feels comfortable with. And the line between this control being acceptable and dysfunctional is hard to define and varies from child to child.

Anyway, it's late at night, and I set out to make a point in far fewer words than I've already written. My point was this, that I subconsciously let go of a lot of my need to understand everything about his world outside of my own after the first few times I visited his middle school. Much more than with his elementary school, I feel like I have partially turned over the reins of his development to his middle school teachers and staff. I intuitively trust the school to be as caring, as concerned, as supportive and attentive with Matt as we have been as parents.

It is the natural order of things that he separate himself from us somewhat at this point in his life, to go about the difficult business of finding himself. By letting go, by giving him freedom to explore, I see he relaxes, and I can occasionally feel him reaching back to make sure I am still there. And every once in a while, among the casual responses I get to my attempts to hug him, he'll hug with me back with such a fierceness that it brings tears to my eyes, and I know we're going to be fine.

Thanks, Matt's teachers, for being such a key part of Matt's extended family, his community, and his parenting. There are few I would trust with such an important-to-me role, fewer still who could pull it off so well.

P.S. Don't worry about trying to cure him of the procrastination thing—it's genetically coded and irreversible.

■ John, parent of a middle school student

National Board Certification   16

In the end, I forgot the noble reasons that had motivated me to apply for certification from the National Board for Professional Teaching Standards. I was focused on survival. The post office closes at midnight, I told myself, and I have less than ninety minutes to go. I was nearly finished writing, proofreading, and packaging the box of reflective essays, videotapes of my classroom instruction, and samples of student work. My wife and I had set up the exhibits one last time on the living room floor, trying to see if the codes on the written portions of my portfolio matched the accompanying artifacts. With horror, we realized that I had forgotten to copy an artifact that was supposed to document my professional service essay. Because I had left out this piece, I would have to recode all the exhibits. The post office was thirty minutes from my house. Would there be enough time?

Suddenly, I remembered that my father had purchased a copy machine for his home two days before. At 10:50 P.M. I arrived at his house, copied the missing documents, and spread all the pieces on the floor again so I could rearrange and recode them. Then I repackaged everything according to the detailed instructions—this piece here, that piece there, this one on top of that one—and raced out the door.

Driving down northern Virginia's Dulles Toll Road and on to the Washington Beltway this late seemed silly, but the voice inside my head was close to panic, repeating phrases as an unprepared middle school student might do before a big test ("Please don't ask me anything about Hammurabi's laws! Please don't ask me to spell Mesopotamia!"). My own mantra seemed synchronized with the rotation of the tires: "Please stay open, post office, please stay open, please stay open."

I felt like a fool. Surely all the other candidates had finished the process early and were home watching television or sleeping peacefully. I just knew that I was the only teacher racing against the deadline. I pulled into the parking lot of the post office at 11:40 P.M. and was relieved to see that the lights were still on. I parked, grabbed my package, and ran to the door. As I entered the lobby, I stopped and smiled—two teachers from the area were waiting in line to mail their own packages to the National Board for Professional

Teaching Standards. They told me that two others had been there just moments before. I almost cried out with joy: "I am not alone!"

A short time later, after shipping off my ten-pound package, I bid my colleagues farewell and walked out of the post office, feeling numb. Back in the family minivan, I was struck by the silence and the calming release of my burden. It was two minutes before midnight on an icy January night in 1994. Although exhausted, I wanted to do something to celebrate my accomplishment. I stopped at a McDonald's restaurant and bought a vanilla milk shake before heading home to bed.

Why Go Through the Agony?

Participating in the assessment phase of the National Board for Professional Teaching Standards is a profoundly moving experience. The process is rigorous, requiring extended analysis, accountability, and demonstration of high standards of instruction and professionalism. Teachers who have completed the assessment phase claim that it has helped them improve their instructional practices and, more important, increase student achievement. Before I went through the process, I made too many decisions "on the fly." Today, my lessons are focused on excellence and motivated by what's best for each student, not what's easiest for me.

In *What Matters Most: Teaching for America's Future* (National Commission on Teaching and America's Future 1996), Gary Fenstermacher, professor of education at Virginia Tech University, summarizes one of the most important reasons for seeking high professional standards:

> In a time when so many advocate for restructured schools . . . it is more important than ever that teachers have the capacity to appraise their actions, evaluate their work . . . incorporate new theory and research into practice, and possess the skills and understanding needed to explain their work. . . . These reflective capacities are not acquired during evening mini-courses after a full day's work. They are, rather, the outcome of sustained and rigorous study, and of dialogue and exchange with master teacher educators. (42)

My department chairperson encouraged me to pursue National Board certification, and I am a different teacher as a result. In talking with other board-certified teachers, I have found evidence of similar transformations. Colleagues say they shifted from always running the show to letting students direct more of their learning. They developed an interdisciplinary focus instead of concentrating on only one subject. They praised the end of isolation as they discovered the benefits of collaboration. They learned to routinely incorporate the latest research into their instruction and accept the pressures of standards and accountability. And through the National Board certification process, all of us have been inspired to design more innovative and authentic assessments that truly enable students to show what they know.

This is the kind of renewal the National Board for Professional Teaching Standards anticipated when it formed in 1987. This independent organization of teachers and other education stakeholders hoped to simultaneously improve the education profession and student learning, recognizing that higher student achievement requires qualified and effective teachers. As described in *Preparing Teachers for National Board Certification: A Facilitator's Guide* (Steeves and Browne 2000), the board's "mission is to establish high and rigorous standards for what accomplished teachers should know and be able to do, and to develop and operate a national, voluntary system to assess and certify teachers who meet these standards…For the first time, the profession finds itself responsible for defining what it means to be a professional teacher" (ix).

The National Board for Professional Teaching Standards began with the recommendations from *A Nation Prepared: Teachers for the 21st Century* (Carnegie Forum on Education and the Economy 1986). The authors of the report called for the establishment of a board "to establish high and rigorous standards for what accomplished teachers should know and be able to do, and to certify teachers who meet those standards." Today, the National Board for Professional Teaching Standards is governed by sixty-three directors, the majority of whom are practicing teachers. The remaining members include business, political, and educational leaders.

National Board certification is different from state licensing. For one thing, it's voluntary, not mandatory. In addition, teachers are evaluated by peers, not administrators, which creates a collegial tone instead of an adversarial one. The evaluation is for teachers who are far enough along in their careers to have accumulated a wealth of knowledge and experience about their subjects and grade level. Finally, the assessments were designed by teachers, not politicians, which means they are valid indicators of professional excellence.

"For me, what makes the National Board unique is that here, for the first time, we have major education reform initiatives being designed and implemented *by* classroom teachers *for* classroom teachers, instead of being imposed upon them from above," Claire Pelton, former vice chair of the board and a demonstration teacher from San Jose, California, said in a 1995 conversation.

The first assessments were field-tested during the 1993–1994 school year for candidates pursuing certification in the Early Adolescent [ages 11–15] Language Arts and Early Adolescent Generalist categories. About thirteen hundred teachers from one hundred twelve school districts nationwide took part in the testing stage, and five hundred forty—about one-third of the total participants—completed the process. About three hundred teachers sought certification as Early Adolescent Generalist, the designation I pursued. Of those who finished in that category, eighty-one became certified.

During the past decade, however, the number of board-certified teachers has exploded. In 2001 there were about ten thousand applicants for National Board certification, up from about 6,124 the year before. To date, 9,531 teachers have earned the designation.

"The significant increase in the number of teachers seeking National Board certification this year represents a milestone for our organization," Betty Castor, president of the National Board for Professional Teaching Standards, said in a 2000 press release. "We believe the National Board is well on its way of reaching its goal of 100,000 candidates by 2006."

Becoming a Reflective Practitioner and Other Benefits

In the shower. Waiting to fall asleep at tonight. Sitting in the dentist's office. Standing in line at the grocery store. Cleaning the children's rabbit cage. Driving toward a vacation destination and doing everything possible to avoid thinking about it. Our teaching, our classrooms, and our students are never far from our minds. We read something in the newspaper, see something at the movie theater, or hear something worth sharing, and what do we say? "I could use that with my students!" In the search for teaching excellence and student success, we are always looking for a better way.

Professional educators establish structures for reflection and revision of their practices. We are not afraid of what such scrutiny might reveal. When a lesson or approach "bombs" in the classroom, we collect the broken pieces of the lesson and turn it into something constructive the following day. By being reflective, we can demonstrate the very things we wish to inspire in our students: problem solving, risk taking, creativity, and adaptability.

This isn't easy, of course. Such introspection and responsiveness requires concentration and discipline, but the rewards almost always justify the commitment. According to the National Board for Professional Teaching Standards, accomplished teachers critically examine their practices and seek to expand their repertoire, deepen their knowledge, and sharpen their judgment. As a result, they remain dynamic, able to meet the evolving needs of their students.

Teachers think systematically about their practice and learn from experience.
■ Proposition #4, National Board for Professional Teaching Standards

During my own journey toward National Board certification, I began writing commentaries on my teaching and analyzing my decisions and actions each day. I admitted mistakes, considered alternatives, tried different approaches, and reflected on the results in subsequent entries. No other professional development activity has helped me improve as much.

There are benefits to National Board certification beyond pedagogy. I have never been treated with as much respect as I was during and after my candidacy. The general public considers certified teachers accomplished educators who have met rigorous standards and have earned the expertise of other professionals, such as a board-certified physician.

An increasing number of states are aligning their standards and assessments for certification with those of the National Board for Professional Teaching Standards. Many states are requiring videotaped lessons when teachers apply for recertification, and most states automatically extend licenses and certification to teachers who have attained National Board certification. In addition, some states and school districts provide tangible rewards for board-certified teachers, including increased salaries or retirement benefits. For example, my school district pays each candidate's fees (currently $2,300), gives candidates two paid days off to work on the required portfolio, and waives the traditional teacher evaluation cycle for the duration of the certificate, which lasts for ten years. Because I am board-certified, I also get an automatic five-year extension of my Virginia teaching license. The benefits are similar in other states. North Carolina gives board-certified teachers a 12 percent salary increase, pays the fees for those who attain certification, and provides up to three days of release time for candidates to work on their portfolios and prepare for the assessment center exercises. In Florida, successful candidates get a 10 percent salary increase, plus another 10 percent hike if they agree to mentor someone through the certification process.

As a candidate for National Board certification, I learned how to discuss instruction and assessment with colleagues from different grade levels and schools across the nation. I jumped into Internet forums and exchanged ideas with colleagues in Texas, Idaho, North Carolina, and Michigan. I was in my eleventh year of teaching at the time, and I had never had such thoughtful conversations about teaching, outside of a few graduate school courses. My teaching days were so full that I rarely had time for professional dialogue until I found a structure and motivation for doing so.

National Board certification also gives teachers a voice in education policies. School board members and state legislatures call us to ask our opinions. We get invitations to serve on panels that study problems in education, consult on new projects, and design curriculum. In my school district, board-certified teachers serve as clinical faculty, assume leadership roles, embrace accountability, provide in-house expertise, use and share highly effective practices, and bring national recognition to our schools. We have assisted schools in danger of reconstitution, written articles and books, taught at local universities, coached new teachers, and presented at national conferences.

We do this while teaching full course loads and raising families in our community. There are twenty of us now in Fairfax County, Virginia. Imagine what we will be able to do when more board-certified teachers join our ranks!

What's Involved?

There are two major assessments that candidates must complete: a school-site portfolio and a performance at an assessment center. Most candidates arrange their portfolios during September or October, in preparation for the deadline in April or May. It takes about one hundred twenty hours to complete all the requirements, which include analyzing videotapes of your instruction, collaborating with colleagues, writing commentaries, and reflecting on your practice. The portfolio assessments are designed to measure teacher performance accurately against the National Board's standards. The school-site portfolios for middle school certification generally have three activities focusing on instruction, assessment, and engaging students and one activity in which candidates must demonstrate how they work with students' families and the community as well as how they collaborate with other education professionals. In most exercises, the assessors want to see coherent and consistent evidence of the candidate's knowledge of the unique nature of the middle school student, evidence of collaboration with colleagues, and an ability to meet the needs of diverse learners. In addition, the assessors want to see evidence of academic standards in action.

The assessment center activities last eight hours and consist of six thirty-minute exercises and a brief computer tutorial. For some certificates, candidates receive stimulus materials to help them think about their responses in advance. The exercises do not analyze writing ability, so candidates can write in paragraphs, bullets, or phrases. The assessment center activities focus on the candidate's knowledge of subject matter.

Living to Tell the Tale

We've discussed the why and the what of National Board certification. Now, let's take a closer look at the how.

In November 1993, I attended a first meeting of the candidates from Northern Virginia, along with Diane Hughart, my colleague at Herndon Middle School. We were immediately intimidated when the day's speakers showed up. They included a former district Teacher of the Year, a local teacher-writer who served on the National Board for Professional Teaching Standards, the director of professional development in our school district, and Mary Futrell, former president of the National Education Association and now Dean of Education at George Washington University. With the arrival of each new person, my heart sank. I knew I was in the wrong place and began thinking of graceful ways to back out. One way or another, however, all of us found the courage to stay.

Diane and I returned to our classes for the next few weeks wondering if we had bitten off more than we could chew. We began videotaping our lessons in December. We had to turn in our portfolio of assessment responses by January 14—there was no time to waste. The fixed-camera position I initially used to film my lessons couldn't show what was happening throughout the room, we all looked like puppets. So I asked my students to film the class by moving around the room with the camera. They picked up all the nuances, including one student who exclaimed, "Oh [expletive], I didn't know the camera was on!" Another student filmed an entire discussion from directly below my nostrils. Diane told me that one of her students walked up to the camera, opened her mouth, burped loudly, then smiled and walked away. We chose to include these particular segments on the tapes we sent to the National Board, hoping the assessors would understand the peculiar nature of the middle school student.

While we were filming one lesson, a construction crew renovating our school building decided to grind and cut cinder blocks for a new wall five feet from the front door of my portable classroom, located in a trailer in the parking lot. At the same time, several military jets took off from nearby Dulles Airport. Later, the construction crew leveled the ground adjacent to my trailer with three bulldozers. All of this was captured on the tape as I attempted to demonstrate my professionalism. I wondered if it was professional to wish for a giant assessment booklet to fall from the sky and crush the construction crew.

When the seven colleagues from our area who were pursuing certification gathered in January, we were stunned by the differences in the required narrative descriptions of the three-week instructional period. One person's description was nine pages long, and another person wrote just a page-and-a-half. My narrative was sixty pages long. Which one of us had interpreted the directions correctly? Had I been a verbose fool, or would the evaluators consider my response to be comprehensive and scholarly? We contacted the National Board seeking clarification. The representatives responded that each person's interpretation would reveal something about us as professionals. That was a great comfort! (The National Board later developed clearer recommendations because of problems like ours.)

Fast forward to March, when we were gearing up for the assessment center testing, which used to be two days long and now has been streamlined to one. At the assessment center, we were asked to show our identification. Diane laughed and said, "Yeah, like you could pay someone to do this." We spent the day analyzing curriculum, describing our instructional practices, demonstrating our knowledge in different core subjects, and trying to live up to the standards set forth by the National Board. The other candidates were terrific. It was cathartic to share stories about the certification process when we got together between the assessment exercises. By the time we had finished on the second day, we had written for more than fifteen hours.

In the end, three of the seven first-year candidates succeeded. We experienced the inspiration of collaborative efforts, both on the part of the National Board and from each other. We also discovered the vitality of alternative and authentic assessments, gained confidence in our professional skills, and learned what it means to be an excellent educator.

How to Succeed

Here is the best advice that my board-certified colleagues and I can offer about the process.

First, investigate the process thoroughly before committing to it. Decide whether this is the best year to try; you might be better off preparing one year and taking the assessments the following year. Turning in a complete, on-site portfolio is 75 percent of the battle. If you are not successful with any portion, you can "bank" the parts on which you did well and redo the other exercises within two years. It will cost $300 to retake any entry.

Set up a support group immediately. Unsuccessful candidates frequently say they did not finish the portfolio or failed to do it correctly because they lacked supportive colleagues with whom they could share the challenges. Candidate groups can help you keep going when you think all is lost. There are many helpful activities that support groups can share:

- For each of the specific standards for your certificate area, answer the following: What does it mean? Why is it so important? How does it manifest itself in a middle school classroom? Describe how you taught a particular lesson and how you demonstrated academic standards. Make a claim about what you did, cite clear and consistent evidence that you did it, and interpret or demonstrate the impact of your teaching on student learning. Afterward, reflect on the lesson and the standard: What did you learn about your instructional practice as a result of this lesson?
- Discuss why highly accomplished teachers analyze practice in this manner.
- Describe your knowledge of adolescent development and how you get to know your students.
- Describe your formative and summative assessments. Are they authentic? Do they provide useful feedback to students? Are the assessments varied and appropriate? How are they developmentally responsive to students?

- List the ways you contribute to the field of education. Choose one and reflect on how it made a difference in the profession.
- Analyze short videotapes of each other in the classroom. Find evidence of the standards in practice. Again, make a claim, cite the evidence, and comment on the impact on student learning. The following are some sample questions for videotape analysis:

What were your objectives?

How did the instructional context affect your practice?

Why did you make certain decisions?

What is the evidence that your teaching achieved the desired results?

Which sections of the videotaped lesson show the students thinking or achieving in the way you intended?

What happened on the videotape (or in the lesson) that will affect your future interactions with the students?

How does each segment demonstrate or provide evidence for the core propositions?

How did your approach meet the needs of diverse learners? In other words, what teaching challenges did the students present?

How did the segment fit into the larger context of the students' learning?

How would you improve the lesson next time?

How did your knowledge of adolescent learning shape the lesson's design?

- Practice analyzing three students' work samples over time. Choose any work that shows how the students came to understand important concepts through worksheets, labs, quizzes, reflections, tests, projects, videotaped interactions, and teacher anecdotes. What decisions did you make based on your analysis of the work?
- Brainstorm ways that professional teachers think systematically about their practice, and comment on the extent to which you do so. If you don't think about your practices in this way, experiment with one of the suggestions.
- Think about a teacher who made a difference when you were a student. What made him or her such a good teacher? What are the qualities of a highly accomplished teacher in your subject area?
- Learn some effective video documentation techniques.
- Record everything that happens within a particular class or subject for three days. Record all lesson events objectively, without opinion, commentary, or evaluation. Write a reflective commentary on those lessons in paragraph style.

Treat your reflections as a dissertation. In other words, seek advice, get feedback, incorporate research, be tenacious, and revise frequently. Write concisely. It hurts your assessment to exceed the page limitations set by the

National Board for Professional Teaching Standards; the evaluators will read what you've written only up to the stated limit. The portfolio directions have excellent examples. Read them carefully and follow the model.

Keep up with the latest research in education. Read education journals that present state-of-the-art practices. Use the research in your reflections. In addition, consider to what extent you are aware of alternative approaches to instruction and embrace innovation. Supervise a student teacher. Helping someone prepare for the profession is a wonderful way to reflect on what's most important about your work.

Break down each assessment into its component tasks, put them on a time line, then complete them. The portfolio instructions provide a graphic organizer that shows how to do this.

Be an intelligent consumer. Call the National Board offices or check the information on their Web site. There can be multiple interpretations of directions; clarify your reading of them.

Although the National Board requires only three years of actual teaching before the assessment, my colleagues and I suggest five to ten years minimum. We think you need that much practical experience before you can know how to meet the diverse needs of students and provide clear and consistent evidence of academic standards in your practice. If you have fewer years of experience, start preparing for National Board certification by analyzing your instructional practices and their impact on students. Ask colleagues to help you break down what happens in your classroom, from the smallest interactions with students to large unit planning. Sit with a colleague and identify which lessons, decisions, and actions demonstrate academic standards in action.

For more information, tour the Web site for the National Board for Professional Teaching Standards at http://www.nbpts.org. Teachers from every state are listed there. They are willing to be contacted to discuss the experience. You also can call the National Board at 1-800-22-TEACH.

I urge you to consider taking this journey to excellence. It should prove to be one of the most exciting adventures of your career. One final thought: remember to check the closing time of the post office nearest you.

The Truth About Middle School Students $\boxed{17}$

Several of my twelve- and thirteen-year-old students are the oldest children in their families, which means they usually cook dinner and do the laundry because both parents work in the evenings. These students also bathe their young siblings and put them to bed before getting started on their homework.

Last year, one of my students and his family raised about $22,000 for the National Juvenile Diabetes Foundation. He persuaded more than 150 of us to participate in a walkathon with him in Washington, D.C., last May.

The students in my school read more than 2,000 books in four months last year. One of my students is the Web curator for her former elementary school. Two of my students recently performed the national anthem at a local swimming program attended by thousands. Another student is an opera singer who performed at the Kennedy Center. One of our eighth graders recently coordinated the building of an elevated sidewalk through a mud pit at the back entrance to the school.

Bragging? You bet. But I'm sure you could make similar claims about your own students' accomplishments. Why, then, do these achievements so rarely earn accolades from the public? The answer has much to do with how the media, and some politicians, have distorted the community's view of the middle school years. In the summer of 2000, for example, the *Washington Post* ran a weeklong newspaper series about young adolescents, and almost every one of the narrative portraits placed them in an unflattering light. Media reports also have trumpeted the huge increase in sexually transmitted diseases among middle school students in an affluent suburb of Atlanta, Georgia. Other troubling reports might have dominated the news in your neck of the woods.

I don't doubt that these incidents are true. And I'm not advocating that we ignore them. But I'm tired of seeing the reputation of all of our ten- to fourteen-year-olds smeared because of the unfortunate actions of a few. As educators, I believe we must accept some responsibility for changing those misperceptions.

The most evidence of there being intelligent life out there is that they haven't visited us.

What are the 1,200 rules of a new republic? Obey, conform, abstain, reform, tell us everything, resist temptation, avoid situations.

"Always be a first-rate version of yourself instead of a second-rate version of someone else."—Judy Garland

Life is not a journey that starts when you are born; it's all the people who you have touched once you're gone.

The sooner we fall behind, the more time we have to catch up.

I think, therefore I am.

Never trust your brother when he always says, "Do you dare?"

There is a difference between learning from the past and learning about the past.

During the 1999–2000 school year, for an entire month, I posted blank sheets of white paper on the back wall of my classroom. I told my students they could write anything they wanted as long as it would be acceptable to their parents and grandparents, would not violate any school policies, and would not be derogatory to anyone. Students raced to the wall each day to see what was written and to add more to it.

Only in America do people order a double cheeseburger, large fries, and a Diet Coke.

If there is only one person you can please, please yourself.

You never learn to swim by staring at the water.

I have the goodest grammar of all!

Their comments—profound, pithy, honest, absurd, juvenile, and everything in between—are recorded here as they were written. They reveal developing wisdom, deep understanding, and free-thinking energy. Their comments also present much more than the limited view of adolescent development than we usually see in the media.

Soccer is the best sport. No it's not, but it's better than baseball.

How big is the big stick of diplomacy?

I would have written less if I had had the time.

The secret to intelligent life is not my sister.

Money runs everything, but why?

Many people believe that zero brain growth occurs during the middle grades. This is bunk. Recent research has proven that the human brain grows at tremendous rates during early adolescence. The cerebral cortex is very elastic, capable of creating trillions of new nerve pathways each day and reconfiguring itself with each new experience. This period isn't marked only by academic gains. The emotional connections children make during the middle years will directly influence how they handle trust, power, conflict, fairness, and relationships in adulthood.

What's ignorance?

Has anyone solved the Unified Field Theory yet?

The air was heavy with the stench of anarchy. Or was it the smell of free-dom? I had never smelled either before.

The two hardest things to handle in life are failure and success.

I don't get it. I just don't get it.

The difference between a fool and a genius is that the genius knows he has his limits.

Why do we kill people to tell them that killing people is bad?

My wife and I usually choose middle school over high school students when we need babysitters for our six- and seven-year-old children. Why? Young adolescents are ceaselessly conscientious. They are not apathetic in positions of trust. Doing the right thing matters to them. They want to be taken seriously so badly that they often go overboard to make sure they are perceived as responsible. When my students have had challenges at home, such as parents who work three jobs, or personal problems, such as diabetes or failing grades, other middle school students tend to be the most mature and tender sources of help.

How long should my 200-word essay be?

Note to self: Cats are not water-resistant.

Never put your name in someone else's heart because that heart can be broken.

I feel like a block of ice.

We can give our students a brain surge and a soapbox while simultaneously tapping into their desire to perform humane acts, their acute sensitivity to injustice, and their need to feel connected to the world. For example, how about teaching them about logical fallacies? We can let them analyze various articles disparaging their age group by searching for rhetorical tricks such as a false dichotomy in which someone assumes there are only two alternatives or the emotional appeal argument in which someone uses evocative words to manipulate readers' feelings instead of their minds.

Instead of swallowing snide comments about today's students not being able to spell or make change, we can politely dispute them by describing the latest activities in our classrooms. "Oh, did you know that my students have spent the last few weeks comparing President Herbert Hoover's political response to business monopolies during the Depression to the Justice Department's current antitrust actions against Microsoft?" "Would you like to drop by to see the multimedia presentations my students have created, including the enhanced digital photography?" "By the way, did you know that our students run their own television studios and are comfortable speaking and singing in front of thousands?"

At the same time, we also need to remind people that these are children, and children occasionally veer off track. It's called growing up.

You are only young once, but you can always be immature.

Cheese is good.
So are crackers.

A true friend knows your weaknesses and doesn't use them against you.

Don't you think Mr. W. picks the best music? Um, no.

Love is every emotion put into one.

I'm Marvin and I'm depressed.

Why is abbreviation such a long word?

Young adolescents can be absurd, on purpose and by accident. They can get their braces stuck in classroom pillows or glue their armpits so they can't raise their arms without ripping hair—both of which actually happened in my classroom. Sophisticated students will laugh when someone passes gas during a test, and they will ask questions that I answered four seconds earlier: "Take out your pencils and write your name on your paper," I direct them. "Mr. W., what do we write first on our paper?" a student will ask without guile.

As middle-level educators, we must learn to be patient with their quirky growth patterns. Our classes are full of human beings in the making, and we play important roles as their coaches, mentors, and referees.

I have lost track of the students who gave me nothing but frustration and terrible work during their time in my classroom but performed well in high school and college. Either they weren't ready to receive what I had to offer, or I wasn't offering what they needed. But somewhere inside, they were germinating the seeds of what they could become. With each of them, I had to look past those frustrating years and not hold their development against them. What would I have become if I had been held to the labels placed on me as a young adolescent? I don't want to think about it.

Don't eat yellow snow.

Life's beautiful—Enjoy!

When good and evil have their final battle, does it matter if you look good?

Pessimism is bad. It never works.

Only in America can a pizza get delivered to your house faster than an ambulance.

What came first, the chicken or the egg?

Genius is two parts: Having a lot to say and not saying it. You are so right. Amen.

Never pierce your belly button in the dark.

Who am I?

What is popularity? Having lots of friends, dressing like everyone else, having a girlfriend/boyfriend, getting good grades, or being yourself?

Let's go out of our way to write letters to the media. Let's do our part to make sure that the 99 percent of students who do the right thing get just as much attention as the 1 percent who make bad choices. We can flood the media with announcements of their significant achievements and service. We can regularly publish lists of the skills they've mastered. We can make positive predictions for our communities based on what we know about our capable youth. And we can talk about how much we enjoy being in their company. Invite students and parents to do the same.

> There are 3 kinds of people in this world: Those who can count and those who can't count.
>
> Worship the turtle!
>
> I'd like to thank me, myself, and I.
>
> The answer to life's questions is always 49.
>
> When God made me, he was just kidding.
>
> Are humans the end of the chain or have we broken it? Or is evolution still going on?
>
> Remember the holocaust.
>
> Pay no attention to the man behind the curtain.

The graffiti wall is now a permanent fixture in my classroom. So is my commitment to spreading the truth about the outstanding accomplishments of middle school students. I invite you to join in the effort.

Appendix

A   Co-Presenting Techniques

Adapted from an In-service Program by Gayla Moilanen

- **Tag team.** Each person takes responsibility for different portions of the presentation. Presenters do not ever present together.
- **Speak and interject.** One presenter speaks while the other interjects observations, examples, alternative perspectives, questions.
- **Speak and chart.** One presenter speaks and facilitates discussion while the other records comments on a chalkboard, overhead, monitor, or chart.
- **Perform and comment.** One presenter demonstrates or performs a skill, and the other presenter comments on the demonstration.
- **Duet.** Both presenters are on stage at the same time. They might alternate brief content chunks, finish each other's sentences, surprise each other. They use close proximity, and they balance stage use. They cue one another with subtle signals.
- **Human videotape.** One person presents while another pulls out a huge television remote control and points it at the presenter, calling out, "Freeze frame." He turns to the audience and facilitates a discussion about the point the presenter was making: "What did we hear her say?" "Do we buy that?" "Let's break it down into smaller chunks . . ." "Let's rewind the tape a few seconds and hear her say it again to see if we're correct." He then presses "rewind" to review the last portion or "play" to continue the presentation. Presenters can take this farther and "fast-forward" the person to the conclusion of her presentation so students can see the end goal, then "rewind" the tape (and person) to the beginning to start the presentation.

B Sponges

"Sponges" are particularly effective strategies when you are concerned with time, being on task, or preparing students for thinking. Sponge activities soak up loose time with purposeful experiences. Some of the better ones I've used include the following. (Many of these were passed along by Fairfax County Public Schools' Office of Staff Development and Training.)

- Write three questions on the board related to today's lesson.
- Graffiti posters with specific prompts around the room (students go to each one and respond).
- In-Out Game. Don't reveal the category—just start giving clues (such as the parts of a cell): "Mitochondria are in my club, but Mighty Mouse is not. Endoplasmic reticulum is in my club, but endoskeletons are not. A nucleus is in my club, but nuclear warfare is not." Students determine the classification the teacher's statements exemplify, then confirm their hypothesis by offering one of their own. If it fits the pattern, the teacher invites them to be part of the club. The game continues until everyone is a member— everyone "gets in."
- Collect feedback from students.
- As you put away materials, be thinking about . . .
- (As you pass out tests) The first question on the test will be . . .
- (If finished early) What wasn't tested on the test?
- (As you collect tests) I asked three questions about the causes of the spread of the Ebola virus. What might a fourth question be, and think of someone to call on to answer it.
- Be ready to say three ways in which the Civil War and Revolutionary War are exactly the same . . .
- In the Manner of the Word. One student leaves. The rest of the class determines an adverb. The other student returns and tries to guess the adverb by asking students to perform pretend tasks "in the manner of the word." Good tasks are ones that have multiple steps, such as ordering a pizza, changing a tire, changing a diaper, making a pizza, building a campfire.
- Write down an alternative title to the book.
- Who would you cast in the role of _____ in this book and why?
- Use a new term in two situations, one correct and one incorrect. Students discern which is which.
- Come up with as many words you can think of that mean the opposite of _____.

C Ideas for Practicing and Using Vocabulary Terms

- **Forms.** Get blank copies of any forms students will encounter in the real world and have them fill out the forms using the vocabulary terms. Examples: a will, a checkbook, tax forms, employment applications, hotel registrations, loan applications, wedding applications, car registrations, medical insurance forms, accident reports, time sheets.

- **Restaurant menu.** Names of items include the vocabulary word, and descriptions of items convey the term's meaning. Example: Antecedent Apple Pie—A dessert so good, it's best served before the meal.

- **Game clues.** Choose familiar board games, car games, or television game show formats.

- **Taboo cards.** Students write the word at the top of an index card, then list the five terms most associated with the word. Students try to get their teammates to say the word without using any of those terms.

- **Art collage.** Use all the words in the list.

- **Shape spellings.** Students write the words so as to convey the meaning of the word. Examples: *tall* written in tall, skinny letters, *conflict* written with each half of the word leaning toward each other or breaking apart, *germination* written with each letter sprouting from soil, *fraction* written as frac/tion.

- **Vocabulary rummy.** Play it just like the card game, except the cards are the vocabulary terms written on index cards. Make up combinations that groups of students are striving for in each hand: words that express all steps in mitosis, nouns and pronouns, words associated with a pentagonal prism (five, edges, faces, vertices), words that describe the Industrial Revolution. When someone calls out "Vocabulary Rummy," he must defend his choices with his playing partners.

- **"Wanted Dead or Alive" poster.** All descriptions and images include the proper uses of the words.

- **Conversation.** Dialogue between two famous people in which they both use the vocabulary terms.

- Rap or folk song.

- Newspaper article.

- Rules to a new board game.

- Illustrated dictionary for younger children.

- Movie poster.

- CD-ROM cover and insert.

- Eulogy.

- **Bumper stickers.** You can display these slogans on a real car bumper in your room or in the school. Make sure the meaning of the word is clear. For example, "Clean up the *environment*—Our surroundings are borrowed from our children!"

D Summarization Techniques

- **3-2-1.** Teachers ask students to write three of something, two of something, then one of something. For example, students might explain *three* things they learned in the lesson that they hadn't known before, *two* areas in which they are still confused, and *one* way the topic can be applied or *one* thing about which they'd like to know more. The criteria for listing items at each level are up to the needs of teacher and the lesson, but it's important to make the category for listing three times easier than the category for listing one item.

- **Carousel brainstorming.** Posters with words and topics about the lessons ahead are displayed around the room. Students move to each poster and record their response to whatever's written on the poster.

- **Exclusion brainstorming.** The teacher writes the topic on an overhead or chalkboard followed by a series of words, some of which fit with the topic and others that do not. Students draw a line through the excluded words and circle those that relate to the topic. Students explain why they excluded and included certain words.

- **Exit cards.** Before leaving class, students write responses to three or four questions on index cards or half-sheets of paper. The questions review core understandings from the lesson. Sample: What are the major phases of mitosis? The cards are used for diagnosis and planning for the next lesson.

- **Graphic organizers.** Students complete teacher-designed organizers or create their own.

- **Human body or stick figure outline.** Students do a life-sized outline of the body of one member of their table group, then draw and color in "Characteristics of [insert topic of the lesson]" in the corresponding locations on the body. For instance, you may want to focus on characteristics of a good writer, reader, scientist, mathematician, artist, historian, or citizen. You may want to examine systems of government, math concepts, art techniques, or types of circuitry. Parts of the body symbolize the attributes of the topic. For example, how is each of the following body parts like the checks and balances of the U.S. government?—hand, heart, mind, legs, feet, stomach, lungs, blood, ears, joints, mouth, skin, circulatory system, endocrine system. If time, materials, and groupings don't allow for the large body outlines, students can draw stick figures and do the same thing in groups or as individuals.

- **Jigsaws.** A larger grouping of material is broken into component pieces. Individuals or small groups study different pieces, then report their findings to the whole group. By the time all individuals or groups have shared, everyone has the complete picture.

- **Luck of the draw.** Each day, students rewrite their notes or learning from the lesson in preparation for summarizing for the class tomorrow. Then in tomorrow's class, the teacher pulls one name from a hat to read his or her summarization and facilitate a short review before the day's new learning.

D	Summarization Techniques *(continued)*

- **PQRST.** Used for text reading. Sequence:

  P   *Preview* to identify main parts.

  Q   Develop *questions* to which you want to find answers.

  R   *Read* the material.

  S   *State* (or *summarize*) the central idea of theme.

  T   *Test* yourself by answering questions (or *teach* the material to someone else).

- **Synectics.** (See next page, Appendix D1.)

- **Test notes.** Students record all they know about a topic on one side of a 3 x 5 inch index card. Decide whether they are allowed to use those index cards as they take the test.

- **Think-pair-share.** Students think individually (using art, writing, or just sitting quietly) about a topic or an issue, then share their thinking with a partner. Partners then offer two or three salient points to the larger class that come from their sharing.

- **Word splash.** Identify a content piece you want students to read and study. Determine the key facts, words, and concepts you want students to learn as a result of studying the material. Then "splash" those words across a sheet of paper by writing them at cock-eyed angles all over the sheet. You might want to carry a bucket containing the words written on posterboard, trip as you cross the room, and let the words scatter across the floor or desktops. Ask student to help you put them back together. Give each table group or individual student a copy of the words, and ask students to put the words together so that they make sense. Wild connections will be made, especially since it's new material and students have no frame of reference. Once done, pass out the content material and ask students to read it, looking for the relationship among the key facts, words, and concepts. Ask them to see if their initial understanding was correct. Then, as small groups or individually, students arrange the words properly, and share their new sequence of connections with the class. The class decides if a particular group's (or individual's) interpretation of the content is correct or if it needs revision. Word splash is based on an idea from Dorsey Hammond, Professor in Reading and Language Arts at Oakland University in Rochester, Michigan.

D1 Illuminate, Reflect, and Summarize with Synectics

Synectics was designed by William J. Gordon, who defines it as "the joining together of different and apparently irrelevant elements," or put more simply, "making the familiar strange." Using the basic sequence, students:

1. Learn a topic.
2. Describe the topic, focusing on descriptive words and critical attributes.
3. Identify an unrelated category to compare to the descriptions in #2. ("Think of a sport that reminds you of these words. Explain why you chose that sport.")
4. Write or express the analogy between the two. ("The endocrine system is like playing zones in basketball. Each player or gland is responsible for his area of the game.")

Important: Students are very creative. Just because we cannot see the analogies right away doesn't mean the students can't either. They often see connections and differences we do not see.

In 4-Square Synectics, the class brainstorms four objects from a particular category (for example: kitchen appliances, household items, the circus, forests, shopping malls). Then, in small groups, students brainstorm what part of today's learning is similar in some way to the objects listed. Finally, they create four analogies, one for each object, then share their analogies with the class.

Example: How is the human digestive system like each household item below?

kitchen sink	old carpet
microwave oven	broom

Example: How is the Pythagorean Theorem like each musical instrument below?

piano	full drum set
electric guitar	trumpet

E   Spelling Bee "de Strange"

A = Achoo!

E = Thpht!!!

O = Oink! Oink!

I = Ribbit!

U = Ooh-la-la!

F Human Bingo

Can make a strange noise with his or her body	Can make into a polynomial: $(X+1)(X+3)$	Can demonstrate titration	Can solve $4\ 2/3$ $-\ 1\ 4/5$	Knows 2 products of photosynthesis
Can define "_____"	Knows 3 causes for the Civil War	Knows the capitals of countries in South America	Knows 3 conflicts in *No Promises in the Wind*	Knows 4 main stages of mitosis
Can import a picture from Internet and insert it into a report	Can perform 3 approved gymnastic moves	Free Space	Knows 4 basic passes in basketball	Knows personal pronoun, third person, objective, plural
Can sing part of any song by CCR	Knows the difference between meiosis and mitosis	Knows 6 things to consider when making difficult decisions	Knows the differences between squid and octopus	Knows formula for area of a triangle
Knows what comes next: J, F, M, A, M, ?	Can name 24 bones with the proper terms	Can draw the sequence of energy transfer in ecosystems	Can perform "_____"	Can list 3 differences between WWI and WWII

G Behavior Analysis

Academia Nuts Team, Herndon Middle School

Name: Date:
Period: Teacher:

A. Describe what you did that resulted in the teacher's request for you to complete this form: (Use the back, if needed.)

B. How did the incident(s) make you feel?

   How do you think others felt?

C. Which class expectation or rule did this action break?

D. What will you do to make sure such behavior doesn't occur again? (More than one idea, please.)

E. What will you do to rebuild our trust in you? (Check as many as you think are necessary to rebuild our trust and for you to learn from your mistake.)

   ___ verbal apology to injured person(s)   ___ letter written to parents

   ___ phone call to parents from you   ___ phone call to parents from teacher

   ___ service to the classroom   ___ service to the school
        (cleaning, organizing, etc.)   (picking up trash, cleaning, etc.)

   ___ after-school detention   ___ before-school detention

   ___ letter of apology   ___ parental accompaniment to class

   ___ removal from enjoyable class activity   ___ essay on related topic
        (field trip, food, etc.)   (chosen with teacher)

   ___ expulsion   ___ sitting alone for a while

   ___ removal from cafeteria for lunch period(s)   ___ discussion with principal

   ___ in-school suspension (crisis)   ___ pay for the damages with own money

   ___ other:

Student Signature: Teacher Approval:
Parent Signature:
Additional Comments:

H Student-Designed Teacher Progress Report

As much as you need to know how you are doing, I need to as well. I would like to learn how to be a better teacher. Let me know in what things I am doing well and in what things I need to improve. Let this be your grading scale:

4 = Achieves excellence
3 = Achieves excellence with some small exceptions
2 = Achieves excellence with some significant exceptions
1 = Doesn't achieve excellence, major improvement needed
0 = Doesn't even come close to achieving excellence (failure)

Use the back of the sheet for comments. Please be as helpful as you can by providing explanations for some of the grades. Both you and your parents are invited to evaluate my performance. If you feel unable to evaluate me in a certain area, leave it blank.

Evaluation of: _____

Activity/Skill	Student	Parent
Teaching writing		
Teaching reading		
Teaching vocabulary		
Teaching grammar, punctuation, spelling		
Teaching how to think		
Deals with paperwork		
Organization		
Handwriting quality on the chalkboard		
Creativity		
Courteous and polite		
Is aware of things in other classes		
Accepts corrections from students		
Appropriate talking speed in lessons		
Lessons are clear, easy to follow		
Treats everyone equally		
Energy level		
Builds trust		
Score sheets (rubrics)		
Grades fairly		
Motivates students to do their best		
Physical classroom atmosphere		
Disciplines well		
Treats students as individuals		
What is taught is useful		
Treats students with respect		
Uses a variety of teaching methods		
Patience		
Knowledge of subjects		
Gives feedback on how you're doing		
Controls temper		
Makes learning interesting		

Explanations and further evaluations (use back if necessary):

Plan for Differentiated Instruction Lesson on Writer's Voice

Inviting and Thinking Activities

- Read essential understandings: There are specific tools to create voice. Word choice and sentence structures are two of them; voice takes time to develop.
- Posted: "You have to be clever to survive middle school." Students are to rewrite the sentence in as many different ways as possible within three minutes. Then students share with partner, choosing the most unique/creative way of stating it. Share this one with the class.
- Students then get into groups of two, three, or four, selected by multiple intelligences (determined prior to class by survey and other assessments). This class has a majority of students demonstrating strong musical and kinesthetic proclivities. Task for students: Describe a moment using only one-syllable words. Choices: a moment in sports, a moment in a music performance, a moment in school. (These choices are based on multiple intelligences as well as the meaningful context of school.) Once done, these are shared with the larger class. These are collected and posted on "one-syllable" wall.

Setting Context for the Lesson

- Review what was done yesterday as well as essential understandings.

Presenting the Agenda/Itinerary

- Posted on the chalkboard in restaurant menu style:

  Appetizers—[Insert introductory activities]
  Entrées—Review and revise assignment, long/short sentence, word substitution, passage analysis, word lists, jargon
  Desserts—3-2-1 summary

Applying Learning Models/Experiences That Best Fit Students' and Lesson's Needs

- Whole class: Give feedback from me on the analysis part of assignment.
- Move to readiness groups (Introductory and Advanced).
- In groups: Share pieces and get feedback on what was done to create the voice of each piece. Student revises analysis based on group input and resubmits piece with analysis.
- Whole group regathers. Activity: long sentence, short sentence. (Model physical length of sentences getting shorter to increase tension and pace—suspense story example—students try example after model is shared.)
- Post: "Jake moved at a slow pace." Then substitute *tortoiselike, plodding, shuffling, leisurely, sluggish,* and *methodical* for the word *slow.* How does the meaning change? Can we really substitute words indiscriminately? [From *After the End* by Barry Lane.]
- Read passage from textbook (p. 50 in textbook, "The Third Level," first paragraph) silently, then with different interpretations, as if punctuation had been slightly rearranged and tone changed.

Plan for Differentiated Instruction Lesson on Writer's Voice (continued)

- Begin mural word lists—action words, describing words, cool phrases.
- (If time) Depending on the audience and our purpose, we change the words: jargon—parachute drop is a predawn vertical insertion, secondhand cars are experienced cars, a hospital death is a therapeutic misadventure, an airplane crash is an involuntary conversion of a 727 (told to stockholders) [*After the End* by Barry Lane].
- (If time) Voice comparisons by two groups. Students have read and analyzed voice in these two stories. Back into original groups for discussion:

  Advanced group: "My Furthest Back Person: The Inspiration for Roots," pp. 39–45; "The Iceman," pp. 223–226.

  Introductory group: "Into Thin Air," pp. 218–219; "Stepping Out with My Baby," pp. 431–433.

  Assignments:

  Find any speech from American history and rewrite its sentiments to be read by a literary character.

  Write a letter to a neighbor sincerely apologizing—you broke their window. [and]

  Write a letter to a sibling apologizing for something you're not sorry for doing. Compare the tones.

  All students: maintain the writer's voice journal.

End of lesson Summary/Closure

- Whole-class discussion (I record on the board, students record in learning logs) "Strategies (Tools) for Creating a Strong Writer's Voice." This becomes a running menu of ideas.
- Students write personal response to Why does writer's voice take time to develop?

Advance Look at the Next Lesson

- Share sentiments from "Give Me Liberty or Give Me Death" speech as rewritten and stated by Harry Potter.

Copyright © 2001 Rick Wormeli. *Meet Me in the Middle: Becoming an Accomplished Middle-Level Teacher.* Stenhouse Publishers.

J   Lesson Design for Differentiating Instruction

Suggested Planning Sequence

1. Identify your objectives. What are the essential and enduring content and skills you want your students to master?

2. Identify your students with unique needs, and determine what they will need in order to achieve the same level of learning.

3. For identified students, modify the content, process, or product. (Remember, this can be done over time, not always within the one lesson.)

4. Identify your formative and summative assessments. How will you provide useful feedback along the way and at the unit's end?

5. Design the learning experiences and alternative pathway experiences that support identified objectives for all students.

6. Run a mental tape of each step in the lesson sequence. Check lesson(s) against criteria for success for differentiated instruction. Make revisions as necessary.

7. Ask a colleague to review your plan and make suggestions.

8. Obtain/create materials needed.

9. Conduct the lesson.

10. Evaluate and revise plans for tomorrow's lesson.

Suggested Components of a Differentiated Instruction Lesson

1. Inviting and thinking activities

2. Setting context for the lesson

3. Presenting agenda/itinerary

Apply learning models (or hybrids thereof) that best fit students' and lesson's needs.

4. Learning experiences: modalities, intelligences, styles, content, skills, resources, momentum, seating, whole/small group/individual, applications of learning, dimensions of learning, students constructing meaning, teaching for understanding, clerical versus learning experiences

5. "Sponges" and motivators

6. Assessment (formative, summative, useful)

7. End of lesson summary/closure

8. Advance look at next lesson

Differentiated Lesson Checklist

- Essential and enduring content and skills (mastery vs. coverage)
- Differentiate process, product, or content
- Students' strengths used

J   Lesson Design for Differentiating Instruction *(continued)*

- Teaching up (not middling)
- Students know "the big picture"
- Anchor activities clear
- Students know how to get help
- Lesson(s) vivid
- As authentic to life as possible
- Students are constructing meaning for themselves
- Subjects integration
- Embedded assessment(s)
- Learners engaged, not passive
- Movement used
- Beginning and end substantive
- Balance of whole/small/individual activities, direct instruction vs. seatwork
- Multiple modalities and media

Lesson/Unit

Lesson/Unit	Differentiated
1. Inviting and Thinking Activities	
2. Setting Context and Objectives	
3. Presenting Agenda/Itinerary	
4. Learning Experiences	
5. Sponges	
6. Assessment (formative/summative/useful)	
7. End of Lesson Summary/Closure	
8. Advance Look at Next Lesson	

K Anchor Activity Differentiated Lesson

Activity/Group _____

Activity/Group _____

Anchor Activity

Activity/Group _____

Activity/Group _____

L   Ebb and Flow Differentiated Lesson

Beginning Activites   Middle Activities   Ending Activities

Whole-Group Instruction	Small-Group Activities	Individual Activities

Direct Instruction

Seatwork

M | *The Outsiders* Project

Three Scenes on Video

Name: Period: Date:
Score: Grade:

Three Scenes	Script	Video Presentation
Three scenes portrayed	Clearly written	Video shown to the class
The scenes that are chosen are important to the story, places where the direction of the story hangs in the balance	Accurately portrayed the scenes from the book	Clean-looking video: steady camera, no background distractions, no "snow" from editing, proper lighting and sound, clear/good view of actors
	Few or no mistakes with spelling, grammar, capitalization, punctuation	Effective opening—"Hook" your audience
	Used proper script format	Effective ending—Leave us with something thoughtful
	Must be submitted in advance (for approval)	Includes a brief reading from the book (practice beforehand/choose something dramatic)
		Includes appropriate props, sounds, costumes
		Included credits (can be filmed on posters and cards, or electronically)
		Running time: 3–12 minutes

Note to parents and students: Anything circled indicates areas for improvement.

4.0 = The writer demonstrates *excellent* understanding and skill. The preceding characteristics describe the writer's work.

3.0 = The writer demonstrates *good* understanding and skill. Most of the listed characteristics describe the writer's work—a few are missing or done improperly.

2.0 = The writer demonstrates *somewhat* of an understanding and skill. Approximately three-quarters of the listed characteristics describe the writer's work—one-quarter of the characteristics are missing or done improperly.

1.0 = The writer demonstrates *little or no* understanding or skill. Few of the listed characteristics describe the writer's work—more than one-quarter of the characteristics are missing or done improperly.

0.0 = Not completed or unscorable.

M The Outsiders Project (continued)

Musical Score for Character

Name: Period: Date:
Score: Grade:

Content	Music Component	General
Music successfully expresses a character's experiences and growth (or change)	Piece has basic elements of musical scores (measures, counts, refrains, notes)	Music is performed live or on tape (audio or video)
Experiences are accurate for the character in the story	Music is appropriate for the content (match mood of topic with mood of music)	Score is written and submitted
		Score is original work specifically written to portray a character from *The Outsiders*

Note to parents and students: Anything circled indicates areas for improvement.

4.0 = The writer demonstrates *excellent* understanding and skill. The preceding characteristics describe the writer's work

3.0 = The writer demonstrates *good* understanding and skill. Most of the listed characteristics describe the writer's work—a few are missing or done improperly.

2.0 = The writer demonstrates *somewhat* of an understanding and skill. Approximately three-quarters of the listed characteristics describe the writer's work—one-quarter of the characteristics are missing or done improperly.

1.0 = The writer demonstrates *little or no* understanding or skill. Few of the listed characteristics describe the writer's work—more than one-quarter of the characteristics are missing or done improperly.

0.0 = Not completed or unscorable.

M   *The Outsiders* Project *(continued)*

Interview with Expert on Gangs

Name: Period: Date:
Score: Grade:

Content	Interview Component	General
Student obtained responses that were substantive, yielding solid information	Questions were appropriate: on topic, mature, eliciting good responses	Method of presenting interview to the class was appropriate
Expert was indeed an expert	Student conducted self with maturity and proper interview manners	Length was appropriate
Information obtained was accurate		Loud enough to be heard
	Interview questions submitted in advance for approval	For live interviews, proper arrangements made with school, teacher, and interviewee

Note to parents and students: Anything circled indicates areas for improvement.

4.0 = The writer demonstrates *excellent* understanding and skill. The preceding characteristics describe the writer's work.

3.0 = The writer demonstrates *good* understanding and skill. Most of the listed characteristics describe the writer's work—a few are missing or done improperly.

2.0 = The writer demonstrates *somewhat* of an understanding and skill. Approximately three-quarters of the listed characteristics describe the writer's work—one-quarter of the characteristics are missing or done improperly.

1.0 = The writer demonstrates *little or no* understanding or skill. Few of the listed characteristics describe the writer's work—more than one-quarter of the characteristics are missing or done improperly.

0.0 = Not completed or unscorable.

The Outsiders Project *(continued)*

Socratic Seminar: Gangs

Students prepared by reading *The Outsiders,* witnessing an interview with Officer Bailey (on gangs), and reading and discussing an article on local gangs.

Seminar Questions

How does a community know it has a gang problem?

Should we feel sorry for gang members or angry? Why?

Is it appropriate for police to follow and be overly strict with people who claim to be gang members?

Does being poor cause students to do poorly in school, and does being rich cause students to do well in school?

Are rumbles a good way to settle gang rivalries if they prevent frequent impulsive fights?

Why do human beings feel the need to form gangs?

What can schools do to stop gangs?

How do we keep youth from joining gangs?

How do we get gangs to disband?

How do you talk to a friend who's in a gang?

Does a good writer have to live or experience the events in a story in order to write about them well?

Are people destined to play certain roles in society? If so, how do you break out of an undesirable role?

Female gang members who have children say they do not want their children to be in gangs. What effect do families have on gang desirability?

Why were there no parents in the novel? How would they have changed the story?

What are gang stereotypes? Are they true?

Question Starters

Why is this called . . . ?

Why would someone want to . . . ?

What is meant by . . . ?

Why does the author call it . . . ?

Are you saying that . . . ?

Anyone disagree with . . . ?

Where in the text do you find support for . . . ?

Is your life similar, different, more of . . . than . . . ?

What would Jefferson think of our student government?

What is . . . about?

How is . . . really about . . . ?

Who is . . . ?

Have we answered . . . ?

What do you mean by . . . ?

N   Meeting of Minds

Based on the PBS television show with Steve Allen

Imagine getting the United States' great historical figures together in one room to discuss important issues of modern times. The divergent perspectives would drive lively debate. With the collective wisdom, audiences would be entertained and ideas would be illuminated. Don't imagine any longer. It's coming to Rachel Carson Middle School and you're part of it.

The Crusaders Team will present a "Meeting of Minds" in which selected groups of students will portray great historical figures of United States history who've been called together to discuss today's issues and to debate complex ideas. In the moderated conversation, researched information about the individuals and their perspectives will be presented. Each team has 6–8 members and will be divided into the following specialty groups:

- Historical figure (1 person)
- Set design and creation (1–3 people)
- Costume design and creation (1–3 people)
- Research life and contributions (all members)

The whole team will determine the historical figure's responses to modern world issues, cite evidence for how the group determined the figure's responses to today's issues, and critique the achievement of all group members.

Unit Sequence by Week (Subject to Modification, Done in Tandem with Other Units of Study)

	Monday	Tuesday	Wednesday	Thursday	Friday
1	Explain the process and product; listen to tapes; read scripts from original Steve Allen show	Students into teams of 6–8; identify historical figures; identify roles on teams; more examples	Identify modern topics; research; design/create costume; design/create set	Research; design/create costume; design/create set	Research; design/create costume; design/create set
2	Research; design/create costume; design/create set	Research; design/create costume; design/create set	Teams determine figure's response to questions and evidence for their interpretations	Teams determine figure's response to questions and evidence for their interpretations	Debate/discussion structure and tips
3	Script show	Script show	Rehearse	Rehearse	Rehearse
4	Rehearse	Performance during school hours, evening for parents and community	Critique of process and team members' celebration		

Copyright © 2001 Rick Wormeli. *Meet Me in the Middle: Becoming an Accomplished Middle-Level Teacher.* Stenhouse Publishers.

Tsunami Team Weekly Schedule—
Rachel Carson Middle School

Monday	Tuesday	Wednesday	Thursday	Friday
A	D	B	E	C
B	E	C	A	D
Lunch/Activity	Lunch/Activity	Lunch/Activity	Lunch/Activity	Lunch/Activity
C	A	D	B	E
Elective	Elective	Elective	Elective	Elective
Elective	Elective	Elective	Elective	Elective

The first two core periods of the day are 72 minutes apiece. Lunch/Activity is a normal-length period (lunch = 30 minutes, activity period = 17 minutes). The third core period of the day is 97 minutes long. The elective courses are 47 minutes apiece, and they meet every day.

Note that every group of students has each subject three times a week, twice for 72 minutes and once for 97 minutes.

Also note that each group of students encounters the subjects at different parts of the day. For example, Joe Student will have math first period on Monday, in the afternoon on Tuesday, and mid-morning on Thursday. At some point during the week, therefore, Joe will encounter math class when he is mentally awake and alert.

P   Structure of the Text

Enumeration

Definition: Listing information, facts, characteristics, features

Signal words: to begin with, second, then, most important, in fact, for example, several, numerous, first, next, finally, also, for instance, in addition, many, few.

Time Order

Definition: Putting facts, events, concepts into sequence using time reference to order them

Signal words: on (date), now, before, when, not long after, as, after, gradually.

Comparison/Contrast

Definition: Explaining similarities (comparison) and differences (contrast)

Signal words: however, as well as, not only/but also, while, unless, yet, but, on the other hand, either/or, although, similarly, unlike.

Cause/Effect

Definition: Showing how things happen (effect) because of other things (cause)

Signal words: because, therefore, as a result, so that, accordingly, thus, since, consequently, this led to, nevertheless, if/then.

Problem/Solution

Definition: Shows the development of a problem and its solution

Signal words: same as for Cause/Effect.

To read and understand a textbook or informational writing, determine which of these five structures is being used. Then, create a mental graphic organizer or actually draw a graphic organizer to visualize and connect the information. Then fill in the organizer with the information.

Another way to look at each type of structure is to see it graphically (through pictures). Imagine for a moment the structure of Cause/Effect. As a picture that whole concept might look like this:

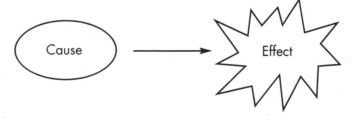

P Structure of the Text *(continued)*

Consider the definitions of the other structures. Draw what you think each one might look like:

Comparison/Contrast	Problem/Solution

Enumeration	Time Order

Colleague Teacher Program— Herndon Middle School

Orientation Agenda

- **Breakfast**
- Introductions: name, year of entry, special interests, why a teacher?
- Colleague teacher program

  Survival kits
  Mentors
  Video observation and reflection
  On-site professional library
  Get-togethers
  Professional development survey
  Standing invitation to drop by any time

- **Break, if needed**
- Other important resources and structures

  TPEP—summary
  Teaching Materials Preparation Center at South Lakes High School and Chapel Square
  Universities, credit unions, and administrative offices
  Professional library
  Maintaining sanity (paradoxical commandments)
  Argus posters for education
  Emergency substitute plan

- Instruction

  Unique characteristics of middle school learners
  Middle school concept
  Assessment suggestions
  Homework guidelines
  Grading policies
  Actions that extend knowledge and reasoning
  New teacher training program—lesson planning panel handout

- **Break, if needed. Lunch?**
- People to know [include names and room numbers]

  Finance officer
  Guidance director
  Assistant principals
  Learning disabilities coordinator
  Computer coordinator
  Media services
  Clinic aide/nurse's aide
  Administrative secretaries

Colleague Teacher Program—
Herndon Middle School *(continued)*

- School practices
  Teacher handbook
- School culture

  Diversity
  Faculty
  Lounges
  Tour of the school
  Auto tour of boundary areas (optional)

Letter to Staff

To: All new staff members   Date:
From: Rick

You did it! Your first week at Herndon Middle School! I hope all is well. I don't know about those eighth-grade students, but the seventh-grade students are terrific!

    Two things: First, we will have a first "gathering" to share food and reflections (and a little bit of business) next week. It will be on _____ from 2:45 p.m. to 3:45 p.m. in Room _____. We will discuss several topics, including parent conferences, the School Plan, and Back to School Night. Administrators will (I hope) be there to hear your stories of success and strangeness, as well as your concerns. Please plan to join us if you can. We are asking each person to bring snacks to share (something sweet, or something such as veggie sticks, crackers and cheese, fruit). Bring enough for 6 or more people. Drinks will be supplied.

    Second, please take a moment and check all appropriate statements below. Then cut this section off and place it in my box by the end of the day or on Monday morning.

    Have a great weekend! Do something outrageous!

Name: Date:

_____ Everything is fine.

_____ I have a question or concern.

_____ I still have some equipment needs. I need:

_____ As of right now, I can attend the September _____ meeting for new staff members.

_____ I'm lost and I already ate my bread crumbs.

R Teacher Survival Kit

To make sure that you have a wonderful year, we have included the following items in your survival kit:

- Rolaids—for when you need relief
- aspirin—for life's little headaches
- Smartees—for you and for those students who forgot how knowledgeable they really are
- Band-Aids—to heal the blows to your ego and index finger
- Stars—to wish upon
- An eraser—to take care of any mistakes
- A balloon "smiley face"—to remind you to keep your sense of humor
- A rubber band—to remind you to be flexible and to stretch
- LifeSavers—for when you think all is lost
- Paper clips—to keep it all together
- Tissues—to dry your tears and for those of us who pretend to be tough, uh, um, this is to blow your nose. Yeah, that's it.
- Bread crumbs—in case you have problems finding your way around the building, try leaving a trail of these.

S Professional Development Survey for New Staff Members

Depending on your experience level, you may be interested in discussions and/or training in the topics listed below. As needs warrant or as opportunities arise, we'll get you the information you need or at the very least, get you connected with someone who has experience in that area. Please return this to Rick Wormeli (Room _____) as soon as possible.

Name of Staff Member

Subject(s) Taught

Room Number

Mark the blank next to each item that is of interest to you. You may check as many as you wish. If there are items you consider rather urgent, please let us know.

_____ parent conferences
_____ reading teacher
_____ ED students
_____ attendance procedures
_____ interims
_____ dealing with diversity
_____ teaming
_____ CRISIS center
_____ the PTA
_____ the Program of Studies
_____ teacher schedules
_____ record keeping
_____ creativity
_____ homework
_____ conflict resolution
_____ dealing with workload
_____ AFT (teacher union)
_____ snow days/delayed op.
_____ observing other teachers
_____ copying machines
_____ guidance department
_____ faculty committees
_____ the master schedule
_____ planning
_____ the school board
_____ Apple Fed. Credit Union
_____ block scheduling
_____ the HMS community

_____ the Media Center
_____ cafeteria
_____ the computer lab
_____ grading scale
_____ lesson plans
_____ integrated approaches
_____ supplies
_____ the administration
_____ electives
_____ student schedules
_____ use of videos
_____ the school plan
_____ prof. dev. catalog
_____ school rules/regs.
_____ EASE (empl. support)
_____ field trips
_____ reflective practitioner
_____ acronyms
_____ faculty portfolios
_____ taking time off
_____ sponsoring clubs/org.
_____ certification
_____ school calendar
_____ teacher burnout
_____ VMSA
_____ mentors
_____ LD students
_____ discipline strategies
_____ report cards
_____ alternative assessment

_____ parent phone calls
_____ cooperative learning
_____ seating arrangements
_____ school newspaper/ yearbook
_____ back to school night
_____ substitute teachers/ folders
_____ laser disc use
_____ make-up work policies
_____ teacher evaluation
_____ religious holidays
_____ NEA (teacher union)
_____ middle school stud. behaviors
_____ education publications
_____ snacks/soda machines
_____ instructional round- tables
_____ student recognition
_____ middle school pro- gramming
_____ the professional library
_____ contacting the news media
_____ retirement
_____ attending conferences
_____ other

T   Parents' Quick Reference

English 7 Policies and Practices—Crusaders Team

Grading Scale

A = 4.0-3.7   C+ = 2.6-2.2   D = 1.1-1.0
B+ = 3.6-3.2   C = 2.1-1.7   F = 0.9 or lower
B = 3.1-2.7   D+ = 1.6-1.2

If a particular assessment is more clearly expressed by percentages or points, it will be done that way for your child, but the score will be weighted more heavily than quizzes and homework. Assignments that are given checks or zeros count no more than 10 percent of your child's overall academic grade. Checks and zeros describe the extent of your child's practice with the content and skills, not mastery thereof. Be assured, however, that a check means your child has a good grasp of the content or skill intended; otherwise a check minus or a zero will be recorded.

Personal growth as well as mastery of English skills and knowledge are more important than grades. Please help your child keep perspective on his or her achievement. While we focus on academics, we will also build stable and compassionate individuals. In this class, our school's Mission Statement is fully recognized:

> Within a safe and nurturing community, the students, staff and parents of Rachel Carson Middle School seek to foster personal and academic excellence, treat one another with dignity, respect our environment, embrace diversity, and develop character that merits trust and honor. We encourage positive risk taking and perseverance in pursuit of our goals.

Redoing Assessments (Tests, Quizzes, Projects, Writings, and Assignments)

At teacher discretion, any assessment may be redone if the student did not completely master the intended content or skills, *and* the student has demonstrated sincere effort to prepare for the assessment the first time it was given. Rigorous relearning or review in preparation for the second attempt will qualify a student to redo an assessment. Redoing assessments is a privilege, not something to be taken for granted. Students must redo assessments within one week of their return; otherwise the original grade stands. The higher grade between the original attempt and the second attempt will be recorded, *not* an average of the two grades. Occasionally, assessments cannot be redone, but instead students may correct their mistakes and receive half credit for each item they correct. Students must redo assessments on their own time, not during direct teaching time in our class. In order to redo any test, major project, major writing or quiz, students must first submit the original work signed by a parent and requesting the retest or redo opportunity.

Make-Up Work

Students are expected to contact their homework partners (study buddies) to determine missing work when absent, or they may access our class's homework Web site on schoolnotes.com,

Copyright © 2001 Rick Wormeli. *Meet Me in the Middle: Becoming an Accomplished Middle-Level Teacher.* Stenhouse Publishers.

Parents' Quick Reference *(continued)*

described below. They may also stay after school to record missing assignments, get explanations, and work on make-up assignments. They are allowed the same number of days they were gone to make up the work, unless a note is received from parents requesting more time. If you have access to e-mail, don't forget to use it to get caught up quickly. School: 925-3600 Mr. Wormeli's e-mail: rwormeli@erols.com.

Homework

There is a list of all homework assignments made for each period posted on the homework board (a surfboard) in our room. Students should be encouraged to review that list regularly. If you or your child would like to see the homework for the day (posted after school), please access schoolnotes.com on the Web and enter our school's zip code: 20171. Once there, find my name, click on it, and the day's homework will be listed. You can go directly to the homework listing for our class using http://schoolnotes.com/20171/wormeli99.html.

No homework is ever assigned on weekends or holidays in our English class. Those times are reserved for students to be with their families, relax, get exercise, and come back ready to learn on the next school day. At their discretion, students may choose to work over weekends and holidays on long-term projects, rough drafts, or their student choice books. If a student is working beyond his or her normal bedtime on homework, please tell him or her to stop and go to bed. Sleep and health will do more for a student's education than finishing assignments when the student is tired. In these situations, parents need to send in a note asking for a brief extension of completion time in order for students to receive full credit. Please be aware of the student's need to manage his/her life such that homework is a priority—sports, music, church, Scouts, visits from relatives, time with friends, and family events are just some of the things that can make a student too tired to do homework each night. Creating balance is a vital skill to learn while in middle school.

Student Papers

Papers with no names are put into a "No Name, No Credit" tray. A student may check the tray and upon finding his/her work, write his/her name on it and resubmit it. The tray is emptied into the trash every few weeks. Once assignments are evaluated by Mr. Wormeli, they are placed in a tray called "Papers to Be Returned to Students." If a student hasn't had a paper returned in a while, he or she should check there.

Writing Portfolios

A Writing Portfolio contains the final versions of student writings, reflections on those writings, and the student's progress and goals this year. It is the most valid statement of the students as writers and thinkers. Students will place all graded writing in these portfolios after they are reviewed by Mr. Wormeli. These collected works are kept on bookshelves in our classroom. Please feel free to stop by and view your child's portfolio at any point in the year, or send in a note and we'll send it home for your review. We will send it home for official parent review at the end of each semester.

| T | Parents' Quick Reference *(continued)* |

Visiting

You are encouraged to visit our English classroom any day you wish. If you want to see your child's class, be sure to ask him or her when English class meets. The front office folks are very careful to prevent interruptions to our class, so they will want to confirm your visit with me before letting you proceed to Room C107. Please be sure to call ahead to make sure they know you are coming. They'll check with me if I haven't already told them about your visit, and they'll provide you with a visitor's badge.

Contacting Teachers

Our school number is 925-3600. I can be contacted through e-mail at rwormeli@erols.com. This is my home e-mail address and I check it each evening between 9 and midnight. The school's address is Rachel Carson Middle School, 13618 McLearen Road, Herndon, VA 20171.

Extra Supplies?

Keep your eyes and ears open for extra paper, pens, pencils, markers, erasers, tape, scissors, hole-punches, and staplers! We maintain an in-class supply center that frequently needs replenishing. We're also looking for puzzles. We're looking for problem-solving puzzles (written or using manipulatives or physical objects) on which students can work if they finish assignments early or for use during our "Puzzle Day" activity period. Put your name on the puzzle if you want it returned to your family.

Want to Volunteer?

Send in a note stating your name, your child's name, your phone number, and your interest in volunteering. Indicate whether you can do work only in your home, or if you're available to help at school. We'll contact you with a list of possibilities given your availability, and get you started right away.

U Letter to Parent

Date:

Dear _____,

    I disrupted _____ class today with my talking and/or inattention. I did it repeatedly, even after I was asked by my teacher to stop talking and/or pay attention. My actions prevented me and my classmates from learning all that we could have learned in today's lessons. I know that this is not the kind of behavior you expect from me and I am sorry for the frustration I have caused. One action I plan to take in order to not repeat this behavior is

A record of my disruptions in this class is maintained by my teacher. Please contact him/her to see how I am improving two weeks from today.
    Sincerely,

    (Student's Name)

Parent Signature:

Date:

Contact phone number(s):

☐ Check here if you would like to speak with the teacher concerning this behavior. This is optional.

V Letter to Parent

I Didn't Have My Homework Today . . .

Name:

Subject:

Date:

Missing Assignment:

Explanation:

Parent/Guardian Name:

   Home Phone:

   Work Phone:

References

Armstrong, T. 2000. *Multiple Intelligences in the Classroom.* 2d ed. Alexandria, VA: Association for Supervision and Curriculum Development.

Asimov, Isaac. 1966. *Fantastic Voyage.* Madison, WI: Turtleback Books.

Atwell, Nancie. 1990. *Coming to Know: Writing to Learn in the Intermediate Grades.* Portsmouth, NH: Heinemann.

Bach, Richard. 1970. *Jonathan Livingston Seagull.* New York: Simon and Schuster.

———. 1977. *Illusions: The Adventures of a Reluctant Messiah.* New York: Delacorte.

Baumrind, D. 1980. "New Directions in Socialization Research." *American Psychologist* 35: 639–652.

Beker, Jerome. 1960. "The Influence of School Camping on the Self-Concepts and Social Relationships of Sixth-Grade School Children." *Journal of Educational Psychology* 51 (6): 352–356.

Bell, R. Q. 1979. "Parent, Child, and Reciprocal Influences." *American Psychologist* 34: 821–826.

Bennett, Dean, and John Padalino. 1989. "The Role of Environmental Education in Programs for Youth-At-Risk." *Contemporary Education* 60 (3): 153–155.

Bloom, Benjamin. 2000. *A Taxonomy for Learning, Teaching, and Assessing: A Revision of Bloom's Taxonomy of Educational Objectives,* ed. Lorin Anderson. New York: Longman.

Bloom, Mark, Diana Vivian Morgan, and Catherine Winters. 1988. "Mutual Motivation." *Health* 20: 32–40.

Boga, Steve. 1997. *Orienteering.* Mechanicsburg, PA: Stackpole Books.

Boreen, Jean, Donna Niday, Mary K. Johnson, and Joseph Potts. 2000. *Mentoring Beginning Teachers: Guiding, Reflecting, Coaching.* Portland, ME: Stenhouse.

Bronfenbrenner, Uri. 1985. "The Parent/Child Relationship and Our Changing Society. In *Parents, Children, and Change,* ed. L. E. Arnold, 45–58. Lexington, MA: Lexington Books.

Brooks, Jacqueline Grennon, and Martin G. Brooks. 1993. *In Search of Understanding: The Case for Constructivist Classrooms.* Alexandria, VA: Association for Supervision and Curriculum Development.

Canady, Robert Lynn, and Michael D. Rettig. 1996. *Teaching in the Block.* Larchmont, NY: Eye on Education.

Carnegie Forum on Education and the Economy. 1986. *A Nation Prepared: Teachers for the 21st Century.* New York: Carnegie Corporation.

Covey, Steven. 1989. *The Seven Habits of Highly Effective People*. New York: Simon and Schuster.

Crompton, John L., and Christine Sellar. 1981. "Do Outdoor Education Experiences Contribute to Positive Development in the Affective Domain?" *Journal of Environmental Education* 12 (4): 21–29.

Dunn, Rita, and Kenneth Dunn. 1993. *Teaching Secondary Students Through Their Individual Learning Styles*. Boston: Allyn and Bacon. See also http://www.learningstyles.net/.

Fluegelman, Andrew, ed. 1976. *The New Games Book*. New York: Headlands Press Book, Doubleday.

Frank, Marjorie. 1988. *If You're Trying to Teach Kids How to Write, You've Gotta Have This Book!* Nashville, TN: Incentive Publications.

Freeman, Carol G. 1996. *Living with a Work in Progress: A Parent's Guide to Surviving Adolescence*. Westerville, OH: National Middle School Association.

Fuller, Barbara. 1989. "Reaching Out from the Inner City." *Sierra* 74 (4): 50–54.

Gardner, Howard. 1993. *Frames of Mind: The Theory of Multiple Intelligences*. New York: Basic Books. Reissued. See also http://www.angelfire.com/oh/themidas and http://pzweb.harvard.edu/pis/hg.htm.

Gennaro, Eugene, Ann Sigford, and Patricia Heller. 1983. "A Course in Winter Ecology at a Nature Center for Middle School Children and Their Parents." *Journal of Environmental Education* 14 (4): 23–25.

Goodrich, Heidi. 1996/1997. "Understanding Rubrics." *Educational Leadership* 54 (4): 14–17.

Gregorc, Anthony. 1979. "Learning/Teaching Styles." *Educational Leadership* 36: 234–236.

———. 1998. *The Mind Styles Model*. Columbia, CT: Gregorc Associates. See also http://www.gregorc.com/.

Griswold, Philip. 1986. "Family Outing Activities and Achievement Among Fourth-Graders in Compensatory Education Funded Schools." *Journal of Educational Research* 79 (5): 261–266.

Hackmann, Donald. 1995. "Ten Guidelines for Implementing Block Scheduling." *Educational Leadership* 53 (3): 24–27.

Harrison, Allen F., and Robert M. Bramson. 1984. *The Art of Thinking*. New York: Berkley Publishing Group. See also http://www.inq-hpa.com/.

Harvard-Smithsonian Center for Astrophysics. 1987. *A Private Universe* (video). See http://www.learner.org/.

Hazelworth, Maureen, and Beth Wilson. 1990. "The Effects of an Outdoor Adventure Camp Experience on Self-Concept." *Journal of Environmental Education* 21 (4): 33–37.

Hersey, Paul, and Kenneth Blanchard. 1996. *Management of Organizational Behavior: Utilizing Human Resources*. Paramus, NJ: Prentice Hall. See also http://www.situational.com/.

Horn, Jack C. 1985. "The Running Bond." *Psychology Today* 19: 74.

Jacobson, Cliff. 1999. *Basic Essentials, Map and Compass*. 2d ed. Guilford, CT: Globe Pequot Press.

Jensen, Eric. 1995. *Super Teaching*. San Diego, CA: The Brain Store.

———. 1998. *Teaching with the Brain in Mind*. Alexandria, VA: Association for Supervision and Curriculum Development.

———. 2000. *Brain-Based Learning*. San Diego, CA: The Brain Store.

Josephson Institute. 2000. *2000 Report Card: The Ethics of American Youth*. Marina del Ray, CA: Josephson Institute. See also http://www.josephsoninstitute.org/survey2000/survey2000-pressrelease.htm.

Kain, Daniel L. 1998. *Camel-Makers: Building Effective Teacher Teams Together*. Westerville, OH: National Middle School Association.

Keirsey, David. 1998. *Please Understand Me II: Temperament, Character, Intelligence*. Del Mar, CA: Prometheus Nemesis Book Co. See also http://www.keirsey.com/ and http://www.cpp-db.com/.

Kjellström, Björn 1994. New rev. ed. *Be Expert with Map and Compass: The Complete Orienteering Handbook*. New York: Hungry Minds.

Kriegel, Robert. 1991. *If It Ain't Broke, Break it! And Other Unconventional Wisdom for a Changing Business World*. New York: Warner Books.

Kushel, Gerald. 1994. *Reaching the Peak Performance Zone*. New York: American Management Association Publishers.

Lavoie, Richard. 1989. *How Difficult Can This Be? The F.A.T. City Workshop* (video). Washington, DC: WETA. See http://www.LDonline.org/.

———. 1997. *When the Chips Are Down* (video). Washington, DC: WETA. See http://www.LDonline.org/.

Lazear, David. 1991. *Seven Ways of Teaching: The Artistry of Teaching with Multiple Intelligences*. Arlington Heights, FL: Skylight Publishing.

LeDoux, John. 1996. *The Emotional Brain: The Mysterious Underpinnings of Emotional Life*. New York: Simon and Schuster.

Lewin, Roger. 1997. *Bones of Contention: Controversies in the Search for Human Origins*. Chicago: University of Chicago Press. See also http://www.cyber-nation/victory/quotations/authors/quotes_lewin.

Markowitz, Karen, and Eric Jensen. 1999. *The Great Memory Book*. San Diego, CA: The Brain Store.

Martin, Katherine. 1985. "The Family That Jogs Together." *Ms.* 14 (July): 99–103.

Marzano, Robert. 1992. *A Different Kind of Classroom: Teaching with Dimensions of Learning*. Alexandria, VA: Association for Supervision and Curriculum Development.

Marzano, Robert, J. McTighe, and D. Pickering. 1993. *Assessing Student Outcomes: Performances Using the Dimensions of Learning Model*. Alexandria, VA: Association for Supervision and Curriculum Development.

McBride, B. A., and R. J. McBride. 1990. "The Changing Roles of Fathers." *Journal of Home Economics* 82 (3): 6–10.

McCarthy, Bernice. 1987. *The 4-MAT System*. 3d ed. Wauconda, IL: About Learning. See also http://www.aboutlearning.com/.

McTighe, Jay. 1996/97. "What Happens Between Assessments?" *Educational Leadership* 54 (4): 6–7.

Middle School Teaming Facts. 1998. Battle Creek, MI: Kellogg Foundation.

National Commission on Teaching and America's Future. 1996. *What Matters Most: Teaching for America's Future*. Kutztown, PA: Kutztown Publishing.

Norton, Jim. 2001. *Practical Skepticism* (Web site). See http://members.aol.com/jimn469897/skeptic.htm.

O'Neil, John. 1995. "Finding Time to Learn." *Educational Leadership* 53 (3): 11–15.

Parks, Sandra, and Howard Black. 1990. *Organizing Thinking: Graphic Organizers.* Pacific Grove, CA: Critical Thinking Books and Software.

Pinker, Steven. 1997. *How the Mind Works.* New York: W. W. Norton.

Popkin, Michael H. 1990. *Active Parenting of Teens.* Marietta, GA: Active Parenting Publishers.

Prescriptions for Success in Heterogeneous Classrooms. 1995. Westerville, OH: National Middle School Association.

Project WILD. 2001. K–12 conservation and environmental curriculum, first developed in 1983 by Western Regional Environmental Council. See http://www.projectwild.org/.

Randi, James. 1982. *Flim-Flam! The Truth About Unicorns, Parapsychology, and Other Delusions.* Amherst, MA: Prometheus Books.

Rief, Linda. 1992. *Seeking Diversity.* Portsmouth, NH: Heinemann.

Rogers, Spencer, and Shari Graham. 1998. *The High Performance Toolbox: Performance Tasks, Assessment Designs, Rubrics, Checklists, and Grading, Parental Support, Quality Student Work, Reaching Standards.* Evergreen, CO: Peak Learning Systems. See also http://www.peaklearn.com/.

Rogers, Spence, Jim Ludington, and Shari Graham. 1998. *Motivation and Learning: Practical Teaching Tips for Block Schedules, Brain-Based Learning, Multiple Intelligences, Improved Student Motivation, Increased Achievement.* Evergreen, CO: Peak Learning Systems. See also http://www.peaklearn.com/.

Sagan, Carl. 1996. *The Demon-Haunted World: Science as a Candle in the Dark.* New York: Random House.

Saphier, Jon, and John D'Auria. 1993. *How to Bring Vision to School Improvement.* Acton, MA: Research for Better Teaching.

Saphier, Jon, and Robert Gower. 1997. *The Skillful Teacher.* Acton, MA: Research for Better Teaching.

Scherer, Marge. 1998/99. "Is School the Place for Spirituality? A Conversation with Rabbi Harold Kushner." *Educational Leadership* 56 (4): 18–22.

Schurr, Sandra L. 1994. *Dynamite in the Classroom: A How-to Book for Teachers.* Westerville, OH: National Middle School Association.

Shermer, Michael. 1997. *Why People Believe Weird Things.* New York: Freeman.

Sloane, Paul. 1992. *Lateral Thinking Puzzlers.* New York: Sterling. The first of a series.

Sousa, David. 1995. *How the Brain Learns: A Classroom Teacher's Guide.* Reston, VA: National Association of Secondary School Principals.

Steeves, Kathleen, and Barbara Browne. 2000. *Preparing Teachers for National Board Certification: A Facilitator's Guide.* New York: Guilford Publications.

Sweeny, Barry. http://www.teachermentors.com/index.html.

Sylvester, Robert. 1995. *A Celebration of Neurons: An Educator's Guide to the Human Brain.* Alexandria, VA: Association for Supervision and Curriculum Development.

Thurston, Cheryl M. 1991. *Ideas That Really Work! Activities for English and Language Arts.* Fort Collins, CO: Cottonwood Press.

Tomlinson, Carol Ann. 1995. *How to Differentiate Instruction in Mixed-Ability Classrooms*. Alexandria, VA: Association for Supervision and Curriculum Development.

———. 1999. *The Differentiated Classroom: Responding to the Needs of All Learners*. Alexandria, VA: Association for Supervision and Curriculum Development.

Ward, William Arthur. See http://www.bgsu.edu/colleges/edhd/programs/MentorNet/Handbook.

Wenglinsky, Harold. 2000. *How Teaching Matters*. Princeton, NJ: Educational Testing Service.

Who's Who Among American High School Students. 1998. Lake Forest, IL: Educational Communications. See also http://www.honoring.com/.

Wiggins, Grant. 1996/1997. "Practicing What We Preach in Designing Authentic Assessments." *Educational Leadership* 54 (4): 18–25.

Willis, Scott, ed. 1996. "Can Schools Eliminate Tracking So That All Students Benefit?" *ASCD Newsletter* 38 (7).

Winebrenner, S. 1992. *Teaching Gifted Kids in the Regular Classroom: Strategies Every Teacher Can Use to Meet the Needs of the Gifted and Talented*. Minneapolis: Free Spirit Publishing.

Wolfe, Pat, and Ron Brandt. 1998. "What Do We Know from Brain Research?" *Educational Leadership* 56 (3): 8–13.

Zinsser, William. 1989. *Writing to Learn*. New York: Harper and Row.

Index

Other Stenhouse Books for Middle School Teachers

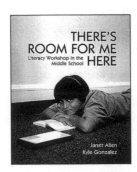

There's Room for Me Here
Literacy Workshop in the Middle School

Janet Allen and Kyle Gonzalez

What do you do with students who cannot or will not read and write? This portrait of Kyle Gonzalez's middle school classroom offers teachers theory-based strategies for helping those students become motivated and successful readers and writers. You will see how one middle school teacher sets up her literacy classroom, offers intervention and support for struggling students, and assesses their progress. Rich in description of Kyle's successes, the book also looks honestly at why some practices were ineffective in her setting.

With Janet's and Kyle's practical and detailed suggestions for creating a literate environment, you'll learn how to establish a literacy workshop, use read-alouds as well as shared, guided, and independent reading and writing, and instill reading and writing practices that help students read content-specific texts.

There's Room for Me Here includes record-keeping forms, extensive bibliographies of literature and professional materials, resource information, and samples of strategy lessons all embedded in this engaging story of a teacher's first three years building a literacy workshop in her classroom.

"We Want to Be Known"
Learning from Adolescent Girls

Edited by Ruth Shagoury Hubbard, Maureen Barbieri, and Brenda Miller Power

A flurry of recent studies shows how concerned teachers and parents are about adolescent girls. What's been missing in the research are practical strategies for changing the curriculum and building communities that help girls grow up secure and strong. This book, written by teacher researchers throughout the country, documents successful innovations. The writers show through the stories of their classrooms how they changed as they watched and listened to girls. Everything from including strong female role models in math and science, to developing service learning programs, to considering the special needs of minority girls, is presented in down-to-earth, teacher-to-teacher prose.

You'll find detailed explanations of how to start discussion groups for girls, ferret out books that have strong women characters, and help male colleagues understand girls' needs. *"We Want to Be Known"* also includes some eloquent poems and essays written by young adolescent girls. This writing is a fascinating window into girl-culture and is suitable for read-alouds and discussions with students about growing up female in America. The book concludes with extensive annotated bibliographies of recommended books compiled by teachers and young girls.

You can read these books and many other
Stenhouse titles on-line at **www.stenhouse.com**.